ACCOUNTING FOR BEGINNERS

(ALL-IN-ONE)

Financial & Managerial Accounting for Beginners — Statements, Bookkeeping, Taxes & Cash Flow

BENJAMIN ADDAMS

GRAPEVINE BOOKS

Published by
GRAPEVINE BOOKS

www.grapevinebooks.com
email: contact@grapevinebooks.com

Ordering Information:
Quantity sales: Special discounts are available on quantity purchases by corporations, associations, and others.
For details, reach out to the publisher.

First published by Grapevine Books, 2025

Contents

Contents

Understanding Accounting: Why It's Essential

Accounting is the backbone of every business. Without it, companies would lack the clarity they need to understand their financial standing, make informed decisions, and set long-term goals. Think of accounting as the language of business—it helps organizations track financial transactions, manage cash flow, and assess their financial health. For anyone who is starting a business or planning to grow one, accounting is the key to ensuring financial stability and long-term success.

Why Accounting Matters

Accounting provides vital insights into the operations of a business. It helps you understand where your money is coming from and where it's going. By keeping accurate records, businesses can analyze profitability, plan for taxes, and ensure they stay compliant with local regulations. Without accounting, business owners would be flying blind, unsure of whether they are on track to meet their financial goals.

For example, when you launch a product or service, you need to know if it's generating revenue that exceeds the costs. Revenue analysis through accounting helps you assess whether you're operating efficiently. Expenses, including fixed and variable costs, are tracked to ensure your business isn't overspending. Profitability ratios reveal how much you earn after expenses, and they're crucial for growth decisions.

Building a Financial Foundation

The most fundamental aspect of business success is financial planning. Proper accounting helps create a clear picture of where a company is headed. Using basic financial statements like the Income Statement, Balance Sheet, and Cash Flow Statement, you gain a snapshot of the company's performance. The Income Statement helps measure the profitability of your business by comparing revenues and expenses, while the Balance Sheet gives an overview of what your business owns and owes. These documents are essential for making sound business decisions and ensuring that you remain solvent and profitable.

A solid accounting foundation also allows businesses to secure funding or investment. When investors or banks look at a company, they need confidence that the business is financially healthy and capable of generating returns. Clear financial statements backed by accurate accounting practices offer this reassurance. Without a financial roadmap, investors would hesitate to back a business, fearing risk and uncertainty.

Common Accounting Mistakes to Avoid

Many small businesses make simple accounting errors that can snowball into bigger issues. One common mistake is failing to separate personal and business finances. Keeping business transactions separate ensures clearer accounting and prevents personal finances from affecting business performance. Another mistake is neglecting tax obligations. Businesses often forget to account for taxes properly, leading to penalties or cash flow issues.

In addition, not maintaining accurate accounts payable and accounts receivable can disrupt cash flow. Businesses need to track outstanding invoices and payments to ensure they maintain a healthy cash cycle. Many businesses fail because they cannot meet their short-term liabilities due to poor cash flow management.

How This Book Works

Welcome to Accounting for Beginners (All-In-One)! This book is designed to provide you with everything you need to get started with financial and managerial accounting, even if you have no prior experience. The goal is to make accounting accessible by breaking down complex concepts into simple, easy-to-understand terms and providing real-world examples to illustrate the principles.

A Step-by-Step Approach

Each chapter is structured to introduce essential concepts gradually. We start with the basics—financial statements, bookkeeping, and cash flow—and move on to more advanced topics like taxes and business analysis. Every chapter builds on the one before it, so you will never feel lost. The book is also peppered with practical examples that demonstrate how accounting is used in everyday business scenarios.

For instance, when we discuss the Income Statement, we'll first explain what it is and how to read it. Then, we'll walk you through creating an Income Statement for a small business. The idea is for you to learn by doing, so you gain hands-on experience as you go.

Clear, Concise Explanations

Accounting can be overwhelming, especially for those who are just starting. That's why this book avoids jargon and complicated formulas. Instead, we focus on providing you with clear definitions and step-by-step guides that make understanding even the most complex concepts simple.

Each section includes a glossary of key terms to reinforce your understanding, and we encourage you to revisit these terms as you progress. The goal is to build your confidence as you go, ensuring you can handle basic financial tasks on your own by the end of the book.

For All Learners

Whether you're learning on your own, working through a class, or managing a small business, this book is tailored to suit your needs. The writing style is engaging, beginner-friendly, and designed to keep you motivated as you learn. If you have no prior background in accounting, you'll find that the content gradually eases you into more advanced topics.

Getting the Most Out of This Guide

Learning accounting for the first time can feel overwhelming, but with the right approach, this guide will become one of the most useful resources on your desk. Whether you are a business owner, a student, or someone curious about financial literacy, this book is structured to help you build confidence step by step. Accounting is not simply about numbers. It is about understanding the financial story behind every decision a business makes. To truly benefit from this guide, it helps to know how to move through the chapters, how to apply what you learn, and how to practice the skills that will set you up for long term success.

Before you begin, remember that accounting is learned through consistent exposure. The more often you interact with the concepts in this guide, the easier everything will become. Think of learning accounting like learning a new language. You would not expect to speak fluently after the first lesson. Instead, you learn through repeated contact with vocabulary, examples, and real situations. The same is true here. Each chapter builds on the previous one, giving you a complete and connected understanding of how the pieces of accounting fit together.

Use Real Examples While You Read

One of the most effective ways to understand accounting principles is by pairing them with real situations. Throughout the guide, you will see examples from small businesses, side hustles, online shops, and service based companies. When you encounter examples like these, pause and imagine how the concept would apply to your own situation. If you run a business or plan to start one, picture your own expenses, your customer payments, or your inventory. If you are a student, think about a business you know well or have studied before.

For instance, when we introduce revenue, take a moment to list out the types of revenue your business or hypothetical business might earn. When we discuss assets, try identifying the assets you own, such as a laptop, office equipment, or inventory. The more you connect the examples to your real environment, the faster the concepts will begin to make sense.

Review the Key Terms in Each Chapter

Every chapter contains essential vocabulary. Words like equity, liabilities, cash flow, and retained earnings will appear repeatedly throughout the book. When these terms show up, take a moment to review the definition provided. If you need to, return to the glossary at the back of the book. The repetition is intentional. These words form the foundation of accounting, so familiarity with them is crucial.

A helpful strategy is to keep a notebook next to you while you read. Write down new terms, along with short definitions in your own words. You can even include a simple example beside each term. For example:

Liability: An amount a business owes.

Example: A loan from the bank.

Writing things down helps reinforce what you learn and improves long term retention.

Make Use of the Tables and Charts

Throughout the guide, you will find tables that organize information like account types, differences between cash and accrual accounting, or categories of financial statements. These tables are included to simplify your learning experience. When you come across one, take a minute to study the format. The tables allow you to compare concepts quickly, helping you understand subtle differences that might be confusing if explained only in text form.

Here is an example of a simple table you will see in the book:

Account Type	Examples	Purpose
Asset	Cash, Inventory, Equipment	Shows what the business owns
Liability	Accounts Payable, Loans	Shows what the business owes
Equity	Owner Capital, Retained Earnings	Shows ownership value

Whenever you feel stuck, return to these visual aids. They are built to clarify, organize, and reinforce the most important concepts.

Practice the Skills as You Learn Them

Accounting becomes meaningful when you apply it. Each chapter contains exercises that allow you to practice what you learned. These include small tasks like categorizing transactions, identifying assets and liabilities, or preparing a short section of a financial statement. You do not need to complete every exercise immediately, but try to work through as many as you can. Consistent practice is the difference between simply reading accounting and actually understanding it.

For example, after reading about journal entries, try writing a few on your own. When the book explains cash flow, take a moment to draft a small cash flow summary for a typical week in your business or personal finances. These exercises transform passive reading into active learning.

Complete the Assessments at the End of Each Chapter

Every chapter ends with an assessment designed to help you measure your understanding. These assessments are not meant to trick you. Instead, they guide you in recognizing which parts you grasp well and which sections you may want to revisit. If you miss a question, review the explanation provided. Understanding why an answer is correct is more important than getting everything right on the first attempt.

Treat the assessments as checkpoints rather than tests. They serve as gentle reminders of the concepts you have learned, helping you solidify the information before moving on to new material.

Take Your Time With the Financial Statements

Many beginners find financial statements intimidating at first. Statements like the Income Statement, Balance Sheet, and Cash Flow Statement contain a lot of information. Do not feel pressured to understand everything immediately. As you progress through the guide, you will revisit these statements several times, each time gaining a deeper understanding.

A helpful approach is to look at a sample statement and identify familiar parts. For example, find total revenue or total expenses on an Income Statement. On a Balance Sheet, locate assets, liabilities, and equity. As you become comfortable with these sections, the statements will begin to feel more intuitive.

Stay Consistent and Review Often

To get the most out of this guide, consistency is key. Even reading one or two sections each day can create strong momentum. Frequent exposure helps the concepts stick, especially when paired with regular practice.

If you find a chapter particularly challenging, do not hesitate to revisit it later. Accounting concepts often make more sense once you see how they connect in later sections.

Use This Guide as a Reference Tool

Once you complete the book, it can still serve as a valuable reference. If you start a business and need to remember how to categorize expenses, you can revisit the chart of accounts section. If tax season approaches and you want to refresh your understanding of deductions, return to the tax chapter. The guide is designed to support you long after your first read.

Learning accounting is one of the most empowering steps you can take for your financial future. With patience, practice, and the structured approach this guide provides, you will gain the skills needed to understand your financial information, make smart decisions, and build a stable foundation for whatever goals you pursue.

Chapter 1: Accounting: The Language of Business

The Core Functions of Every Business

In every business, regardless of size or industry, there are three core activities that drive operations: financing, operating, and investing. These functions form the foundation of a business's financial system and are essential to understanding the flow of money within a company. Whether you're managing a small startup or running a large corporation, accounting practices help keep these functions organized, measurable, and aligned with business goals.

In this section, we'll break down each of these functions, explain their significance, and show how accounting tracks and supports each of them. By the end, you'll understand how they relate to your business's financial health and how accounting keeps the balance in check.

Financing: Raising Money to Support the Business

Financing involves acquiring money to run or expand a business. For most businesses, this function begins with the entrepreneur's personal investment, such as savings, or by raising money from external sources. Financing also includes loans, investments from venture capitalists, and funds raised from issuing **shares** (equity financing).

Internal financing occurs when owners or stakeholders inject capital into the business from their personal savings. This form of financing is common among small businesses or startups that cannot yet access larger funding sources. For instance, an entrepreneur might use their personal funds to cover initial expenses like office rent, equipment purchases, and inventory.

External financing, on the other hand, refers to money borrowed from outside sources, such as loans or bonds, or money received from investors. This external funding is often necessary for businesses looking to scale operations quickly, build infrastructure, or expand into new markets. Unlike equity financing, which involves selling part of the company, debt financing requires the business to repay the borrowed funds with interest.

When a company takes on financing, it also creates a **liability** on its balance sheet. The most common liabilities include accounts payable (money owed to suppliers) and loans or bonds that need to be repaid. Businesses use accounting practices to track and manage this debt.

Operating: Managing Day-to-Day Business Activities

Once the business has acquired the necessary funds, the next core function is operating. Operating refers to the daily activities required to run the business, such as producing goods or services, selling to customers, managing inventory, and maintaining equipment. This is where businesses earn their revenue and manage

their expenses.

Operating activities can be divided into two categories:

1. **Revenue generation**: This includes all activities related to selling goods or services to customers. Whether it's a retail store selling products, a service-based business offering professional services, or an online business generating income from e-commerce, operating revenue is the lifeblood of a business. Businesses track revenue to determine how well they are meeting their sales goals, assess the impact of marketing strategies, and understand the demand for their products or services.
2. **Expense management**: Every business must manage its expenses, which include both fixed and variable costs. Fixed costs, such as rent, insurance, and salaries, are incurred regardless of how much the business produces or sells. Variable costs, such as the cost of raw materials, shipping, and commissions, change in proportion to sales or production levels. Managing expenses is crucial because it directly affects profitability. Businesses that spend more than they earn will find themselves in financial trouble.

Accounting plays a critical role in operating by recording and classifying transactions. For example, bookkeepers track daily sales and purchases, ensuring that the financial statements reflect the current state of the business. The income statement, for example, helps business owners see how much revenue was generated and how much was spent in the process, highlighting net profit or net loss.

Investing: Acquiring Assets to Grow the Business

Once the business is operational, the next function is investing. Investing involves acquiring resources that will help the business grow and generate future returns. These investments could be in the form of **physical** assets, such as property, machinery, and equipment, or **intangible** assets like intellectual property and software.

The purpose of investing is to make the business more productive and efficient, enabling it to increase its revenue in the future. For example, a manufacturing business may invest in a new machine that will increase production capacity and reduce costs. An online retailer might invest in a more efficient inventory management system to improve product delivery times and customer satisfaction.

In the early stages of a business, investing often comes in the form of small purchases, such as a computer or tools necessary for the business. As the company grows, the investment might shift towards acquiring larger assets, such as commercial real estate or advanced machinery, to support increased demand and expand operations.

Investing activities are reflected in the **balance sheet**, where assets are listed. These investments typically represent the most significant expenditures a business makes. However, while investing is essential for growth, it's crucial that these investments are strategically chosen. Poor investment decisions can drain a business's cash flow and leave it struggling to meet day-to-day expenses.

For example, imagine a startup investing heavily in marketing before building a strong customer base. While marketing is important, such an investment can lead to cash flow problems if the revenue doesn't keep up with the advertising costs. Proper accounting and financial planning ensure that investing activities are aligned with the business's financial capabilities and long-term goals.

How Accounting Helps Track and Manage These Core Functions

Accounting acts as the **record-keeper** for all these activities. In every business, the three core functions are continuously monitored and adjusted based on financial data and performance. Financial statements provide the blueprint for understanding the effectiveness of each function:

1. **The Income Statement**: Tracks revenue and expenses, showing whether the business is profitable. It reveals whether the company is generating enough revenue to cover its expenses and still make a profit.
2. **The Balance Sheet**: Shows the business's assets, liabilities, and equity at any given point in time. It provides a snapshot of the company's financial health and helps assess whether the business has enough assets to cover its liabilities.
3. **The Cash Flow Statement**: Tracks the inflow and outflow of cash, ensuring that the business has enough liquidity to meet its daily needs. A positive cash flow is crucial for sustaining operations, paying off debt, and investing in growth.

By keeping detailed records and using these financial reports, businesses can analyze their financial performance and make data-driven decisions. Whether a company needs to cut costs, invest in growth, or raise more capital, accounting helps provide the information necessary to make those decisions confidently.

Good accounting practices help ensure that each of these core activities works in harmony. They provide business owners and managers with the financial information necessary to make strategic choices, optimize operations, and ensure long-term success. Accounting is not just a technical function; it is an essential tool for understanding and guiding the direction of the business.

As we proceed through this guide, you will learn how accounting plays a role in each of these activities and how to use financial statements to make smarter, more confident business decisions.

Branches of Accounting

Accounting is a broad field with various specialized branches that cater to different aspects of financial management. While the core principles of accounting remain the same across industries, each branch focuses on specific areas of financial record-keeping, reporting, and analysis. Understanding these branches helps business owners, accountants, and financial professionals apply the right techniques and tools to manage their financial information effectively.

1. Bookkeeping: The Foundation of Accounting

Bookkeeping is the process of recording daily financial transactions in a systematic manner. It forms the foundation of the entire accounting process, as all other branches depend on the accuracy and organization of these initial records. Bookkeepers are responsible for tracking all the incoming and outgoing transactions, including sales, purchases, receipts, and payments.

Bookkeeping typically involves:

- **Recording Transactions**: This includes entering financial data into ledgers, journals, or accounting software, ensuring every transaction is captured accurately.
- **Classifying Transactions**: Once transactions are recorded, they need to be categorized into appropriate accounts, such as sales, expenses, assets, or liabilities.
- **Maintaining a Chart of Accounts**: A chart of accounts is a list of all the accounts used by a business to classify financial transactions. It helps bookkeepers stay organized and ensure consistency in the accounting process.

For example, if you own a retail store, a bookkeeper would track every sale made, record any inventory purchases, and maintain records of any business expenses. These activities provide the data necessary for generating the financial statements that a company uses to assess its performance.

While bookkeeping is often seen as a **routine task**, it is crucial for keeping financial data organized and accessible. Without accurate bookkeeping, the entire accounting process could fall apart, leading to errors in financial reporting and potential legal issues.

2. Financial Accounting: Reporting to Stakeholders

Financial accounting involves the preparation of financial statements that summarize a company's financial performance and position. It is primarily concerned with providing information to external stakeholders such as investors, creditors, and regulatory bodies. The primary financial statements prepared in financial accounting include the Income Statement, Balance Sheet, and Cash Flow Statement.

The main objective of financial accounting is to present an accurate picture of a business's financial health and performance over a specific period. This helps external stakeholders make informed decisions regarding investments, loans, or business partnerships.

Key aspects of financial accounting include:

- **Accurate Reporting**: Financial accounting adheres to Generally Accepted Accounting Principles (GAAP) or International Financial Reporting

Standards (IFRS), ensuring that financial statements are prepared consistently and transparently.

- **External Focus**: Unlike other branches of accounting, financial accounting is focused on external reporting. It provides a snapshot of a company's financial status and ensures that external parties can trust the company's financial information.
- **Compliance**: Companies must comply with legal and regulatory requirements when preparing financial statements. This includes tax reporting, audits, and filings with government agencies such as the Securities and Exchange Commission (SEC).

For example, if a company is looking to attract investors, the financial statements prepared by the accounting team will show whether the company is profitable, its current liabilities, and its ability to generate cash flow. These statements play a critical role in the investment decision-making process.

3. Managerial Accounting: Internal Decision Making

Managerial accounting, also known as **management accounting**, focuses on providing financial information to internal stakeholders, such as business owners, managers, and department heads. Unlike financial accounting, which is aimed at external reporting, managerial accounting supports strategic decision-making within the company.

Managerial accounting helps management evaluate the company's financial performance, plan for the future, and make day-to-day decisions. Key activities in managerial accounting include:

- **Budgeting and Forecasting**: Managerial accountants work closely with managers to create budgets that outline expected revenues and expenditures. These budgets guide business decisions and help monitor financial performance against actual results.
- **Cost Analysis**: Managerial accountants track and analyze costs to ensure the company is operating efficiently. They break down costs into **fixed** and **variable costs**, helping managers understand the cost structure of the business and identify areas for improvement.
- **Variance Analysis**: This process compares budgeted or forecasted performance against actual performance. Variance analysis helps managers identify discrepancies, understand their causes, and take corrective actions to stay on track.
- **Performance Evaluation**: Managerial accounting tools, such as **cost-volume-profit (CVP)** analysis, help evaluate business performance. These analyses assess the relationship between sales, production costs, and profitability, enabling managers to make data-driven decisions.

For example, a manager might use **break-even analysis**—a tool in managerial accounting—to determine the sales volume needed to cover fixed and variable costs. This information helps in setting pricing strategies and forecasting future profitability.

While financial accounting focuses on historical data, managerial accounting looks ahead. It provides businesses with the insights they need to improve performance, optimize operations, and increase profitability.

4. Tax Accounting: Ensuring Compliance with Tax Laws

Tax accounting is a branch of accounting that focuses on ensuring a business's compliance with tax laws and regulations. Tax accountants specialize in preparing tax returns, calculating tax liabilities, and advising businesses on tax strategies to minimize their tax burdens.

Tax accounting is governed by strict rules and laws set by local, state, and federal governments. This branch of accounting focuses on:

- **Tax Filing**: Tax accountants prepare and file tax returns for individuals, businesses, and other organizations. They calculate tax liabilities based on income, deductions, and credits available under tax laws.
- **Tax Deductions and Credits**: Tax accountants help businesses identify potential deductions and credits that can reduce their tax liabilities. These may include deductions for business expenses, such as rent, supplies, or employee salaries, and credits for activities like research and development or sustainable business practices.
- **Tax Planning and Strategy**: Tax accountants also provide guidance on tax-efficient strategies. This involves helping businesses structure their transactions, investments, and operations in a way that minimizes taxes while remaining compliant with the law. Proper tax planning can lead to significant savings for the business over time.
- **Compliance**: Tax accountants ensure that businesses adhere to tax laws, avoiding penalties, audits, or fines. This includes staying up to date on tax code changes and ensuring that all filings are completed correctly and on time.

For instance, if a company is planning to purchase new equipment, a tax accountant may advise on the most tax-efficient way to handle the purchase—whether through financing, leasing, or expensing it in the year of purchase.

Bookkeeping: The Basics

Bookkeeping is often the first step in the accounting process, but don't be fooled. Its importance cannot be overstated. Accurate and reliable bookkeeping is the foundation of every successful business, large or small. It involves recording every transaction the business makes, from sales and expenses to investments and loans. Without effective bookkeeping, a business cannot produce accurate financial statements, track cash flow, or make informed decisions. In this chapter, we will cover the essentials of bookkeeping: what it is, its key components, and how to do it effectively.

What is Bookkeeping?

Bookkeeping is the process of systematically recording all the financial transactions of a business. It is the groundwork upon which financial statements are built, helping business owners, managers, and accountants track the money coming in and going out of the business. Essentially, bookkeeping allows a business to maintain an accurate record of its financial activities, ensuring that financial reports are accurate and up to date.

The primary goal of bookkeeping is to ensure that every transaction is properly recorded, classified, and summarized in a way that is easily accessible. Bookkeepers use various tools, such as journals, ledgers, and accounting software, to document transactions and ensure that everything is accurate.

Key Components of Bookkeeping

Bookkeeping involves several key components, which include:

Recording Transactions: The first step in bookkeeping is recording all business transactions. These transactions include sales, purchases, payments, and receipts. Each transaction needs to be documented, detailing the amount, date, and nature of the transaction. This is typically done using accounting software or a paper-based system.

Categorizing Transactions: After recording transactions, the next step is categorizing them. Expenses and revenues are categorized into different accounts, such as rent, supplies, or sales revenue. Categorizing transactions makes it easier to track and report financial data. For example, expenses related to advertising might be recorded separately from those related to utility bills.

Maintaining a Chart of Accounts: The Chart of Accounts (COA) is a detailed list of all the accounts used by a business to classify its financial transactions. The COA is the foundation of bookkeeping, helping organize transactions into categories such as assets, liabilities, equity, revenue, and expenses. Each category is assigned a specific account number, making it easier to find and manage the records.

General Ledger: The general ledger is the master record of all financial transactions in a business. It contains detailed information about all the accounts in the Chart of Accounts. The general ledger serves as a central place to record and summarize financial activity, providing a comprehensive overview of the business's financial status.

Trial Balance: The trial balance is a summary of all the general ledger accounts, listing their balances at a specific point in time. It helps ensure that the books are balanced, meaning that the total of the debit entries matches the total of the credit entries. A trial balance is typically prepared at the end of an accounting period to verify the accuracy of the financial records before preparing financial statements.

The Bookkeeping Process

The bookkeeping process generally follows a set sequence of steps. While the process may vary slightly depending on the business and its accounting method (cash or accrual), the general process remains the same:

I. Record Transactions.

Every transaction that occurs in the business—whether it's a sale, purchase, or payment—needs to be recorded. For each transaction, the bookkeeper will write down the date, the amount, and the accounts affected.

Example: A business sells a product for $500. The transaction would be recorded as follows:

- Debit **Accounts Receivable** (Asset) for $500
- Credit **Sales Revenue** (Income) for $500

II. Classify Transactions

After recording, transactions are classified into the appropriate accounts. This ensures that financial data is organized correctly for later reporting.

Example: The $500 from the sale is classified as sales revenue, and the customer owes the business money, so it is recorded in Accounts Receivable.

III. Post to the General Ledger

After classifying the transactions, the bookkeeper will post them to the general ledger. Each transaction is transferred to its corresponding ledger account, such as accounts receivable, accounts payable, or sales revenue. This process allows for easy tracking of each account's balance.

IV. Prepare a Trial Balance

Once the transactions are posted, the next step is to prepare a trial balance. The trial balance ensures that all the credits and debits balance correctly. If the trial balance does not balance, the bookkeeper must find and correct the errors before moving forward.

V. Generate Financial Statements

After verifying the trial balance, the bookkeeper can prepare the financial statements: the Income Statement, Balance Sheet, and Cash Flow Statement. These statements are based on the data in the general ledger and trial balance.

VI. Close the Books

At the end of each accounting period, the bookkeeper will close the books by transferring the temporary accounts (such as revenue and expenses) to permanent accounts, such as retained earnings. This process resets the temporary accounts for the next period.

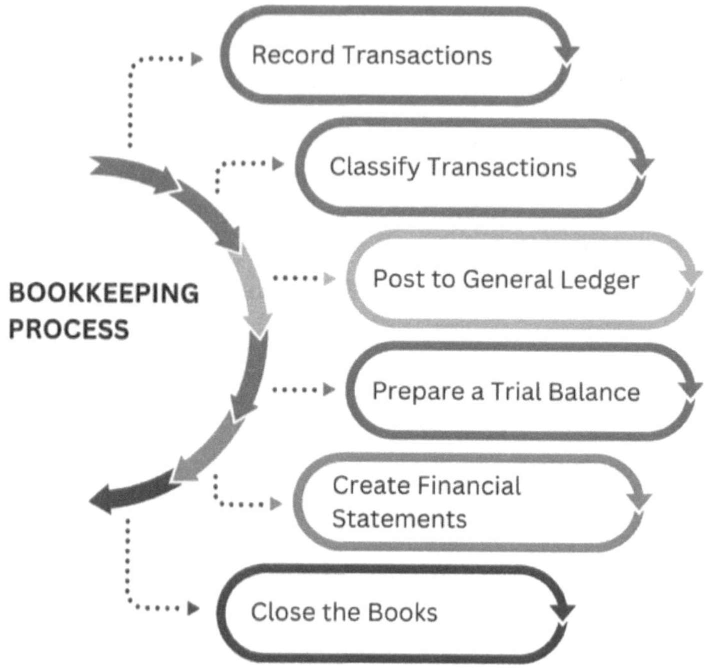

Bookkeeping Methods: Cash vs. Accrual

When it comes to bookkeeping, businesses can choose between two primary methods: **cash accounting** and **accrual accounting**. The method you choose affects how and when transactions are recorded.

Cash Accounting	Accrual Accounting
Transactions are recorded when cash is received or paid.	Transactions are recorded when they occur, regardless of when cash changes hands.
Revenue is recognized only when payment is received.	Revenue is recognized when it is earned, even if payment is received later.
Expenses are recorded when they are paid.	Expenses are recorded when they are incurred, not when they are paid.
Simpler and easier to track, ideal for small businesses.	More complex, provides a more accurate representation of a business's financial health.

Cash Accounting	Accrual Accounting
Easier to track the actual cash flow since transactions are recorded only when cash changes hands.	Can provide a distorted view of cash flow since revenues and expenses are recorded regardless of cash transactions.
Often used by small businesses and individuals due to its simplicity.	Used by larger businesses and those with more complex financial operations.
A sale in January is recorded in February when payment is received.	A sale in January is recorded in January, even if payment is received in February.
Provides a simpler snapshot of cash inflow and outflow.	Provides a more comprehensive picture of the company's financial performance, including accounts receivable and payable.
Typically results in simpler tax reporting. However, taxes are paid when cash is received.	Tax reporting is more detailed and may result in taxes being owed even before cash is actually received.
May not give a clear picture of a company's profitability and financial position if significant credit sales or purchases are involved.	Provides a more accurate reflection of a company's financial health, even if payment has not yet been made.
Suitable for businesses with simpler operations and those that don't carry large inventories or have significant credit transactions.	Suitable for larger businesses or those with more complex financial structures, including inventory and credit.

The Role of Bookkeepers in Business

Bookkeepers play a crucial role in ensuring that the financial data is accurate, organized, and accessible. Their responsibilities extend beyond simply recording transactions—they also provide insights into the financial health of the business. Bookkeepers work closely with accountants to prepare for audits, generate financial statements, and ensure tax compliance. The key responsibilities of a bookkeeper include:

- **Daily transaction recording**: Ensuring that all financial transactions are recorded promptly and accurately.
- **Account reconciliation**: Comparing the business's records with bank statements to ensure accuracy.
- **Expense management**: Tracking business expenses and making sure that spending stays within budget.
- **Payroll processing**: Calculating employee wages, withholding taxes, and ensuring timely payroll distribution.

Bookkeeping Best Practices

To ensure the effectiveness of bookkeeping, businesses should follow some best practices:

- **Maintain accurate records**: Always record transactions as soon as they occur, and ensure all receipts, invoices, and other documentation are kept for reference.
- **Separate personal and business finances**: Avoid mixing personal and business accounts. This practice helps ensure the accuracy of financial records and simplifies tax preparation.
- **Use accounting software**: Accounting software like **QuickBooks** or **Xero** can help automate bookkeeping tasks and ensure greater accuracy.
- **Review financial statements regularly**: Regularly review your financial reports to monitor cash flow, expenses, and profitability.

Financial Accounting

The primary goal of financial accounting is to provide a true and fair representation of a company's financial performance and position. This helps external stakeholders, such as investors, creditors, and regulatory bodies, make informed decisions about whether to invest in, lend money to, or do business with the company.

At its core, financial accounting provides answers to three essential questions:

1. **What is the company's financial performance?**

   This includes determining how much revenue the company earned, what expenses it incurred, and whether it made a profit or a loss.

2. **What is the company's financial position?**

   This involves understanding what the company owns (assets), what it owes (liabilities), and the owners' equity in the business.

3. **What is the company's cash flow situation?**

   This focuses on understanding the inflows and outflows of cash, which is essential for assessing whether the company can meet its short-term financial obligations.

Key Financial Statements

Financial accounting relies heavily on three primary financial statements, which provide detailed insights into the company's financial performance and position. These statements include:

I. Income Statement

The Income Statement summarizes a company's revenues, expenses, and profits over a specific period (typically a month, quarter, or year). This statement shows whether the company is generating enough income to cover its expenses and still make a profit. It is often referred to as the **Profit and Loss Statement** because it reveals how much profit or loss a company has made during the reporting period.

- **Revenue**: The total amount of money earned from sales of goods or services.
- **Expenses**: The costs incurred in running the business, including operating expenses, cost of goods sold (COGS), salaries, rent, and taxes.
- **Net Profit or Loss**: The bottom line of the income statement, which is calculated by subtracting total expenses from total revenue. If revenues exceed expenses, the company has a net profit; if expenses exceed revenue, the company has a net loss.

Example:

- Revenue: $500,000
- Expenses: $350,000
- **Net Profit**: $150,000

The income statement is important because it helps assess the profitability of a business, which is a key factor for investors and creditors.

II. Balance Sheet

The **Balance Sheet** provides a snapshot of a company's **financial position** at a specific point in time. It details what the company owns (assets), what it owes (liabilities), and the equity invested by the owners. The balance sheet follows the accounting equation:

Assets = Liabilities + Owner's Equity

Assets: Resources owned by the company that are expected to bring future economic benefits. Assets are classified into two categories: **current assets** (e.g., cash, accounts receivable) and **non-current assets** (e.g., property, equipment, intellectual property).

Liabilities: Obligations that the company must settle in the future, such as loans, accounts payable, and accrued expenses. Liabilities are also divided into **current liabilities** (e.g., accounts payable, short-term debt) and **non-current liabilities** (e.g., long-term debt, pension obligations).

Owner's Equity: The residual interest in the assets of the business after deducting liabilities. This represents the owners' stake in the business and is often referred to as **shareholder equity** in corporations. It can include **retained earnings**, which are profits that have been reinvested into the business rather than paid out as dividends.

Example:

Assets: $1,000,000

Liabilities: $600,000

Owner's Equity: $400,000

The balance sheet is important because it provides insight into a company's financial health and its ability to meet short- and long-term obligations. A strong balance sheet with more assets than liabilities is a sign of a financially stable business.

3. **Cash Flow Statement**

The Cash Flow Statement tracks the movement of cash in and out of the business during a specified period. Unlike the income statement, which records revenues and expenses based on accrual accounting, the cash flow statement focuses solely on actual cash transactions. This is critical for understanding a company's ability to meet its day-to-day financial obligations and manage liquidity.

The cash flow statement is divided into three sections:

Operating Activities: This section shows the cash generated or used by the company's core business operations, such as cash received from customers and cash paid to suppliers and employees.

Investing Activities: This section includes cash spent on buying or selling long-term assets, such as property, equipment, and investments.

Financing Activities: This section shows the cash flows associated with borrowing or repaying debt, issuing stock, and paying dividends to shareholders.

Example:

Operating Activities: Cash Inflow: $200,000, Cash Outflow: $150,000

Investing Activities: Cash Outflow (for new equipment): $50,000

Financing Activities: Cash Inflow (loan received): $100,000

The cash flow statement is important because it helps determine the liquidity of a business and its ability to generate cash for expansion, debt repayment, and other financial needs.

Accounting Principles and Standards

Financial accounting is governed by certain accounting principles and standards to ensure consistency, transparency, and accuracy in financial reporting. These include:

1. **Generally Accepted Accounting Principles (GAAP)**: In the United

States, companies must adhere to GAAP, a set of standards and guidelines developed by the **Financial Accounting Standards Board (FASB)**. GAAP ensures that financial statements are prepared consistently and transparently, making it easier for stakeholders to compare financial performance across companies.

2. **International Financial Reporting Standards (IFRS)**: Outside the United States, companies typically follow **IFRS**, a set of global accounting standards issued by the **International Accounting Standards Board (IASB)**. IFRS shares many similarities with GAAP but also has some differences, particularly in areas like asset valuation and revenue recognition.
3. **Accrual Basis of Accounting**: Financial accounting generally follows the **accrual basis**, which means that revenue and expenses are recognized when earned or incurred, not when cash is received or paid. This method provides a more accurate picture of a company's financial health, as it accounts for transactions as they occur, regardless of cash flow timing.
4. **Consistency**: Financial statements must be prepared using consistent methods from year to year. If a company changes its accounting methods, it must disclose the reasons for the change and its impact on the financial statements.

The Importance of Financial Accounting for Stakeholders

Financial accounting is essential for providing **reliable financial information** to external stakeholders, including:

Investors: Investors rely on financial statements to assess a company's profitability, financial position, and growth potential. They use these statements to determine whether the company is a good investment opportunity.

Creditors and Lenders: Banks and other creditors use financial accounting data to evaluate the company's ability to repay loans or credit. Lenders assess the company's cash flow, profitability, and financial stability before granting credit.

Regulatory Agencies: Government agencies, such as the Securities and Exchange Commission (SEC), require publicly traded companies to file accurate and transparent financial statements to protect investors and ensure compliance with tax and financial regulations.

Management: While managerial accounting focuses on internal decision-making, financial accounting provides management with a clear overview of the company's financial health, enabling them to make informed decisions regarding growth, investments, and cost control.

Managerial Accounting: Making Informed Decisions

Managerial accounting plays a pivotal role in helping business owners and managers make informed decisions that drive the success of the business. Unlike financial accounting, which focuses on providing information for external stakeholders such as investors and creditors, managerial accounting is designed for **internal decision-making**. It helps businesses analyze their financial performance, set budgets, manage costs, and plan for future growth. The goal is to provide actionable insights that assist in improving the company's profitability and operational efficiency.

In this section, we'll explore what managerial accounting entails, how it differs from financial accounting, and the key tools and techniques used by managers to make strategic decisions. We will also cover the importance of cost management, budgeting, and variance analysis—essential components of managerial accounting that contribute to better decision-making.

What is Managerial Accounting?

Managerial accounting involves the collection, analysis, and interpretation of financial data to help managers make well-informed business decisions. This branch of accounting is more **forward-looking** than financial accounting, focusing not only on recording past transactions but also on forecasting future outcomes and guiding decisions that affect business operations.

The key difference between managerial accounting and financial accounting is that managerial accounting is internal to the company, whereas financial accounting focuses on reporting to external stakeholders. Managerial accounting is dynamic and provides insights that help businesses plan, control, and analyze their financial performance in real time.

Some examples of managerial accounting activities include:

- **Cost analysis** to determine the expense of producing goods or services.
- **Budgeting** to set financial goals and allocate resources effectively.
- **Forecasting** to predict future financial outcomes.
- **Variance analysis** to compare budgeted amounts to actual performance.

Key Tools and Techniques in Managerial Accounting

Managerial accounting relies on several key tools and techniques that help managers make informed decisions. These tools help businesses evaluate performance, plan for the future, and manage costs effectively. Let's take a look at the most common tools and techniques used in **managerial accounting**:

I. Cost-Volume-Profit (CVP) Analysis

Cost-Volume-Profit (CVP) analysis, also known as break-even analysis, is a technique used to understand how changes in cost and volume affect a business's operating profit. CVP analysis is crucial for determining the break-even point, which is the level of sales at which total revenue equals total costs—resulting in neither a profit nor a loss.

CVP analysis helps businesses understand the relationships between:

Fixed costs: Costs that do not change regardless of the level of production or sales (e.g., rent, salaries).

Variable costs: Costs that vary depending on the level of production or sales (e.g., materials, commissions).

Sales price: The amount earned from each unit sold.

By understanding these relationships, businesses can determine how many units they need to sell to cover their costs and generate a profit.

For example, if a company sells a product for $50, with variable costs of $20 per unit and fixed costs of $10,000, CVP analysis would help the business calculate the break-even point, the number of units that need to be sold to cover both variable and fixed costs.

II. Costing Methods: Job Order and Process Costing

Job Order Costing and Process Costing are two methods used to allocate costs to products or services. Both are important tools in managerial accounting for managing and controlling costs.

- **Job Order Costing**: This method is used when products are made based on specific customer orders. Costs are traced and allocated to individual jobs or batches. For example, a custom furniture manufacturer uses job order costing to track the costs of labor, materials, and overhead for each unique piece of furniture.
- **Process Costing**: This method is used when products are produced in a continuous flow, and individual units are not easily distinguishable from one another. Process costing is common in industries like oil refining or food production. Costs are accumulated by department or process and then allocated to the units produced during that period.

Both costing methods help businesses determine the **cost per unit** of production, which is essential for pricing, budgeting, and profitability analysis.

III. Budgeting: Planning for Financial Success

Budgeting is one of the most important aspects of managerial accounting. It involves creating a financial plan for the business that sets goals for revenue, expenses, and profitability. Budgets act as a financial blueprint, guiding decisions on how resources should be allocated across different areas of the business.

The two main types of budgets in managerial accounting are:

- **Operating Budgets**: These budgets cover the daily expenses of running a business, such as salaries, materials, rent, and utilities. They help businesses plan for the short-term, typically for a month, quarter, or year.
- **Capital Budgets**: These budgets are used for long-term investments,

such as purchasing new equipment, expanding facilities, or launching new products. Capital budgets help businesses assess the feasibility and financial impact of large investments.

By comparing budgeted figures to actual performance, businesses can determine whether they are on track to meet their financial goals or if corrective actions are needed.

IV. Variance Analysis

Variance analysis is a technique used to compare actual performance to budgeted performance. By examining the differences (or variances) between what was expected and what actually occurred, managers can identify areas where performance deviated from expectations. This analysis helps businesses determine why the variance occurred and what corrective actions need to be taken.

There are two main types of variances:

- **Favorable Variance**: This occurs when actual revenue is higher than expected or actual costs are lower than budgeted. A favorable variance is a positive indicator of business performance.
- **Unfavorable Variance**: This occurs when actual revenue is lower than expected or actual costs are higher than budgeted. An unfavorable variance may signal problems that need to be addressed, such as overspending, poor sales performance, or inefficiency in operations.

For example, if a business budgeted $5,000 for materials but actually spent $6,000, it would have an unfavorable variance of $1,000. By analyzing the cause of this variance, such as higher material costs or poor purchasing decisions, the business can take steps to prevent similar issues in the future.

Cost Management: Keeping Expenses in Check

Effective cost management is a key component of managerial accounting. By carefully tracking and controlling costs, businesses can improve their profitability and remain competitive in the market. Managerial accountants use various techniques to manage and allocate costs efficiently.

Some common cost management techniques include:

Activity-Based Costing (ABC): This method allocates overhead costs based on the activities that drive those costs. For example, if a company manufactures multiple products, ABC helps allocate overhead costs (such as utilities and salaries) based on which products require more resources.

Standard Costing: Standard costing involves setting a predetermined cost for each unit of production and comparing the actual cost to the standard cost. This helps businesses identify inefficiencies and control expenses.

Cost-Volume-Profit Analysis (CVP): As mentioned earlier, CVP analysis helps businesses understand how changes in costs, sales volume, and pricing affect profitability. It is a valuable tool for businesses to make strategic pricing, production, and sales decisions.

The Role of Managerial Accounting in Strategic Decision-Making

Managerial accounting provides businesses with the information they need to make informed strategic decisions. Whether it's expanding into a new market, investing in new technology, or launching a new product, the insights gained from managerial accounting help business leaders assess the financial feasibility and long-term impact of these decisions.

For example, when considering whether to launch a new product line, a business would use CVP analysis to determine how many units it needs to sell to break even and become profitable. Similarly, budgeting helps ensure that the company has the necessary resources to support the new product launch and that expenses are kept in line with expected revenues.

Tax Accounting Essentials

Tax accounting is a crucial branch of accounting that focuses on ensuring a business complies with tax laws and regulations. Every business, whether it's a small startup or a large corporation, must understand the tax implications of its financial activities. Tax accounting helps businesses calculate tax liabilities, prepare tax returns, and ensure compliance with local, state, and federal tax laws. In this section, we will cover the essentials of tax accounting, including the types of taxes businesses are subject to, common tax strategies, and the role of tax accountants in managing business taxes.

Tax accounting is the process of preparing tax returns, calculating taxes owed, and ensuring compliance with tax regulations. Unlike financial accounting, which focuses on providing information to external stakeholders like investors and creditors, tax accounting is focused on ensuring that a business adheres to tax laws and minimizes its tax burden while staying within legal boundaries.

Tax accountants specialize in understanding complex tax laws and applying them to a business's financial situation. Their role is to help businesses calculate their tax obligations, identify deductions, and make sure they are in compliance with all relevant tax codes. This can involve corporate taxes, income taxes, payroll taxes, and sales taxes—depending on the type of business.

STARBUCKS' COMPLIANCE ADJUSTMENT

In 2012, Starbucks faced public scrutiny regarding its tax strategy in the UK, where it was revealed that the company had paid minimal tax despite earning substantial revenues.

CHALLENGES

- Facing Public Backlash Over Tax Strategies
- Ensuring Tax Compliance Amid Complex Regulations

OBJECTIVES

OPTIMIZE TAX STRATEGIES

Ensure compliance with tax laws while minimizing tax liabilities.

IMPROVE TRANSPARENCY

Respond to public scrutiny by ensuring greater transparency in tax reporting.

RESULT AND BENEFITS

- Starbucks revamped its tax reporting to ensure clearer and more transparent financial disclosures.
- By changing its tax practices, Starbucks improved its reputation and regained consumer confidence.
- Starbucks implemented tax strategies that aligned with regulations while reducing future liabilities.

Types of Taxes Businesses Face

Businesses face several different types of taxes, each of which has its own rules, regulations, and compliance requirements. Below are the most common types of taxes that businesses must account for:

I. Income Taxes

Income tax is the tax levied on a business's profits. This is one of the most common and significant taxes for businesses. Businesses are required to pay income tax on their net income, which is calculated by subtracting expenses (such as salaries, rent, and materials) from revenue.

- **Sole Proprietorships** and **partnerships** are taxed on the owner's personal income tax return, meaning they do not file separate tax returns for the business.
- **Corporations**, on the other hand, are taxed separately from their owners. This means the business files its own tax return, and the income is taxed at the corporate tax rate.

Corporate income tax rates vary by country, region, and the size of the business. For example, in the U.S., corporations pay a flat **21% federal tax rate**, though state and local taxes may also apply.

II. Payroll Taxes

Payroll taxes are taxes withheld from an employee's paycheck and paid to the government by the employer. These taxes include:

- **Social Security**: A federal tax that provides benefits for retirees, the disabled, and survivors.
- **Medicare**: A tax that funds the Medicare program, which provides health care for those over the age of 65 or with certain disabilities.
- **Unemployment Taxes**: Employers are also required to pay federal and state unemployment taxes to fund unemployment benefits.

Payroll taxes are a significant responsibility for businesses because they must both withhold and match the employee's contribution. Employers are responsible for ensuring that these taxes are calculated and paid correctly, both for the employee's portion and the employer's portion.

III. Sales Taxes

Sales tax is a tax levied on the sale of goods and services. The consumer typically pays the sales tax at the time of purchase, but the business is responsible for collecting and remitting the tax to the government.

- **Sales tax rates** vary depending on the state or country. In some regions, sales tax is **applicable only to certain types of goods** (e.g., tangible products), while in others, it applies to most goods and services.
- **Sales tax compliance** is critical because businesses must collect the right

amount of tax, file returns regularly, and remit the collected taxes to the tax authorities.

Many states also require businesses to obtain a sales tax permit to legally collect and remit taxes.

IV. Property Taxes

Property tax is a tax levied on real estate and personal property owned by a business. In the U.S., businesses are required to pay property taxes on real property (e.g., land and buildings) and sometimes on personal property (e.g., machinery, equipment, and furniture). Property taxes are generally assessed by local governments and can vary significantly based on the property's value and location.

V. Excise Taxes

Excise taxes are taxes imposed on specific goods and services. These are typically indirect taxes paid by the manufacturer or seller, who may pass the cost onto consumers. Common excise taxes apply to products such as gasoline, tobacco, and alcohol.

Businesses that manufacture, import, or sell goods subject to excise taxes must ensure compliance with reporting and payment requirements.

Key Tax Accounting Strategies

Tax accounting involves more than just ensuring compliance with tax laws—it also includes strategies that help businesses minimize their tax liabilities. Below are some of the most common tax strategies used by businesses:

I. Tax Deductions

Tax deductions reduce the amount of taxable income a business reports. Certain business expenses can be deducted from a business's income, which in turn reduces the business's tax liability. Common tax deductions include:

- **Operating expenses**: These are costs necessary for running the business, such as rent, salaries, utilities, and supplies.
- **Depreciation**: Businesses can deduct the cost of certain assets (e.g., equipment or property) over time, as these assets lose value.
- **Interest on business loans**: Interest payments on loans taken to finance business activities can be deducted.
- **Professional fees**: Fees paid to accountants, lawyers, and consultants are generally deductible.

II. Tax Credits

Tax credits are another way businesses can reduce their tax liabilities. Unlike deductions, which lower taxable income, tax credits reduce the actual amount of tax owed. Examples of tax credits available to businesses include:

- **Research and Development (R&D) Tax Credit**: Businesses that invest in R&D activities may qualify for this tax credit.

- **Energy Efficiency Tax Credits**: Some governments offer tax credits to businesses that make energy-efficient upgrades to their facilities.

Tax credits are generally more beneficial than deductions because they directly reduce the tax liability rather than just lowering taxable income.

III. Tax Deferral Strategies

Tax deferral allows businesses to postpone paying taxes until a future period. This strategy can be particularly helpful for improving cash flow or financing growth. Common tax deferral strategies include:

- **Retirement Plans**: Contributions to certain types of retirement plans, like a 401(k), may be deferred until the employee withdraws the funds.
- **Deferred Income**: Businesses can defer income recognition to future periods, particularly in cases of long-term contracts or sales where the revenue will be earned over time.

IV. Choosing the Right Business Structure

The structure of a business (e.g., sole proprietorship, partnership, corporation, LLC) significantly affects how it is taxed. Businesses may choose their structure based on tax implications:

- **Sole Proprietorships** and **Partnerships** are taxed on the owner's personal income tax return, which may result in simpler tax filing and lower overall tax rates for small businesses.
- **Corporations** are taxed separately from their owners, and the business pays taxes on its income. However, corporations may also be eligible for certain tax breaks and deductions that sole proprietors and partnerships are not.
- **LLCs** (Limited Liability Companies) offer flexibility in taxation, as they can choose to be taxed as a sole proprietorship, partnership, or corporation.

Choosing the right structure is a critical decision that impacts how much tax the business will pay and how tax laws are applied to its operations.

The Role of Tax Accountants

Tax accountants play an essential role in ensuring that businesses comply with tax laws and optimize their tax positions. They are responsible for:

- **Preparing and filing tax returns**: Tax accountants ensure that tax returns are prepared accurately and submitted on time to avoid penalties.
- **Advising on tax planning**: They help businesses develop strategies to minimize taxes, including recommending deductions, credits, and other tax-saving opportunities.
- **Navigating tax laws**: Tax accountants stay updated on changes to tax laws

and regulations and help businesses adapt to new rules.

- **Representing the business in case of an audit**: If a business is audited by tax authorities, tax accountants represent the company and ensure that the audit process is smooth.

Whether you are just starting your business or looking to optimize your existing tax strategy, understanding tax accounting is key to managing your company's finances efficiently.

The Accounting Cycle: Understanding the Flow

The accounting cycle is a systematic process used by businesses to track and record financial transactions. It ensures that all transactions are properly documented, classified, and summarized to prepare accurate financial statements. The cycle is essential for maintaining financial accuracy and transparency, allowing businesses to manage their operations efficiently and comply with regulatory requirements.

In this section, we will break down the accounting cycle step by step, explaining each phase and its role in the overall process. Whether you are running a small business or managing a large corporation, understanding the accounting cycle is fundamental for making informed financial decisions and maintaining accurate records.

What is the Accounting Cycle?

The accounting cycle is a repetitive series of steps that companies follow to record their financial transactions and generate financial statements. This cycle occurs over a specific accounting period—usually a month, quarter, or year—and ends with the preparation of financial reports, such as the Income Statement, Balance Sheet, and Cash Flow Statement.

The cycle is designed to ensure that each transaction is accurately recorded and classified, that financial information is consistently summarized, and that reports are prepared in accordance with generally accepted accounting principles (GAAP) or International Financial Reporting Standards (IFRS). It also helps businesses identify discrepancies, correct errors, and provide reliable financial data to internal and external stakeholders.

The Steps of the Accounting Cycle

The accounting cycle consists of eight main steps, each of which plays a crucial role in ensuring the accuracy and completeness of financial records. Let's walk through these steps:

1. Identifying and Analyzing Transactions

The first step in the accounting cycle is identifying and analyzing financial transactions. Every business activity that involves a financial exchange must be recorded. These transactions may include:

- **Sales** of goods or services
- **Purchases** of inventory or assets
- **Payments** of expenses
- **Receipts** from customers
- **Loans or investments**

Each transaction must be analyzed to determine what accounts are affected and whether the transaction involves a **debit** or a **credit**. For example, when a business sells a product, the revenue account is increased, and the accounts receivable or cash account is also impacted.

Example: A company sells products for $1,000 on credit.

- **Debit**: Accounts Receivable (Asset) +$1,000
- **Credit**: Sales Revenue (Income) +$1,000

2. Recording Transactions in the Journal

After transactions are identified and analyzed, they are recorded in a journal. This process is known as journalizing. The journal serves as the initial point of entry for all financial transactions, providing a chronological record of events.

Each journal entry contains a date, a description of the transaction, and the accounts affected (with debits and credits). Transactions are recorded using the double-entry system, which ensures that for every debit entry, there is an equal and opposite credit entry.

Example Journal Entry:

- **Date**: January 1st
- **Debit**: Accounts Receivable (Asset) $1,000
- **Credit**: Sales Revenue (Income) $1,000

3. Posting to the General Ledger

Once the transactions are recorded in the journal, the next step is to post them to the general ledger. The general ledger is a collection of accounts used to categorize and summarize the business's financial transactions. Each account in the general ledger has a unique balance and reflects the cumulative total of all journal entries related to that account.

Posting from the journal to the ledger allows the business to track how each account is affected by transactions over time. The ledger helps identify the **balance** of each account at any given point.

Example: Posting the journal entry for sales:

- **Accounts Receivable**: Debit $1,000 (increases asset)
- **Sales Revenue**: Credit $1,000 (increases income)

4. Preparing an Unadjusted Trial Balance

Once all journal entries have been posted to the general ledger, the next step is to prepare an unadjusted trial balance. The trial balance is a list of all the accounts in the general ledger, along with their balances (either debit or credit). The trial balance ensures that the total **debits** equal the total **credits**, serving as a preliminary check for accuracy.

If the debits and credits do not match, it indicates that an error has occurred in the journalizing or posting process, and adjustments are needed.

Example: A trial balance might show:

- **Total Debits**: $10,000
- **Total Credits**: $10,000

5. Making Adjusting Entries

At the end of the accounting period, adjusting entries are made to ensure that the financial statements reflect the true financial position of the business. Adjusting entries are necessary for accrual accounting because certain revenues and expenses may not have been recorded yet, or the timing of revenue and expense recognition needs to be adjusted.

Common types of adjusting entries include:

- **Accrued Revenues**: Revenue earned but not yet received or recorded.
- **Accrued Expenses**: Expenses incurred but not yet paid or recorded.
- **Deferred Revenues**: Revenue received in advance of providing goods or services.
- **Prepaid Expenses**: Payments made in advance for expenses that will be incurred in future periods.

These adjustments ensure that the Income Statement and Balance Sheet are accurate and reflect the correct timing of revenue and expenses.

6. Preparing an Adjusted Trial Balance

After the adjusting entries are made, the next step is to prepare an adjusted trial balance. This version of the trial balance reflects the changes made by the adjusting entries and is used to verify that the debits and credits are still balanced after adjustments.

The adjusted trial balance is a critical step because it provides the final balances

that will be used to prepare the company's financial statements.

7. Preparing Financial Statements

Once the adjusted trial balance is prepared, the next step is to use this data to prepare the business's financial statements. The financial statements are the core outputs of the accounting cycle and include:

- **Income Statement**: Shows the business's profitability by detailing revenues, expenses, and the net income or loss for the period.
- **Balance Sheet**: Displays the company's assets, liabilities, and equity at a specific point in time.
- **Cash Flow Statement**: Summarizes the company's cash inflows and outflows, showing how cash was generated and used during the period.

Financial statements are essential for internal decision-making and are also required for external reporting to investors, creditors, and regulatory agencies.

8. Closing the Books

The final step in the accounting cycle is to **close the books** for the accounting period. Closing the books involves resetting the temporary accounts—such as **revenues** and **expenses**—to zero so that they can begin the next accounting period with a clean slate. This process involves transferring the balances from the income statement to the **retained earnings** account on the balance sheet.

After closing the books, the company is ready to start the accounting cycle again for the next period. The **closing entries** ensure that the financial statements for the period are finalized and accurate, and any profit or loss is transferred to retained earnings.

Understanding the accounting cycle helps business owners and managers gain better insights into their company's financial position, make data-driven decisions, and plan for the future. It is a fundamental process that keeps financial operations organized, transparent, and reliable.

Accounting Principles: A Foundation for Everything

Accounting principles form the bedrock upon which all accounting practices are built. They provide a standard set of guidelines that ensure financial statements are accurate, reliable, and consistent across businesses and industries. These principles help maintain the integrity of financial reporting, making it easier for stakeholders—including investors, creditors, regulators, and management—to understand and compare financial information.

In this section, we will explore the fundamental accounting principles that govern the way businesses record and report their financial activities. These principles serve as the foundation for accounting practices worldwide, ensuring that financial information is presented clearly, fairly, and in compliance with regulations. We'll cover the Generally Accepted Accounting Principles (GAAP) and the International Financial Reporting Standards (IFRS), as well as the core concepts that guide accounting decisions.

What are Accounting Principles?

Accounting principles are rules or guidelines that accountants follow to record and report financial transactions. These principles are essential because they help standardize accounting practices, ensuring that financial statements are consistent and understandable. Accounting principles are designed to protect stakeholders by ensuring that financial data is presented accurately and fairly.

The two primary sets of accounting standards that guide businesses around the world are:

1. **Generally Accepted Accounting Principles (GAAP):** These principles are used in the United States and are developed by the Financial Accounting Standards Board (FASB).
2. **International Financial Reporting Standards (IFRS):** These standards are used internationally and are developed by the International Accounting Standards Board (IASB).

While there are some differences between GAAP and IFRS, both aim to provide transparency, consistency, and comparability in financial reporting. The fundamental accounting principles are largely similar across both standards.

The Core Accounting Principles

The core accounting principles that businesses follow are designed to ensure that financial data is both reliable and relevant for decision-making. Let's examine these principles in more detail.

I. The Revenue Recognition Principle

The Revenue Recognition Principle dictates that revenue should be recognized when it is earned, regardless of when cash is received. This principle helps businesses recognize income at the time it is generated, rather than when payment is made. The timing of revenue recognition is crucial because it impacts the accuracy of financial reporting.

Example: If a business provides a service in March but does not receive payment until April, the revenue should still be recognized in March when the service was provided, not when the payment was received. This ensures that the income is recorded in the period it was earned, providing a more accurate representation of the business's financial performance.

II. The Matching Principle

The Matching Principle states that expenses should be recognized in the same period as the revenues they help generate. This principle is important because it ensures that financial statements reflect the true profitability of a business by matching costs with associated revenues.

- **Example**: If a business incurs advertising costs in January that are directly related to sales made in February, the advertising expenses should be recorded in February, even though the payment for the advertising was made in January. This ensures that the costs are matched with the revenue they helped generate.

III. The Cost Principle

The Cost Principle (also known as the Historical Cost Principle) dictates that assets should be recorded at their original cost at the time of purchase, rather than their current market value. This principle provides a clear, objective way to value assets, ensuring consistency in financial reporting.

- **Example**: If a company buys a building for $500,000, the building will be recorded on the balance sheet at that price, regardless of any changes in the market value over time. If the market value increases or decreases, the asset is still reported at the original cost, unless it is sold or otherwise disposed of.

IV. The Full Disclosure Principle

The Full Disclosure Principle requires that all relevant financial information be disclosed in the financial statements or in the notes to the financial statements. This principle ensures that users of financial statements have access to all the information they need to make informed decisions.

- **Example**: If a company is involved in a lawsuit, the financial statements must disclose the potential financial impact of the lawsuit, even if the outcome is uncertain. This provides transparency and allows investors and creditors to assess the potential risks associated with the business.

V. The Consistency Principle

The Consistency Principle states that businesses should use the same accounting methods and procedures from one period to the next. This principle ensures that financial statements are consistent over time, making it easier for stakeholders to compare performance across periods.

- **Example**: If a business uses the straight-line method to depreciate its assets in one year, it must continue to use the same method in future periods. If the business changes its depreciation method, it must disclose the change and explain why it was made.

VI. The Conservatism Principle

The Conservatism Principle dictates that accountants should choose methods that result in lower profits and asset valuations when there is uncertainty. This principle ensures that financial statements are cautious, recognizing potential losses sooner than gains. The goal is to avoid overestimating assets or revenue and underestimating liabilities or expenses.

- **Example**: If a company is unsure whether an account receivable will be paid, the business would record a doubtful accounts expense to reflect the potential loss. On the other hand, if the business expects a future gain, such as from a pending lawsuit settlement, it would not record the gain until it is more certain.

VII. The Economic Entity Principle

The Economic Entity Principle states that the financial activities of a business must be separate from the financial activities of its owners, employees, and other businesses. This principle ensures that personal transactions do not affect the financial statements of the company.

- **Example**: If a business owner withdraws money from the business for personal use, this transaction should be recorded as an owner's drawing and should not be mixed with business expenses or income. Keeping personal and business finances separate ensures that financial statements accurately reflect the company's operations.

VIII. The Going Concern Principle

The Going Concern Principle assumes that a business will continue to operate for the foreseeable future. This principle allows businesses to defer the recognition of certain expenses, such as depreciation, over time, rather than recognizing them all at once.

- **Example**: If a company purchases a building that will be used for many years, the cost of the building is spread over its useful life rather than being recorded as a single expense in the year of purchase. The going concern assumption allows businesses to allocate costs in a way that reflects the long-term nature of their operations.

IX. The Monetary Unit Principle

The Monetary Unit Principle assumes that business transactions can be measured and expressed in terms of money. This principle simplifies financial reporting by allowing businesses to focus on monetary values rather than non-monetary aspects.

- **Example**: A company may own equipment, land, or intellectual property, but these assets are reported in terms of their monetary value. The company's financial statements are based on dollars, euros, or other currencies, providing a standard unit for comparing financial performance.

Accounting principles are essential because they ensure that financial information is reliable, consistent, and comparable across businesses. These principles provide the foundation for generating accurate financial statements, making them crucial for stakeholders who rely on this data to make informed decisions. Whether you're an investor analyzing a company's performance, a business owner tracking profitability, or a financial analyst preparing a report, understanding and following these principles ensures that the financial information you work with is both credible and meaningful.

By adhering to these accounting principles, businesses can not only ensure compliance with regulations, but they can also build trust with external stakeholders. Furthermore, these principles help businesses make strategic financial decisions, plan for growth, and evaluate operational effectiveness. In short, accounting principles are the backbone of financial reporting and the foundation of everything related to the world of business accounting.

Chapter 2: Financial Accounting

The Income Statement: What It Tells You

The Income Statement is one of the most important financial statements a business can prepare. It provides a summary of a company's revenues, expenses, and profits over a specified period, typically a month, quarter, or year. Also known as the Profit and Loss Statement (P&L), the Income Statement helps business owners, investors, creditors, and other stakeholders understand how efficiently a business is generating profit from its operations.

In this section, we'll dive deep into the components of the Income Statement, explore how to read and interpret it, and discuss its importance in assessing a company's financial performance. We'll also look at how the Income Statement fits into the broader context of financial reporting and decision-making.

What is the Income Statement?

The Income Statement is a financial report that shows a company's financial performance over a specific period. It summarizes:

- **Revenue**: The total income earned from business activities, such as sales of goods and services.
- **Expenses**: The costs incurred to generate revenue, including operational costs like rent, utilities, wages, and materials.
- **Net Income (Profit or Loss)**: The bottom line of the Income Statement, which is calculated by subtracting total expenses from total revenues. If revenue exceeds expenses, the company has made a profit; if expenses exceed revenue, it results in a loss.

The Income Statement is a crucial tool for understanding the **profitability** of a business. It allows businesses to assess their overall financial health, set future budgets, and make data-driven decisions. It is also used by external stakeholders—such as investors, lenders, and creditors—to evaluate the company's ability to generate profits and manage expenses.

The Key Components of the Income Statement

The Income Statement is generally divided into several key sections:

1. Revenue

Revenue, often referred to as **sales**, is the total amount of money a business earns from its primary operations. It's the starting point of the Income Statement and represents the funds earned from selling products or services before any costs are deducted. Revenue is typically recognized when it is earned, regardless of whether cash has been received.

There are two main types of revenue:

- **Operating Revenue**: This is the income generated from the core business activities, such as selling products, providing services, or performing activities central to the company's business model. For example, a restaurant earns revenue from selling food and drinks.
- **Non-operating Revenue**: This includes income from activities that are not part of the core business operations. Examples include interest income, rental income, or gains from the sale of assets.

It's important to distinguish between gross revenue (total income from all sources) and net revenue (gross revenue minus returns, allowances, and discounts). Businesses often report net revenue to reflect the actual income after deductions.

2. Cost of Goods Sold (COGS)

The Cost of Goods Sold (COGS), also known as cost of sales, represents the direct costs incurred in producing or purchasing the goods and services sold by the business. COGS includes expenses such as raw materials, direct labor costs, and manufacturing overhead that can be directly attributed to the production of goods or services.

For a retail business, COGS would include the cost of purchasing inventory that is sold to customers. For a manufacturing company, COGS would include the cost of raw materials, labor costs associated with production, and factory overhead costs.

Formula for COGS:

Understanding COGS is critical because it directly affects a business's gross profit. A high COGS relative to sales can indicate inefficiency or rising production costs, while a low COGS relative to sales can suggest better profit margins.

3. Gross Profit

Gross Profit is the difference between revenue and COGS. It represents the amount of money left over after the direct costs of producing goods and services have been deducted from revenue. Gross profit shows how efficiently a business produces and sells its products or services.

Formula for Gross Profit:

$$\text{Gross Profit} = \text{Revenue} - \text{COGS}$$

A business's gross profit margin is a key indicator of profitability. It can be calculated by dividing gross profit by revenue and multiplying by 100 to get the percentage.

Gross Profit Margin formula:

A higher gross profit margin indicates that a company is able to produce its goods or services at a relatively low cost compared to the price it charges customers.

4. Operating Expenses

Operating expenses include all costs that are not directly tied to the production of goods or services but are necessary for running the business. These expenses can be divided into two categories:

- **Selling, General, and Administrative Expenses (SG&A)**: This includes costs related to marketing, advertising, salaries, rent, office supplies, and administrative expenses. SG&A is typically the largest operating expense for many businesses.
- **Depreciation and Amortization**: Depreciation accounts for the wear and tear on physical assets like equipment and buildings, while amortization applies to the reduction in value of intangible assets, like patents or goodwill.

$$\text{Operating Expenses} = \text{SG\&A} + \text{Depreciation} + \text{Amortization}$$

Operating expenses are deducted from gross profit to calculate operating income. Managing operating expenses is critical for improving a company's bottom line.

5. Operating Income

Operating income, also known as operating profit, represents the company's profit from its core business operations. It is calculated by subtracting operating expenses from gross profit. Operating income is a critical measure of the company's profitability, as it excludes non-operating income and expenses.

$$\text{Operating Income} = \text{Gross Profit} - \text{Operating Expenses}$$

Operating income shows how well the company is performing in its main business activities, independent of other factors like interest or tax expenses. It's a good indicator of the company's ability to generate profit from its regular business operations.

6. Other Income and Expenses

This section of the Income Statement includes any **non-operating** items that do not directly relate to the company's core business activities. These may include:

- **Interest Income**: Earnings from investments, cash deposits, or loans made by the company.
- **Interest Expense**: The cost of borrowing money, typically from loans or bonds.
- **Gains or Losses** from the sale of assets: Any gains or losses from selling assets such as property or equipment.

These items are added to or subtracted from operating income to calculate net income. Other income and expenses give a more complete picture of a business's overall financial health.

7. Net Income (or Net Loss)

The final line of the Income Statement is Net Income (or Net Loss), which represents the company's total profit or loss after all revenues, expenses, gains, and losses have been accounted for. It is often referred to as the **bottom line** because it's the final figure on the statement.

Net income is a critical measure of profitability and is often used to evaluate a company's performance. It is also used to calculate earnings per share (EPS) for publicly traded companies, which is a key metric for investors.

The Importance of the Income Statement

The Income Statement is an essential tool for business owners, managers, investors, and other stakeholders. It provides valuable insights into the company's ability to generate profit from its core operations and manage costs effectively.

For business owners and managers, the Income Statement helps identify areas where costs can be reduced and revenue can be increased, thus improving profitability. It also provides a clear picture of operating efficiency.

For investors and creditors, the Income Statement is a key indicator of whether a business is worth investing in or lending to. Positive net income indicates a business's ability to generate profit, while consistent losses may indicate financial instability.

APPLE INC. - ANALYZING THE INCOME STATEMENT

Despite significant growth, Apple faced challenges in maintaining its high profit margins due to rising component costs (e.g., semiconductor shortages).

CHALLENGES

- Revenue Volatility
- Managing Operating Expenses

OBJECTIVES

TRACK PROFITABILITY OVER TIME

This is the primary goal, using the Income Statement.

EVALUATE OPERATIONAL EFFICIENCY

Ensure costs are managed relative to all income generated.

RESULT AND BENEFITS

- In 2021, Apple's total revenue was $365.8 billion, a 33% increase from the previous year.
- Apple's operating income for 2021 was $108.9 billion,.
- Apple's clear, transparent Income Statement helped maintain strong investor confidence, as reflected in its stock price increase of 35% in 2021.

Statement of Owner's Equity

The Statement of Owner's Equity (also called the Statement of Changes in Equity) is a financial statement that provides an overview of the changes in the owner's equity within a company during a specific period. It offers insights into the factors that have contributed to the increase or decrease in the owner's equity, which is the residual value of the company's assets after deducting its liabilities.

This statement plays a vital role in helping business owners, investors, and stakeholders understand the financial strength of a business by outlining changes to the owner's equity—particularly in relation to profits, withdrawals, additional investments, and other financial activities.

In this section, we will explore the components of the Statement of Owner's Equity, explain how it's constructed, and demonstrate its importance in understanding a company's financial health and ownership structure.

What is the Statement of Owner's Equity?

The **Statement of Owner's Equity** tracks changes in the ownership interest in a company over a specific period. It shows how the value of the company's equity (ownership value) has changed during the accounting period due to several factors:

- **Net income or loss**: The profit or loss generated by the business during the period, as reported on the **Income Statement**.
- **Owner contributions**: Additional investments made by the owner(s) during the period, which increase equity.
- **Owner withdrawals**: The amount the owner withdraws from the business, which reduces equity.
- **Other changes**: This can include adjustments like dividends (for corporations), revaluation of assets, or changes due to changes in accounting methods.

For sole proprietorships and partnerships, the statement is typically straightforward, showing the changes in the owner's capital account. For corporations, the statement is more complex and may also include stockholders' equity, which reflects common stock, retained earnings, and additional paid-in capital.

The statement provides a bridge between the Balance Sheet and the Income Statement. While the Income Statement shows the company's performance (profit or loss) over time, the Statement of Owner's Equity explains how that performance affected the owner's equity, and how other factors (like contributions or withdrawals) impacted the equity position.

Components of the Statement of Owner's Equity

The Statement of Owner's Equity consists of several key components that help businesses track changes in their owner's equity:

1. **Beginning Owner's Equity**
   The statement starts with the owner's equity at the beginning of the period, which reflects the owner's initial investment and any retained earnings carried over from the prior period. This is the starting point of the calculation, which then adjusts for the various factors affecting equity throughout the period.

Example: If a business starts the year with $50,000 in owner's equity, this will be the opening balance for the statement.

2. **Add: Net Income**
   Net income from the Income Statement is added to the owner's equity, as it reflects the profits earned by the business during the period. Net income increases the owner's equity because it represents the portion of the revenue that remains after all expenses are deducted.

Example: If the business made a net income of $20,000 during the period, this amount will increase the owner's equity.

3. **Add: Owner Contributions**
   Any additional investments or contributions made by the owner into the business during the period are added to the owner's equity. These contributions might include cash or assets that the owner invests in the business to help fund its growth or operations.

Example: If the owner invested an additional $5,000 in cash into the business, this will be added to the equity.

4. **Subtract: Owner Withdrawals**
   Any money or assets that the owner withdraws from the business during the period will be subtracted from the owner's equity. Owner withdrawals could include salaries, dividends, or personal use of business funds.

Example: If the owner withdrew $4,000 during the period, it would be subtracted from the equity.

5. **Add/Subtract: Other Adjustments**
   The statement may also include other adjustments that affect the owner's equity, such as:
   - **Dividends** (for corporations): Payments made to stockholders that reduce the retained earnings, thus reducing total equity.
   - **Revaluation adjustments**: Changes to the value of assets, such as property or equipment, based on fair market value.
   - **Changes due to accounting methods**: If a company changes its

accounting methods (e.g., from cash to accrual), adjustments may need to be made to the equity accounts.

Example: If a business changes its valuation method for inventory, resulting in a $2,000 increase in equity, this would be added to the statement.

6. **Ending Owner's Equity**
After adjusting for net income, contributions, withdrawals, and other changes, the final result is the ending owner's equity. This figure represents the total value of the owner's interest in the company at the end of the accounting period and will be reflected on the Balance Sheet as part of the owner's equity section.

7. **Formula**:

"Ending Owner's Equity"="Beginning Owner's Equity"+"Net Income"+"Owner Contributions"-"Owner Withdrawals"+"Other Adjustments"

Example:

"Ending Owner's Equity"=50,000("beginning equity")+20,000("net income")+5,000("contributions")-4,000("withdrawals")=71,000

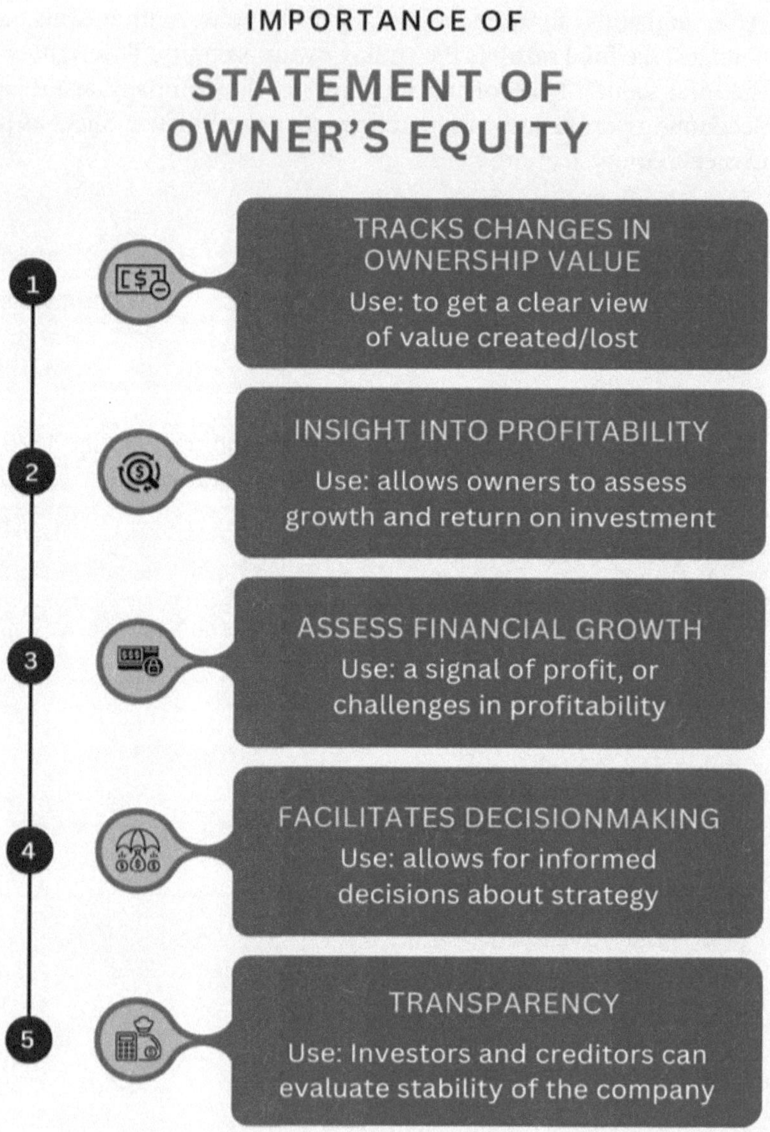
IMPORTANCE OF
STATEMENT OF OWNER'S EQUITY
1
TRACKS CHANGES IN OWNERSHIP VALUE
Use: to get a clear view of value created/lost
2
INSIGHT INTO PROFITABILITY
Use: allows owners to assess growth and return on investment
3
ASSESS FINANCIAL GROWTH
Use: a signal of profit, or challenges in profitability
4
FACILITATES DECISIONMAKING
Use: allows for informed decisions about strategy
5
TRANSPARENCY
Use: Investors and creditors can evaluate stability of the company

Why is the Statement of Owner's Equity Important?

The **Statement of Owner's Equity** serves several critical purposes for both business owners and external stakeholders. Here are the key reasons why it is important:

1. **Tracks Changes in Ownership Value**
This statement shows how a business's financial activities affect the owner's equity over a period of time. By tracking changes in equity, the owner gains a clear understanding of how much value their business is creating or losing.

2. **Provides Insight into Profitability and Growth**
The inclusion of net income in the statement allows owners to see the impact of their company's profitability on their equity position. This helps owners assess whether the business is growing and generating a return on investment.

3. **Helps Assess Financial Health**
The statement of owner's equity provides a snapshot of the financial health of the business. Increases in owner's equity indicate that the business is profitable, efficiently managing costs, and reinvesting in growth. Decreases in equity, however, may signal that the business is facing challenges, such as excessive withdrawals or poor profitability.

4. **Facilitates Financial Decision-Making**
Business owners use the statement to make informed decisions about investments, withdrawals, and business strategy. If a business has experienced significant growth in equity, the owner may decide to expand operations or reinvest in new projects. Conversely, if equity is declining, the owner might look for ways to reduce costs or increase revenues.

5. **Supports Transparency with Investors and Creditors**
For businesses with external investors or lenders, the statement of owner's equity adds transparency to the financial health of the company. Investors can use the statement to assess how profits, investments, and withdrawals impact their ownership value. Creditors may also review this statement to evaluate the company's financial stability before providing loans.

The Statement of Owner's Equity in Different Business Structures

The **Statement of Owner's Equity** varies depending on the type of business entity:

- **Sole Proprietorships**: The statement primarily reflects the changes in the owner's capital account, as the business is owned by one individual. Contributions, withdrawals, and net income are the primary items affecting equity.

- **Partnerships**: Similar to sole proprietorships, but with multiple owners. The statement reflects changes in the capital accounts of each partner. Contributions, withdrawals, and net income are allocated based on each partner's share of the partnership.
- **Corporations**: For corporations, the statement is more complex and reflects the stockholder's equity section, which includes common stock, retained earnings, and additional paid-in capital. Net income and dividends affect the retained earnings, which is a key component of stockholder equity.

The Balance Sheet: A Snapshot of Financial Health

The Balance Sheet is one of the most important financial statements used by businesses and investors to assess a company's financial health. It provides a snapshot of a company's financial position at a specific point in time by showing the relationship between its assets, liabilities, and owner's equity. The Balance Sheet helps determine what a company owns, what it owes, and the value of the ownership stake at that particular moment.

In this section, we will break down the structure of the Balance Sheet, explain each of its components, and discuss how it is used by both internal and external stakeholders to evaluate a business's financial stability and performance.

What is the Balance Sheet?

The Balance Sheet, also known as the Statement of Financial Position, is a financial statement that lists a company's assets, liabilities, and equity at a specific point in time. It provides a clear picture of the company's financial position, offering insights into its ability to pay its debts, manage its resources, and generate value for its owners or shareholders.

The Balance Sheet is divided into three main sections:

1. **Assets**: What the company owns or controls and expects to provide future economic benefits.
2. **Liabilities**: What the company owes to external parties and is obligated to settle in the future.
3. **Owner's Equity (Shareholder's Equity)**: The residual interest in the company after liabilities are deducted from assets, representing the owner's claim on the business's resources.

The basic accounting equation for the Balance Sheet is:

This equation ensures that the Balance Sheet is always in balance, as every business transaction affects both the assets and liabilities (or equity) of the company.

Components of the Balance Sheet

Let's explore each component of the Balance Sheet in more detail:

1. Assets

Assets are resources that a company owns or controls, with the expectation that they will provide future economic benefits. Assets are classified into two broad categories: current assets and non-current (or long-term) assets.

- **Current Assets**: These are assets that are expected to be converted into cash, sold, or consumed within one year or within the company's normal operating cycle. Common examples of current assets include:

  Cash and Cash Equivalents: Money in hand or in the bank, and highly liquid investments that are easily converted into cash.

  Accounts Receivable: Money owed to the business by customers who have purchased goods or services on credit.

  Inventory: Goods held for sale or raw materials used in production.

  Prepaid Expenses: Payments made in advance for goods or services to be received in the future, such as insurance or rent.

- **Non-Current Assets**: These are assets that the business intends to hold for more than one year or beyond its normal operating cycle. Non-current assets are also known as **long-term assets** and include:

  Property, Plant, and Equipment (PP&E): Tangible, long-term assets like land, buildings, machinery, and equipment used in the production process.

  Intangible Assets: Non-physical assets such as patents, trademarks, copyrights, or goodwill.

  Investments: Long-term investments in other companies, real estate, or financial instruments that are not intended to be sold within the next year.

Example:
A company might list its assets as follows:

Cash and Cash Equivalents: $50,000

Accounts Receivable: $30,000

Inventory: $20,000

Property, Plant, and Equipment: $200,000

Intangible Assets: $10,000

Total assets would then equal the sum of these figures:

$$\text{Total Assets} = 50{,}000 + 30{,}000 + 20{,}000 + 200{,}000 + 10{,}000 = 310{,}000$$

2. Liabilities

Liabilities are the company's debts or obligations that arise during the course of business operations. Liabilities are divided into two categories: **current liabilities** and **non-current liabilities**.

- **Current Liabilities**: These are obligations that the company is expected to settle within one year or within its normal operating cycle. Common examples of current liabilities include:

  Accounts Payable: Money owed to suppliers for goods or services received.

  Short-Term Loans: Loans or credit facilities due for repayment within one year.

  Accrued Expenses: Expenses that have been incurred but not yet paid, such as wages, taxes, or interest.

  Unearned Revenue: Payments received in advance for goods or services that will be delivered in the future.

- **Non-Current Liabilities**: These are obligations that are due beyond one year. Non-current liabilities are often long-term debts or obligations that don't need to be paid in the short term. Examples include:

Long-Term Debt: Loans or bonds that are due after one year.

Deferred Tax Liabilities: Taxes owed in the future, based on differences in tax accounting and financial accounting.

Pension Liabilities: Obligations to provide pension benefits to employees in the future.

Example:
A company might list its liabilities as follows:

Accounts Payable: \$25,000

Short-Term Loans: \$10,000

Long-Term Debt: \$50,000

Deferred Tax Liabilities: \$5,000

Total liabilities would then be the sum of these amounts:

$$\text{Total Liabilities} = 25{,}000 + 10{,}000 + 50{,}000 + 5{,}000 = 90{,}000$$

3. Owner's Equity

Owner's Equity (also known as **shareholder's equity** for corporations) represents the residual interest in the company after liabilities have been deducted from assets. It is essentially the **net worth** of the business and reflects the owner's claim on the company's resources. In other words, it is what is left for the owners or shareholders once all debts have been paid.

The main components of owner's equity are:

- **Contributed Capital**: The amount of money or assets invested by the owners into the business. For corporations, this includes **common stock** and **preferred stock**.
- **Retained Earnings**: The portion of net income that is retained in the business rather than being distributed to the owners or shareholders as dividends. Retained earnings are reinvested in the company for growth or debt repayment.
- **Additional Paid-In Capital**: Amounts paid by shareholders over and above the nominal value of stock.
- **Owner's Draw**: For sole proprietorships or partnerships, any withdrawals made by the owner from the business for personal use.

Formula for Owner's Equity:

$$\text{Owner's Equity} = \text{Total Assets} - \text{Total Liabilities}$$

Example:
If the business has:

Total Assets: $310,000

Total Liabilities: $90,000

The **Owner's Equity** would be calculated as:

$$\text{Owner's Equity} = 310{,}000 - 90{,}000 = 220{,}000$$

How the Balance Sheet Reflects Financial Health

The Balance Sheet is an essential tool for assessing the financial health of a business. It provides a snapshot of the company's financial stability by showing the relationship between its assets, liabilities, and owner's equity. Here's how each component of the Balance Sheet reflects different aspects of a company's financial health:

1. **Liquidity**: The relationship between current assets and current liabilities indicates the company's ability to meet its short-term obligations. If a business has more current assets than current liabilities, it is generally considered to have strong liquidity. This is important for paying off short-term debts and operating smoothly without borrowing excessively.
2. **Leverage**: The balance between liabilities and equity shows how much debt the company is using to finance its operations. A company with too much debt relative to equity may be considered risky, as it may have trouble paying off its obligations. Debt-to-equity ratios are commonly used to assess leverage.

3. **Solvency**: The solvency of a business is determined by its ability to meet long-term obligations. A company with a strong balance of assets over liabilities is more likely to weather financial difficulties and remain solvent in the long term.
4. **Operational Efficiency**: The Balance Sheet helps stakeholders assess the company's efficiency in using its assets. For example, if a company has a large amount of inventory or accounts receivable, it may signal inefficiency or poor cash flow management.

A strong Balance Sheet, with ample assets and manageable liabilities, signals a business's capacity for growth, sustainability, and risk management. By understanding the Balance Sheet's components and their implications, you can gain valuable insights into the long-term financial health of a company.

Statement of Cash Flows: Tracking Money In and Out

The **Statement of Cash Flows** is one of the primary financial statements used to assess a company's liquidity, solvency, and financial flexibility. Unlike the Income Statement or the Balance Sheet, which provide information on profitability and financial position at a point in time, the Statement of Cash Flows focuses on the actual cash inflows and outflows over a specific period. It answers one of the most important questions for businesses and investors: **Where did the money come from, and how was it spent?**

In this section, we will break down the components of the Statement of Cash Flows, explain its purpose and importance, and show how it helps businesses and stakeholders understand the company's cash management practices. We will also explore the three key sections of the Statement of Cash Flows: Operating Activities, Investing Activities, and Financing Activities.

What is the Statement of Cash Flows?

The **Statement of Cash Flows** is a financial statement that tracks the movement of cash and cash equivalents in and out of a business over a given period. It provides insights into how a company generates cash (through operations, investments, or financing) and how it uses that cash (for operating expenses, investing in assets, or paying off debts).

Unlike other financial statements, which may include **accrual-based accounting**, the Statement of Cash Flows focuses on **actual cash transactions**, providing a clear view of how much cash the company has on hand to meet its obligations.

The Statement of Cash Flows is essential for understanding a company's ability to:

- **Pay bills and obligations**: Cash is required to pay creditors, suppliers, employees, and service debt.
- **Invest in future growth**: Companies need cash to fund research and

development, buy equipment, or expand operations.

- **Return value to shareholders**: Cash is necessary for paying dividends or repurchasing stock.

The Three Sections of the Statement of Cash Flows

The Statement of Cash Flows is divided into three main sections, each of which tracks a different source or use of cash. Each of these sections provides insights into different aspects of the company's cash position, helping users understand how the business is generating and using cash.

1. Cash Flows from Operating Activities

The Operating Activities section shows cash flows related to the company's core business operations—those activities that generate revenue and incur expenses. These activities represent the day-to-day operations of the business, such as selling goods or services and paying wages or suppliers.

Cash flows from operating activities include:

- **Cash receipts from customers**: This includes cash collected from the sale of goods or services.
- **Cash payments to suppliers**: This includes payments made for inventory, raw materials, and services necessary for production.
- **Cash payments for operating expenses**: This includes salaries, rent, utilities, and other costs associated with running the business.
- **Cash payments for interest and taxes**: Cash paid for interest on loans and income taxes.

Operating activities are crucial because they reflect the company's ability to generate sufficient cash from its core business operations. Positive cash flow from operating activities indicates that the business can sustain itself without relying on external financing or the sale of assets.

Cash flows from operating activities can be calculated using two methods:

- **Direct Method**: The direct method lists actual cash inflows and outflows. For example, it directly records cash received from customers and cash paid to suppliers.
- **Indirect Method**: The indirect method starts with net income from the Income Statement and adjusts for non-cash items (e.g., depreciation, changes in working capital) to calculate cash provided by (or used in) operating activities.

Example:

Cash received from customers: $100,000

Cash paid to suppliers: $40,000

Cash paid for operating expenses: $20,000

Cash paid for taxes: $5,000

Net cash from operating activities: $100,000 - $40,000 - $20,000 - $5,000 = **$35,000**

2. Cash Flows from Investing Activities

The Investing Activities section shows cash flows related to the purchase and sale of long-term assets, such as property, equipment, investments, and intangible assets. This section reflects how much cash is spent on acquiring assets necessary for business growth or how much cash is generated from the sale of these assets.

Common cash flows from investing activities include:

- **Purchases of property, plant, and equipment (PP&E)**: Cash spent on acquiring new physical assets, such as machinery, buildings, or land.
- **Proceeds from the sale of assets**: Cash received from selling assets, including real estate or equipment.
- **Purchases and sales of investments**: Cash used to buy or receive from selling investments in other companies, stocks, bonds, or securities.
- **Loans made to other entities**: Cash provided to other businesses or individuals in the form of loans.

Investing activities are important for assessing how a company is using its cash to fund future growth. A positive cash flow from investing activities often indicates that the company is selling assets, possibly to raise cash, while a negative cash flow suggests that the company is making new investments or purchases to grow its business.

Example:

Cash used to purchase new equipment: $50,000

Cash received from the sale of an old asset: $10,000

Net cash from investing activities: $10,000 - $50,000 = -$40,000 (net outflow)

3. Cash Flows from Financing Activities

The Financing Activities section shows cash flows related to the company's financial structure—how it raises capital, pays off debt, or returns value to shareholders. This section includes cash flows from activities such as:

- **Issuing or repurchasing stock**: Cash received from issuing new shares or cash used to buy back shares from shareholders.
- **Borrowing or repaying loans**: Cash received from issuing bonds or loans,

or cash used to repay loans or interest.

- **Paying dividends**: Cash paid to shareholders as a return on their investment.

Financing activities are important because they show how the company is managing its capital—whether it's raising funds to expand operations or paying down debt to reduce liabilities. Positive cash flow from financing activities can indicate that the company is raising funds for growth, while negative cash flow may suggest the company is paying off debt or returning money to shareholders.

Example:

Cash received from issuing common stock: $30,000

Cash used to repay a loan: $20,000

Cash paid for dividends: $10,000

Net cash from financing activities: $30,000 - $20,000 - $10,000 = $0

Understanding Cash Flow Net Change

The Net Change in Cash represents the overall change in a company's cash position from the beginning to the end of the accounting period. It is calculated by adding together the net cash flows from the three sections of the Statement of Cash Flows:

"Net Change in Cash"="Net Cash from Operating Activities"+"Net Cash from Investing Activities"+"Net Cash from Financing Activities"

The net change in cash is then added to the beginning cash balance (as shown on the previous period's Balance Sheet) to determine the ending cash balance at the end of the period.

For example, if a company has:

- **Net Cash from Operating Activities**: $35,000
- **Net Cash from Investing Activities**: -$40,000
- **Net Cash from Financing Activities**: $0
- **Beginning Cash Balance**: $50,000

The ending cash balance would be:

"Ending Cash Balance"="Beginning Cash Balance"+"Net Change in Cash"

"Ending Cash Balance"=50,000+(35,000-40,000+0)=50,000-5,000=45,000

This shows that the company's cash position has decreased by $5,000 during the period, primarily due to investments in assets.

Why is the Statement of Cash Flows Important?

The Statement of Cash Flows provides valuable insights into the **liquidity** and cash management of a business. It highlights the company's ability to generate cash from its core operations, manage its investments, and meet its financial obligations. Here are some reasons why the Statement of Cash Flows is crucial:

1. **Liquidity Assessment**: The Statement of Cash Flows helps determine if a business has enough cash to cover its short-term obligations. Cash flow from operating activities is particularly important for assessing whether the business can generate enough cash to fund its daily operations.
2. **Evaluating Cash Management**: By examining cash inflows and outflows from investing and financing activities, stakeholders can assess how the business is managing its long-term growth and financial structure. Positive cash flow from operations indicates that the company can finance its activities from internal resources, reducing the reliance on external funding.
3. **Investor Confidence**: Investors use the Statement of Cash Flows to evaluate the company's financial flexibility and risk profile. A company with strong cash flow from operations is more likely to sustain growth, pay dividends, and weather economic downturns.
4. **Debt Management**: Creditors and lenders use the Statement of Cash Flows to assess the company's ability to repay loans and service debt. Strong cash flow from operations suggests that the company can meet its debt obligations without relying on borrowing or asset sales.

The Statement of Cash Flows is an indispensable tool for understanding a company's cash position and its ability to generate and manage cash. By focusing on actual cash inflows and outflows, it provides stakeholders with a clear and accurate view of the company's liquidity, operating efficiency, and financial flexibility. Whether you are a business owner, investor, creditor, or financial analyst, understanding the Statement of Cash Flows is essential for making informed decisions about the company's future and financial health.

Cash Basis vs. Accrual Basis Accounting

In the world of accounting, two primary methods are used to record and report financial transactions: cash basis accounting and accrual basis accounting. These two methods differ fundamentally in how and when they recognize revenue and expenses, making them essential concepts for understanding a company's financial health and performance. Both methods have their advantages and drawbacks, depending on the nature of the business and its financial goals.

In this section, we will explore the key differences between cash basis and accrual basis accounting, examine when each method is used, and understand the impact of each on financial reporting. By the end, you'll have a clear understanding of

both accounting methods and how they influence the way a business tracks and reports its financial activities.

What is Cash Basis Accounting?

Cash basis accounting is a method of accounting that recognizes revenue and expenses only when cash is exchanged. This means that revenue is recorded when it is received (i.e., when the payment is made) and expenses are recorded when they are paid, not when they are incurred.

Under cash basis accounting, a company's financial transactions are recognized in the accounting period in which the cash is actually received or paid, regardless of when the service is provided or the goods are delivered.

Key Features of Cash Basis Accounting:

Revenue Recognition: Revenue is recorded when cash is received from customers. For example, if a customer pays for a product or service in January, the revenue is recognized in January, regardless of when the product or service was delivered.

Expense Recognition: Expenses are recorded when cash is paid. If a company pays for supplies in cash in March, the expense is recognized in March, even if the supplies were used in February.

Simplicity: Cash basis accounting is relatively simple and straightforward to implement. It is often preferred by small businesses, freelancers, and sole proprietors because it requires minimal record-keeping and offers a clear picture of cash flow.

Example of Cash Basis Accounting:

Let's say a business sells a product for $1,000 in January but does not receive payment until February. Under cash basis accounting:

Revenue is recorded in February, when the cash is received.

Similarly, if the business incurs an expense of $500 in December but does not pay the vendor until January, under cash basis accounting:

The expense is recorded in January, when the payment is made.

Advantages of Cash Basis Accounting:

1. **Simplified Tracking**: Since cash basis accounting tracks cash flow, it is easier to understand and manage for small businesses.
2. **Tax Benefits**: Cash basis accounting allows businesses to defer recognizing income until cash is received. This can help reduce taxable income for the current year if payments are delayed.
3. **Clear Cash Flow Visibility**: Since revenue and expenses are only recorded when cash is exchanged, business owners have a clear view of the cash available for operations at any given time.

Disadvantages of Cash Basis Accounting:

1. **Limited Financial Insight**: Cash basis accounting may not provide an accurate picture of a business's financial health, as it doesn't account for accounts receivable (money owed by customers) or accounts payable (money the business owes).
2. **Inaccurate Matching of Revenues and Expenses**: Since revenue and expenses are recorded when cash is exchanged, they may not be properly matched. For instance, a business may incur significant expenses in one period but not recognize the revenue until a later period, which can distort profitability.

What is Accrual Basis Accounting?

Accrual basis accounting is a method that recognizes revenue when it is earned and expenses when they are incurred, regardless of when cash is received or paid. This method provides a more accurate representation of a company's financial performance because it matches revenue with the expenses incurred to generate that revenue in the same period.

In accrual basis accounting, revenue is recognized when a service is provided or goods are delivered, and expenses are recorded when incurred, not necessarily when payment is made. This method follows the matching principle, which states that expenses should be recorded in the same period as the revenues they help generate.

Key Features of Accrual Basis Accounting:

1. **Revenue Recognition**: Revenue is recognized when it is earned, i.e., when the company provides goods or services, not necessarily when cash is received. For example, if a business provides a service in January but receives payment in February, the revenue is recorded in January.
2. **Expense Recognition**: Expenses are recorded when they are incurred, i.e., when the business receives goods or services, not when payment is made. For example, if a business receives supplies in December but does not pay for them until January, the expense is recorded in December when the goods were received.
3. **Complexity**: Accrual basis accounting is more complex than cash basis accounting, as it requires the tracking of both cash and non-cash transactions, such as accounts receivable and accounts payable.

Example of Accrual Basis Accounting:

Let's say the same business sells a product for $1,000 in January and provides the product to the customer. Under accrual basis accounting:

Revenue is recognized in January, even though the customer doesn't pay until February.

Similarly, if the business incurs an expense of $500 in December for supplies received but does not pay the vendor until January, under accrual basis accounting:

The expense is recorded in December, when the goods were received, not when the payment was made.

Advantages of Accrual Basis Accounting:

1. **More Accurate Financial Picture**: Accrual basis accounting provides a clearer and more accurate picture of a company's profitability, as it matches revenues with related expenses in the same period.
2. **Improved Financial Management**: By recording both accounts receivable (money owed) and accounts payable (money owed to others), accrual accounting helps businesses manage their finances more effectively and track cash flow more precisely.
3. **Required for Larger Businesses**: Larger businesses or businesses that generate significant revenue are typically required to use accrual basis accounting for financial reporting purposes. It is the preferred method for preparing financial statements in accordance with Generally Accepted Accounting Principles (GAAP) and International Financial Reporting Standards (IFRS).

Disadvantages of Accrual Basis Accounting:

1. **More Complex**: Accrual accounting is more complicated to maintain, as it requires tracking accounts receivable, accounts payable, and other non-cash transactions.
2. **Less Visibility into Cash Flow**: Accrual accounting doesn't provide a clear picture of cash on hand, which can be challenging for small business owners who need to manage short-term liquidity.
3. **Possible Tax Implications**: Since accrual accounting recognizes revenue when earned, a business could be required to pay taxes on income that has not yet been received, which may create cash flow problems.

MICROSOFT - ACCRUAL BASIS ACCOUNTING

Microsoft adopts the accrual basis of accounting to provide an accurate picture of its financial performance.

CHALLENGES

- Ensure Compliance with Reporting Standards
- Optimize Financial Management

OBJECTIVES

COMPLIANCE WITH REPORTING STANDARDS

This is a requirement for publicly traded companies.

OPTIMIZE FINANCIAL MANAGEMENT

Microsoft was able to make data-driven decisions.

RESULT AND BENEFITS

- Microsoft reported revenue of $168 billion in fiscal year 2021, with net income of $61.3 billion.
- By using accrual accounting, the company could recognize revenue even before payments were fully received.
- Microsoft presented a detailed set of financial statements that boosted stock prices.

Key Differences Between Cash Basis and Accrual Basis Accounting

Aspect	Cash Basis Accounting	Accrual Basis Accounting
Revenue Recognition	Recorded when cash is received	Recorded when earned, regardless of cash received
Expense Recognition	Recorded when cash is paid	Recorded when incurred, regardless of cash paid
Complexity	Simple, easy to maintain	More complex, requires tracking of receivables/payables
Financial Insights	Provides a limited view of financial health	Provides a more accurate picture of financial health
Matching Principle	Does not follow the matching principle	Follows the matching principle, matching revenues with expenses
Tax Benefits	Allows businesses to delay tax recognition	May require tax to be paid before cash is received

When to Use Cash Basis vs. Accrual Basis Accounting

The choice between cash basis and accrual basis accounting depends on the size of the business, its complexity, and its financial goals.

Cash Basis Accounting is typically used by:

- **Small businesses** and sole proprietors who do not have extensive inventory or complicated transactions.
- **Startups** with limited financial complexity, where managing cash flow is a priority.
- Businesses that operate on a cash-only basis and prefer simplicity.

Accrual Basis Accounting is generally used by:

- **Larger businesses** that have complex transactions, inventories, and longer operating cycles.
- Businesses that are required to follow **GAAP** or **IFRS** for financial reporting purposes.
- Companies that want a more accurate representation of their profitability and financial position.
- Ultimately, both methods have their place in the world of accounting, and choosing the right one depends on the business's specific needs and goals.

Chapter 3: The Accounting Equation

Double-Entry Accounting: The Heart of Financial Accounting

Double-entry accounting is one of the most fundamental concepts in financial accounting. It serves as the foundation for recording every financial transaction that occurs within a business. This system ensures that the accounting equation—Assets = Liabilities + Owner's Equity—remains balanced after each transaction. The double-entry method helps ensure that a company's financial records are accurate, complete, and reflect the true financial condition of the business.

In this section, we'll explore the principles behind double-entry accounting, how it works, and why it's integral to the overall process of financial accounting. We'll also look at how double-entry accounting is applied to the **accounting equation** and the way businesses record their transactions.

What is Double-Entry Accounting?

Double-entry accounting is a system where every transaction is recorded in at least two accounts: one **debit** and one **credit**. The key principle behind this system is that for every debit entry, there must be a corresponding credit entry of equal value. This ensures that the accounting equation is always in balance.

For example, when a company buys office equipment on credit, it increases the asset account (equipment) and also increases the liability account (accounts payable) to reflect the amount owed to the supplier. Both sides of the equation must be equal to ensure the books are balanced.

The equation for double-entry accounting is:

$$\text{Debit} = \text{Credit}$$

This method serves several purposes:

- It helps prevent errors because both sides of the transaction must balance.
- It provides a comprehensive picture of a company's financial activity, reflecting both the sources and uses of funds.
- It enables the preparation of accurate financial statements, including the Income Statement, Balance Sheet, and Cash Flow Statement.

The Basics of Debits and Credits

In double-entry accounting, every transaction affects at least two accounts, with one account being debited and another account being credited. Here's a basic overview of **debits** and **credits**:

Debit	Credit
Increases assets	Increases liabilities

Debit	Credit
Increases expenses	Increases equity (owner's capital)
Decreases liabilities	Increases revenue
Decreases equity (owner's withdrawal)	Decreases assets

For each transaction, one account will be debited, and the other will be credited. The debit is typically used to record the increase in assets or expenses, while the credit is used for increasing liabilities, revenues, or equity.

Examples:

- **Example 1: Purchase of Equipment on Credit**
  If a business purchases equipment worth $5,000 on credit, the accounting entry would be:

  Debit Equipment (Asset) $5,000

  Credit Accounts Payable (Liability) $5,000
  This transaction increases the asset (equipment) and also increases the liability (accounts payable) by the same amount, keeping the accounting equation balanced.

- **Example 2: Earning Revenue in Cash**
  If a business earns $3,000 in cash for services provided, the accounting entry would be:

  Debit Cash (Asset) $3,000

  Credit Service Revenue (Equity/Revenue) $3,000

  This increases the company's cash (an asset) and also increases its revenue (affecting the equity portion of the accounting equation).

How Double-Entry Accounting Relates to the Accounting Equation

The accounting equation is the foundation of all financial accounting and is always in balance:

In double-entry accounting, each transaction affects at least two accounts in a way that maintains this equation. Let's look at how various transactions impact the equation:

Transaction	Impact on Assets	Impact on Liabilities	Impact on Owner's Equity
Sale of goods for cash	+ Cash (Asset)	No change	+ Revenue (Equity)
Purchase of inventory on credit	+ Inventory (Asset)	+ Accounts Payable (Liability)	No change
Payment of wages	- Cash (Asset)	No change	- Expenses (Equity)
Owner invests capital	+ Cash (Asset)	No change	+ Capital (Equity)
Loan repayment	- Cash (Asset)	- Loan Payable (Liability)	No change

In each case, both the debit and the credit sides of the equation balance, keeping the overall equation intact. Whether you're increasing assets, liabilities, or equity, double-entry accounting ensures that every transaction is properly recorded and that the balance sheet remains balanced.

COCA-COLA - FINANCIAL MANAGEMENT

Coca-Cola needs to maintain consistent financial records across multiple jurisdictions, currencies, and accounting systems.

CHALLENGES

- Global Operations and Complex Transactions
- Ensuring Accurate Reporting for Investors

OBJECTIVES

ENSURE ACCURATE FINANCIAL RECORDS

Every transaction is recorded in at least two accounts—debit and credit—to maintain balance.

MAINTAIN COMPLIANCE WITH GAAP AND IFRS

These standards require the use of double-entry accounting.

RESULT AND BENEFITS

- By using double-entry accounting, Coca-Cola can ensure that its financial statements reflect a true and fair view of the company's financial position.
- Coca-Cola's use of double-entry accounting facilitates the efficient preparation of its major financial statements.

The Importance of Double-Entry Accounting

1. **Accuracy and Error Prevention**
   Double-entry accounting helps prevent errors by ensuring that each transaction is recorded twice: once as a debit and once as a credit. If the total debits and credits don't match, an error has occurred, and it can be quickly identified. This system ensures the integrity of financial records, providing confidence in the accuracy of the company's financial statements.

2. **Comprehensive Financial Tracking**
   Double-entry accounting provides a complete record of all financial transactions. Since every transaction affects both sides of the balance sheet (assets, liabilities, and equity), it gives a comprehensive picture of a company's financial health. This holistic view is essential for making strategic business decisions, as it reflects both the resources available to the company and its obligations.

3. **Compliance and Transparency**
   Double-entry accounting is the foundation of Generally Accepted Accounting Principles (GAAP) and International Financial Reporting Standards (IFRS), the two primary frameworks for financial reporting. These standards require the use of double-entry accounting to ensure that financial statements are consistent, comparable, and transparent. This is especially important for publicly traded companies, which must provide accurate and standardized financial information to investors and regulators.

4. **Preparation of Financial Statements**
   Double-entry accounting makes it easier to prepare the three major financial statements:

   Income Statement: Shows profitability by comparing revenues and expenses.

   Balance Sheet: Provides a snapshot of the company's financial position, showing assets, liabilities, and equity.

   Statement of Cash Flows: Tracks the flow of cash in and out of the business, reflecting how operations, investments, and financing activities affect cash balances.

Each of these statements relies on the data recorded through double-entry accounting, making it an essential tool for financial analysis and reporting.

Common Errors in Double-Entry Accounting

While double-entry accounting is designed to ensure accuracy, errors can still occur. Common mistakes include:

1. **Recording Transactions in the Wrong Accounts**
   Sometimes, transactions are entered in the wrong accounts, which can lead to misclassification of assets, liabilities, or equity. For example, recording an expense as an asset can distort the financial statements.
2. **Unequal Debits and Credits**
   One of the most basic errors is when the debits and credits for a transaction do not balance. This usually occurs when an amount is omitted or miscalculated, which can affect the entire financial statement.
3. **Omitting Transactions**
   Missing transactions—whether it's revenue, an expense, or an asset purchase—can result in incomplete financial reporting. Since double-entry accounting tracks every financial event, missing entries can cause significant discrepancies in the financial records.
4. **Overlooking Adjustments**
   At the end of an accounting period, businesses must make adjusting entries to account for accruals, deferrals, depreciation, and other factors. Failing to record these adjustments can result in inaccurate financial reporting.

Double-Entry Accounting in Practice: Real-World Applications

Double-entry accounting is used by businesses of all sizes and across industries. Here's how it's applied in different sectors:

1. **Small Businesses**
   Small businesses often use accounting software like QuickBooks, Xero, or FreshBooks, which are built on double-entry accounting systems. These tools simplify the process of recording transactions, managing accounts, and generating reports, making it easier for small business owners to track their finances.
2. **Corporations**
   Larger corporations require more sophisticated double-entry systems to manage the complexity of their financial transactions. They often use **Enterprise Resource Planning (ERP)** systems like SAP or Oracle, which provide real-time financial data and integrate all aspects of the business—from sales and inventory management to payroll and tax compliance.
3. **Non-Profit Organizations**
   Non-profits also rely on double-entry accounting to ensure that they track

donations, grants, and expenses accurately. Since they are required to maintain transparency for donors and funders, double-entry accounting helps them manage their finances in compliance with regulatory standards.

By using double-entry accounting, businesses can ensure that every transaction is properly recorded, that the accounting equation remains balanced, and that their financial data is reliable for decision-making and reporting purposes. Whether you're managing a small business, a large corporation, or a non-profit organization, understanding and applying double-entry accounting is essential for sound financial management.

Understanding Assets

Assets are one of the key elements on the **Balance Sheet** and represent the economic resources owned or controlled by a business. Assets are essential because they are expected to provide future economic benefits, such as generating revenue, supporting operations, or being used in the production of goods and services. Understanding assets is crucial for assessing a company's financial health and its ability to sustain and grow its operations.

In this section, we will dive deeper into the different types of assets, their classification, and their significance in financial analysis. We will also explore how businesses use and manage assets to maximize their value and support long-term financial goals.

What are Assets?

In accounting terms, assets are defined as anything of value or a resource that a company owns or controls and expects to provide future economic benefits. Assets are an integral part of a company's financial health because they represent the resources available to generate income, meet liabilities, and ensure the company's sustainability.

The accounting equation emphasizes the role of assets in maintaining a balanced financial structure:

$$\text{"Assets"}=\text{"Liabilities"}+\text{"Owner's Equity"}$$

Assets can be tangible, such as buildings or machinery, or intangible, such as patents or trademarks. Regardless of their form, all assets contribute to the company's ability to generate revenue and sustain its operations.

Types of Assets

Assets are typically classified into two main categories: **current assets** and **non-current (long-term) assets**. This classification is based on how easily they can be converted into cash and the length of time over which the benefits are expected to be realized.

Asset Type	Description	Examples
Current Assets	Assets expected to be converted into cash or used up within one year or within the business's normal operating cycle.	Cash, Accounts Receivable, Inventory, Prepaid Expenses
Non-Current Assets	Assets that are expected to provide benefits over a longer period (more than one year).	Property, Plant, and Equipment (PP&E), Intangible Assets, Long-term Investments

Each type of asset serves a different purpose and plays a unique role in the overall functioning of a business.

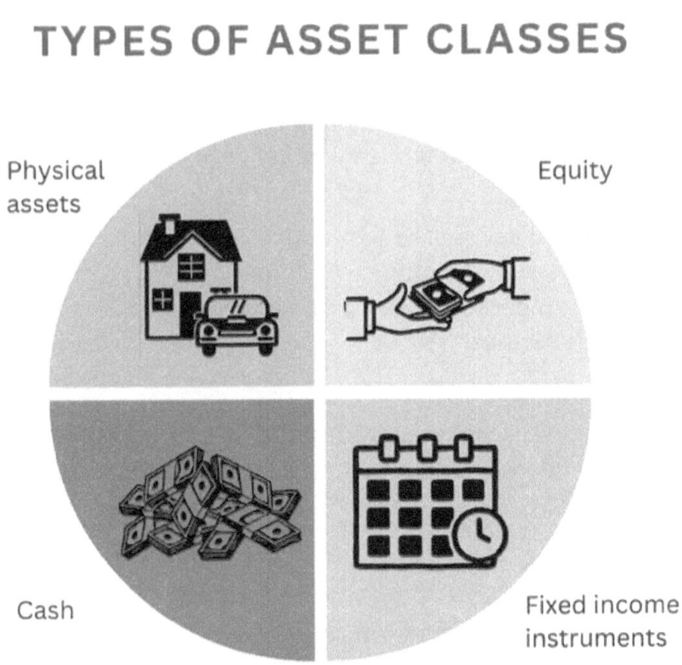

Current Assets: Liquidity and Flexibility

Current assets are the assets that businesses expect to convert into cash or consume within one year or within their normal operating cycle, whichever is longer. These assets are crucial for managing a business's liquidity, which refers to the ability to meet short-term obligations and fund day-to-day operations.

Key Features of Current Assets:

- **Liquidity**: These assets can be easily converted into cash, allowing businesses to maintain smooth operations.
- **Short-Term Benefit**: Current assets are expected to generate cash or provide value within a short time frame.

Components of Current Assets:

1. **Cash and Cash Equivalents**:
   This includes physical cash, bank deposits, and highly liquid investments that are easily converted into cash, typically within 90 days. Cash is the most liquid asset and is essential for meeting immediate financial obligations.
2. **Accounts Receivable**:
   Amounts owed by customers for goods or services provided on credit. Accounts receivable represent future cash inflows and are an essential component of a business's liquidity management.
3. **Inventory**:
   Goods or raw materials held by the business that are intended for sale or use in the production of goods for sale. Effective management of inventory is critical to ensuring that a business has sufficient products to meet customer demand while avoiding excess stock that ties up cash.
4. **Prepaid Expenses**:
   Payments made in advance for goods or services that will be received in the future, such as insurance premiums, rent, or subscriptions. These payments are recorded as assets and are gradually expensed over time as the benefit is realized.

Example:

A company may have $50,000 in cash, $30,000 in accounts receivable, $20,000 in inventory, and $5,000 in prepaid expenses. These current assets are critical for meeting the company's short-term obligations and maintaining smooth operations.

Non-Current Assets: Long-Term Value

Non-current assets, also referred to as long-term assets, represent the company's investments and resources that are expected to provide value for more than one year. These assets are vital for the company's long-term growth and financial stability.

Key Features of Non-Current Assets:

- **Long-Term Benefit**: These assets provide value to the company over a longer period, often several years.
- **Depreciation and Amortization**: Many non-current assets, such as property or machinery, lose value over time through depreciation or amortization.

Components of Non-Current Assets:

1. **Property, Plant, and Equipment (PP&E)**:
   This category includes physical, tangible assets such as land, buildings, machinery, and vehicles that are used in the business's operations. These assets are critical for production, manufacturing, and service delivery.

   Depreciation: PP&E assets are subject to depreciation, which is the gradual reduction in value over time due to wear and tear. Depreciation is recorded as an expense on the Income Statement and reduces the value of these assets on the Balance Sheet.

2. **Intangible Assets**:
   These are non-physical assets that have value due to their legal rights or intellectual property. Common examples include **patents**, **trademarks**, **copyrights**, and **goodwill**. While intangible assets do not have a physical presence, they can generate revenue and provide long-term benefits.

   Amortization: Similar to depreciation, intangible assets are amortized over their useful life to allocate their value as an expense on the Income Statement.

3. **Long-Term Investments**:
   These include investments in stocks, bonds, or other financial assets that the business intends to hold for more than one year. Long-term investments are often made to generate passive income, such as dividends or interest, or to diversify the company's portfolio.

4. **Deferred Tax Assets**:
   These are taxes that a company has overpaid and expects to recover in future periods. Deferred tax assets arise due to temporary differences between accounting and tax treatment.

Example:

A manufacturing company may own a factory building worth $500,000, have machinery worth $200,000, and hold a patent valued at $50,000. These non-current assets are vital for the company's production capabilities and long-term profitability.

The Importance of Managing Assets

Effectively managing both current and non-current assets is essential for a company's operational success and long-term financial health. The following principles highlight why asset management is critical:

1. **Liquidity and Solvency**:
   Proper management of current assets, such as cash, receivables, and inventory, ensures that a business has sufficient liquidity to meet its short-term financial obligations. Solvency, which refers to a company's ability to meet long-term debts, is closely tied to the company's non-current assets, including PP&E and investments.
2. **Profitability**:
   Non-current assets such as machinery and intellectual property directly contribute to a company's ability to generate profits. Effective utilization of these assets can lead to higher production, more competitive products, and increased market share.
3. **Investment Decisions**:
   A company's asset portfolio is a key factor for investors and creditors when evaluating the business. Strong, well-managed assets contribute to a positive perception of the business, enhancing its ability to attract investments or obtain financing.
4. **Depreciation and Amortization Impact**:
   The depreciation of assets like machinery or buildings, and the amortization of intangible assets, affects both the Balance Sheet and Income Statement. Properly accounting for depreciation helps companies avoid overstatement of asset values and provides an accurate picture of financial health.

Asset Valuation and Revaluation

Over time, the value of certain assets may change. For example, property may appreciate in value, while **machinery** may depreciate. Understanding the proper valuation of assets is essential for businesses to make informed decisions regarding asset management, sales, and investments.

1. **Fair Market Value vs. Book Value**:

   Book Value: The value of an asset as recorded in the company's accounting records, which is typically the purchase price minus accumulated depreciation or amortization.

   Fair Market Value: The price at which an asset could be bought or sold in an open market. For some assets, such as real estate, the fair market value may differ significantly from the book value.
2. **Revaluation of Assets**:

Some companies may choose to revalue their assets, particularly if they have appreciated in value. Revaluation is typically done for property and investment assets, and the increased value is reflected in the Balance Sheet. This helps ensure that the company's financial records accurately represent the current value of its assets.

As a business grows, it must continually assess its assets, ensuring that it is using them effectively to generate revenue, reduce costs, and position itself for future success. For investors, creditors, and business owners, understanding the value and role of assets is fundamental to making informed decisions about the company's financial health and future prospects.

Intangible Assets: An Overview

Intangible assets represent non-physical resources that provide long-term value to a company. These assets play a significant role in the company's overall financial health, often contributing to its competitive edge, brand recognition, and market positioning. Unlike physical assets such as buildings or machinery, intangible assets have no physical form but can still have substantial value, especially in industries like technology, media, pharmaceuticals, and entertainment.

In this section, we will explore what intangible assets are, how they are classified, and why they are important in business. We'll also cover the key differences between intangible assets and tangible assets, the challenges in valuing intangible assets, and how businesses report these assets in their financial statements.

What Are Intangible Assets?

Intangible assets are non-physical assets that have value due to the benefits they provide to a company. These assets are often tied to legal rights, intellectual property, or the company's reputation, and they typically generate revenue over an extended period. While intangible assets do not have a physical form, they can significantly influence the company's earning potential, competitive advantages, and growth prospects.

Some key characteristics of intangible assets include:

- **Non-Physical**: Unlike tangible assets like land or equipment, intangible assets cannot be touched or physically measured.
- **Long-Term Value**: Intangible assets provide value to a company over an extended period, often lasting many years.
- **Legal or Contractual Rights**: Many intangible assets, such as patents, trademarks, and copyrights, are protected by law, giving the company exclusive rights to use them.

Examples of Intangible Assets:

- **Patents**: Legal rights granted for inventions, allowing the owner to exclude others from using or selling the invention.
- **Trademarks**: Distinctive symbols, names, or logos that identify and distinguish products or services.
- **Goodwill**: The value of a company's reputation, customer base, and brand loyalty that cannot be easily quantified.
- **Copyrights**: Legal rights granted to creators of original works, such as books, music, and software, to control reproduction and distribution.
- **Franchises**: Rights granted to operate a business using a company's established brand, systems, and intellectual property.

Types of Intangible Assets

Intangible assets can be classified into two main categories: identifiable intangible assets and unidentifiable intangible assets. Let's break down these categories in more detail:

Category	Description	Examples
Identifiable Intangible Assets	These are assets that can be separately identified and valued. They are typically related to intellectual property or contractual rights.	Patents, Trademarks, Copyrights, Franchise Agreements
Unidentifiable Intangible Assets	These assets cannot be easily separated from the company's overall business value. They are usually tied to the company's reputation and relationships.	Goodwill, Customer Relationships, Brand Recognition

Identifiable Intangible Assets:

1. **Patents**:
   Patents are exclusive rights granted to inventors for new inventions, allowing them to exclude others from making, using, or selling the invention for a specific period. Patents can provide a significant competitive advantage, especially in technology and pharmaceutical industries, as they prevent others from copying the inventor's product or idea.
2. **Trademarks**:
   Trademarks are symbols, words, or other identifiers that distinguish a company's products or services from those of others. Trademarks help

build brand recognition and can be crucial for maintaining customer loyalty. They can also be licensed or sold to generate revenue.

3. **Copyrights**: Copyrights protect original works of authorship, such as books, music, and software. The copyright holder has the exclusive right to reproduce, distribute, and display the work, typically for a specific period. Copyrights are valuable in creative industries, where intellectual property is a significant source of income.

4. **Franchise Agreements**: A franchise agreement allows a business to use another company's established brand, systems, and intellectual property to operate a similar business. Franchise agreements are common in industries like food service, retail, and hospitality, where the brand's reputation and systematized approach provide significant value.

Unidentifiable Intangible Assets:

1. **Goodwill**:
Goodwill is the value of a business's reputation, brand recognition, customer loyalty, and other factors that contribute to its ability to generate profits. Goodwill is often recorded when a company acquires another business for more than its fair market value. The excess paid is classified as goodwill. Unlike other intangible assets, goodwill is not amortized but is subject to impairment testing.

2. **Customer Relationships**:
Customer relationships represent the value a company derives from its ongoing relationships with customers. These relationships are difficult to quantify but can provide long-term financial benefits through repeat business, customer loyalty, and referrals.

3. **Brand Recognition**:
Brand recognition is the value associated with a company's established brand. It reflects how well customers can identify a brand and its products or services. Strong brand recognition can lead to customer loyalty, higher sales, and premium pricing.

The Importance of Intangible Assets

Intangible assets play a significant role in the success and growth of a company. While tangible assets like machinery and buildings are important for operations, intangible assets often have a more substantial impact on a company's market value and profitability, particularly in knowledge-based and creative industries.

1. **Competitive Advantage**:
Intangible assets such as patents, trademarks, and goodwill can provide a significant competitive edge. For instance, patents prevent competitors

from copying an innovation, while strong brand recognition allows a company to charge premium prices for its products.

2. **Revenue Generation**:
Intangible assets can contribute directly to revenue. For example, copyrights allow companies to collect royalties from the use of their intellectual property, while franchise agreements can provide a steady income stream from licensing the brand to other businesses.

3. **Market Perception and Company Valuation**:
Intangible assets like goodwill and customer relationships often play a key role in the valuation of a company. Investors and buyers consider the strength of a company's brand, customer base, and intellectual property when assessing its market value. Goodwill, in particular, is often the largest component of a company's market value in acquisitions.

Challenges in Valuing Intangible Assets

Valuing intangible assets is inherently more challenging than valuing tangible assets. While physical assets can be easily appraised based on market value, intangible assets are often based on subjective criteria or legal rights that do not have a straightforward valuation. Here are some common challenges:

1. **Subjectivity**:
The value of intangible assets such as goodwill and brand recognition is difficult to quantify. These assets often depend on factors like market perception, customer loyalty, and reputation, which are not easily measured in financial terms.

2. **Lack of Market Comparisons**:
Many intangible assets, such as patents and copyrights, may not have a direct market for comparison. This makes it difficult to determine their value, especially when they are unique to the company.

3. **Legal and Contractual Limitations**:
The value of some intangible assets is tied to legal rights or contracts, such as patents or trademarks. Changes in laws, legal disputes, or the expiration of contracts can affect the value of these assets.

4. **Amortization and Impairment**:
While tangible assets like machinery and buildings are depreciated over time, intangible assets like patents and goodwill are amortized or tested for impairment. Goodwill, for example, does not have a fixed useful life and is instead subject to annual impairment tests to determine if its carrying value on the Balance Sheet is still justified.

Intangible assets are reported on the Balance Sheet under the non-current assets section, either as individual line items or grouped together. In certain cases, intangible assets like goodwill are only recorded if they have been acquired through a business combination. For intangible assets with a finite life, such as patents and copyrights, amortization is applied over their useful life. This process is similar to depreciation for tangible assets, where the cost is expensed over time. The amortization expense is recorded on the Income Statement and reduces the carrying value of the intangible asset on the Balance Sheet. However, unlike amortizable intangible assets, goodwill and some other intangible assets are subject to annual impairment tests. If the carrying value of the asset exceeds its fair market value, an impairment charge is recorded, reducing the asset's value on the Balance Sheet. Additionally, companies are required to disclose details about their intangible assets in the notes to the financial statements, including their nature, useful life, and any amortization or impairment charges.

Though challenging to value and manage, intangible assets offer unique opportunities for companies to build and maintain competitive advantages. Understanding how to leverage these assets effectively can drive business success, enhance profitability, and increase market valuation. For investors, creditors, and business owners, recognizing and managing intangible assets is essential for making informed financial decisions and ensuring sustainable growth.

Liabilities and Their Impact on Financial Health

Liabilities represent the debts or obligations a company owes to external parties, which arise from past transactions or events and are expected to be settled in the future. Liabilities are a crucial aspect of a company's financial structure, and their management directly impacts a company's financial health, liquidity, and solvency.

In this section, we will explore the different types of liabilities, their role in business operations, and their impact on a company's overall financial health. We will also discuss how liabilities are recorded, how they affect financial statements, and the importance of managing them effectively to ensure long-term business stability.

What are Liabilities?

Liabilities are obligations that require the company to transfer assets, such as cash, goods, or services, to another party in the future. These obligations arise from financial or operational activities like borrowing money, purchasing on credit, or other contractual arrangements.

Liabilities are classified into two main categories based on the timing of when they are due for settlement:

Liability Type	Description	Examples
Current Liabilities	Obligations that are due to be settled within one year or within the company's normal operating cycle.	Accounts Payable, Short-Term Loans, Accrued Expenses, Taxes Payable
Non-Current Liabilities	Obligations that are due after one year or beyond the company's normal operating cycle.	Long-Term Debt, Bonds Payable, Deferred Tax Liabilities

Both current and non-current liabilities are crucial for understanding a company's overall financial position, affecting liquidity, solvency, and capital structure.

Current Liabilities: Short-Term Obligations

Current liabilities represent the debts or obligations that a company must pay within a year or during its operating cycle. Managing current liabilities effectively is critical for ensuring that the business can meet its short-term financial obligations without running into liquidity problems.

Some common types of **current liabilities** include:

- **Accounts Payable**: Amounts owed to suppliers or vendors for goods and services purchased on credit. This is one of the most common short-term liabilities for businesses that purchase inventory or supplies on credit.
- **Short-Term Loans**: Loans or credit lines that need to be repaid within a year. These loans can be used for operational needs or as part of a working capital strategy.
- **Accrued Expenses**: Expenses that have been incurred but not yet paid. Examples include wages, rent, and utilities that accumulate over time but are typically paid later.
- **Taxes Payable**: Taxes owed to the government but not yet paid. These may include income taxes, payroll taxes, and sales taxes.

Impact of Current Liabilities on Financial Health

Managing current liabilities effectively is essential for maintaining liquidity and avoiding financial distress. If a company's current liabilities exceed its current assets (which are used to pay these liabilities), it can face cash flow problems, making it difficult to pay off debts as they come due.

The current ratio is a key financial metric used to assess a company's ability to meet its short-term obligations:

"Current Ratio"="Current Assets" /"Current Liabilities"

A **current ratio** of less than 1 indicates that the company may have difficulty meeting its short-term liabilities, while a ratio above 1 suggests that the company has sufficient current assets to cover its obligations.

Non-Current Liabilities: Long-Term Financial Obligations

Non-current liabilities, also called **long-term liabilities**, are obligations that are due after one year. These liabilities represent the company's long-term debt and other obligations that may require more time to settle. Managing non-current liabilities is essential for ensuring the company maintains its solvency and can continue to grow.

Common examples of **non-current liabilities** include:

- **Long-Term Debt**: Loans or bonds that mature beyond one year. These are often used by businesses to finance expansion, purchase assets, or restructure existing debt.
- **Bonds Payable**: Companies issue bonds to raise capital. The bondholders are paid periodic interest, and the principal amount must be repaid at maturity. Bonds are typically considered long-term liabilities because they have maturity dates of several years or decades.
- **Deferred Tax Liabilities**: Taxes that a company owes but has not yet paid, often due to differences between accounting income and taxable income. These are typically long-term in nature, as they are not expected to be paid within the next 12 months.

Impact of Non-Current Liabilities on Financial Health

Non-current liabilities are crucial for financing long-term growth, but they also represent future obligations that must be carefully managed. High levels of long-term debt can increase a company's financial risk, particularly if it struggles to generate enough cash flow to service the debt.

The debt-to-equity ratio is an important metric for assessing a company's reliance on debt financing:

A high debt-to-equity ratio indicates that the company relies heavily on debt to finance its operations, which can be risky if the company's earnings fluctuate or if interest rates rise. A low ratio, on the other hand, suggests that the company is more financially stable and less dependent on external financing.

"Debt-to-Equity Ratio"="Total Liabilities" /"Owner's Equity"

The Role of Liabilities in Capital Structure

Liabilities play a crucial role in a company's **capital structure**, which refers to the mix of debt and equity financing used to fund its operations and growth. A company's capital structure directly impacts its cost of capital, financial flexibility, and risk profile.

- **Debt Financing**: Taking on debt allows a company to leverage its operations and invest in growth without diluting ownership. However, too much debt can lead to high interest payments and financial strain, particularly during downturns or periods of low revenue.
- **Equity Financing**: Issuing equity (e.g., common or preferred stock) allows a company to raise funds without incurring debt. However, this can dilute ownership and control of the business.

The optimal capital structure strikes a balance between debt and equity, allowing the company to take advantage of the benefits of leverage while managing the risks associated with debt obligations.

Liabilities are recorded on the Balance Sheet under two categories: current liabilities (due within one year) and non-current liabilities (due after one year). They play a significant role in preparing both the Income Statement and the Statement of Cash Flows. On the Income Statement, interest on debt is considered an expense, reducing a company's net income. The higher the debt level, the higher the interest expense, which can negatively affect profitability. In the Statement of Cash Flows, cash flows from financing activities, such as borrowing or repaying debt, are recorded. This statement is essential for tracking how liabilities are being managed, whether the company is raising new capital or repaying existing debt.

Managing Liabilities for Financial Health

Managing liabilities is critical for ensuring the company's financial stability and long-term success. Companies should focus on the following principles when managing liabilities:

1. **Liquidity Management**: Companies must ensure they have enough current assets to meet short-term obligations. Regularly monitoring the **current ratio** and ensuring timely collection of receivables can help maintain liquidity.
2. **Debt Service**: It's essential to manage long-term debt and ensure that the business generates enough cash flow to meet debt payments without jeopardizing operations. Maintaining a manageable **debt-to-equity ratio** ensures the company does not become overly reliant on borrowed funds.
3. **Cost of Capital**: Companies should carefully evaluate the cost of debt relative to the benefits of financing with borrowed funds. High levels of debt can increase the cost of capital and reduce profitability, particularly if interest rates rise.
4. **Debt Refinancing**: Refinancing existing debt at lower interest rates or longer terms can help reduce financial pressure and provide more breathing room for growth. However, businesses must weigh the costs of refinancing against potential savings.

JOHNSON & JOHNSON - MANAGING LIABILITIES

With operations in over 60 countries, J&J's financial management plays a crucial role in maintaining the company's financial health.

CHALLENGES

- Managing Short-Term Liabilities Amid Global Operations
- Long-Term Debt and Financing for R&D

OBJECTIVES

LIQUIDITY FOR SHORT-TERM OBLIGATIONS

By maintaining a healthy current ratio and optimizing working capital.

SUSTAINABLE DEBT PROFILE

J&J aims to maintain an optimal debt-to-equity ratio.

RESULT AND BENEFITS

- Johnson & Johnson has maintained a strong liquidity position, with its current ratio hovering around 1.5 in recent years.
- With a long-term debt of approximately $20 billion and a debt-to-equity ratio of around 0.4, J&J manages its debt load effectively, keeping interest expenses low.

Debits & Credit

At the core of accounting, every financial transaction involves both a debit and a credit, and for every debit, there must be a corresponding credit. This is the fundamental principle of the double-entry accounting system, which ensures that the accounting equation remains balanced:

Assets = Liabilities + Owner's Equity

In this system, debits and credits are used to increase or decrease various types of accounts. Understanding how debits and credits affect different accounts is crucial for proper financial reporting and ensuring that the accounting records are accurate and complete.

Debits and credits are recorded in the general ledger, which organizes all accounts by type. The basic rule is simple: debits increase certain accounts and decrease others, and credits have the opposite effect. This distinction depends on the type of account involved.

The Rules of Debits and Credits

Each type of account is affected differently by debits and credits. The following table outlines how debits and credits affect the four main types of accounts in accounting: assets, liabilities, equity, and income/expenses.

Account Type	Increase with a Debit	Decrease with a Debit	Increase with a Credit	Decrease with a Credit
Assets	Yes	No	No	Yes
Liabilities	No	Yes	Yes	No
Owner's Equity	No	Yes	Yes	No
Revenue/ Income	No	Yes	Yes	No
Expenses	Yes	No	No	Yes

Explanation of Effects on Accounts:

1. **Assets**:

   Debits increase assets because they represent the acquisition of resources.

   Credits decrease assets because they reflect the outflow or disposal of resources.

Example: When cash is received from a customer, the asset account (Cash) is debited (increased).

2. **Liabilities**:

Debits decrease liabilities because they represent payments or settlements of debts.

Credits increase liabilities because they reflect an increase in amounts owed by the company.

Example: When a loan is repaid, the liability account (Loans Payable) is debited (decreased).

3. **Owner's Equity**:

Debits decrease owner's equity, such as when the owner withdraws funds from the business or when expenses are incurred.

Credits increase owner's equity, such as when the company earns revenue or when the owner invests capital in the business.

Example: When the business generates revenue, the equity account (Retained Earnings) is credited (increased).

4. **Revenue/Income**:

Debits decrease income, which usually happens in the case of refunds or returns.

Credits increase income as they reflect earned revenue.

Example: When a service is sold, the revenue account (Service Revenue) is credited (increased).

5. **Expenses**:

Debits increase expenses, as they represent costs incurred by the company.

Credits decrease expenses, though this is less common (e.g., a reversal or correction).

Example: When rent is paid, the expense account (Rent Expense) is debited (increased).

DEBTS AND CREDIT IN DOUBLE ENTRY ACCOUNTING

Account Type	Debit	Credit
Assets	↑	↓
Expenses	↑	↓
Revenue	↓	↑
Liabilities	↓	↑
Equity	↓	↑

Why Debits and Credits Matter in Financial Accounting

Debits and credits are not just mechanical tools for keeping track of transactions—they are essential for ensuring **accuracy** and **balance** in financial accounting. Here's why debits and credits are so important:

1. **Balance and Accuracy**:
   Double-entry accounting ensures that every transaction is recorded accurately by making sure that debits and credits always balance. This balance guarantees that the accounting equation is always satisfied.

2. **Financial Statement Preparation**:
   Accurate debits and credits are essential for preparing the three main financial statements:

   Income Statement: Tracks revenue and expenses to calculate net income.

   Balance Sheet: Reflects the company's assets, liabilities, and equity.

   Statement of Cash Flows: Tracks cash inflows and outflows from operations, investing, and financing activities.

3. **Error Detection**:
   If debits and credits do not balance, it indicates an error in recording the transaction. This error detection ensures that financial records are reliable

and that discrepancies can be identified and corrected.

4. **Comprehensive Financial Picture**:
   Debits and credits ensure that both sides of each transaction are captured. This dual tracking provides a comprehensive picture of how business activities affect financial health, helping business owners and investors make informed decisions.

Common Challenges with Debits and Credits

Even though the principles of debits and credits are simple, mistakes can still occur. Some common challenges include:

1. **Misclassification of Accounts**:
   Sometimes, transactions are recorded in the wrong accounts. For example, a payment for an asset might be mistakenly recorded as an expense. Proper understanding of account types is necessary to avoid such errors.
2. **Overlooking Adjustments**:
   At the end of an accounting period, businesses must make adjusting entries for things like accrued expenses or deferred revenues. Failing to record these adjustments can lead to inaccurate financial reports.
3. **Unequal Debits and Credits**:
   One of the most common errors in accounting is when debits and credits don't balance. This often occurs due to simple mistakes, such as omitting an entry or recording an incorrect amount.

To understand how the principles of accounting are applied in a real-world business setting, let's explore the accounting process for a pet supplies company. This example will walk through key transactions, how they are recorded in the accounting system, and how they affect the company's financial statements. We'll focus on several key accounting concepts, including revenue recognition, expenses, inventory management, and liabilities.

By following the pet supplies company through a series of transactions, we'll demonstrate how double-entry accounting, debits and credits, and other key accounting principles work in practice.

Let's assume the company, Happy Pets Supplies, is a small retail business that sells pet food, toys, grooming products, and accessories. The company also offers some services, such as grooming and pet training. It has been in operation for two years and follows accrual basis accounting.

Key Accounts for Happy Pets Supplies

The company maintains several key accounts, including:

Account Type	Examples of Accounts
Assets	Cash, Accounts Receivable, Inventory, Prepaid Rent
Liabilities	Accounts Payable, Sales Tax Payable, Short-Term Loans
Owner's Equity	Owner's Capital, Retained Earnings
Revenue	Sales Revenue, Service Revenue
Expenses	Cost of Goods Sold, Rent Expense, Wages, Utilities

Transaction 1: Selling Pet Supplies

On January 1, Happy Pets Supplies sells pet food and toys for $2,000 to a customer. The customer pays in cash.

Debit: Cash $2,000 (Increase in asset)

Credit: Sales Revenue $2,000 (Increase in equity)

This transaction increases the company's cash and revenue. Since the sale was made for cash, there is no accounts receivable involved.

Transaction 2: Purchasing Inventory on Credit

On January 3, Happy Pets Supplies purchases pet grooming products worth $1,200 from a supplier on credit.

Debit: Inventory $1,200 (Increase in asset)

Credit: Accounts Payable $1,200 (Increase in liability)

The company's inventory increases, and it now owes the supplier $1,200, reflected in **accounts payable**.

Transaction 3: Paying Rent

On January 5, the company pays $800 for the monthly rent on its store location.

Debit: Rent Expense $800 (Increase in expense)

Credit: Cash $800 (Decrease in asset)

Rent is an ongoing operating expense that reduces the company's available cash. The expense is recorded in the period when it is incurred.

Transaction 4: Providing Pet Grooming Services

On January 7, Happy Pets Supplies provides pet grooming services for $500 to a customer. The customer will pay in two weeks.

Debit: Accounts Receivable $500 (Increase in asset)

Credit: Service Revenue $500 (Increase in equity)

Since the customer hasn't paid yet, the transaction is recorded as an **accounts receivable**, meaning the company expects to receive the payment in the future.

Impact on Financial Statements

Let's now look at how these transactions impact the key financial statements for Happy Pets Supplies:

Income Statement (Profit and Loss Statement)

The Income Statement shows the company's revenues and expenses over a period, ultimately determining whether the company is operating at a profit or a loss.

Revenue	**Amount**
Sales Revenue	$2,000
Service Revenue	$500
Total Revenue	**$2,500**

Expenses	**Amount**
Rent Expense	$800
Wages Expense	$1,000
Cost of Goods Sold	$500
Total Expenses	**$2,300**

| **Net Income** | **$200** |

Balance Sheet

The **Balance Sheet** shows the company's financial position at a specific point in time, listing its **assets**, **liabilities**, and **equity**.

Assets	**Amount**
Cash	$500
Accounts Receivable	$500
Inventory	$700
Total Assets	**$1,700**

Liabilities	**Amount**
Accounts Payable	$0

Liabilities	Amount
Total Liabilities	$0

Owner's Equity	Amount
Owner's Capital	$1,500
Retained Earnings	$200
Total Equity	$1,700

Inventory Management and Cost of Goods Sold (COGS)

Inventory management is critical for any retail business, as it impacts both the balance sheet and income statement. For Happy Pets Supplies, accurate inventory tracking ensures that the correct amount of cost of goods sold is recorded, reflecting the true cost of the inventory that has been sold.

In the example above, the company adjusted its inventory at the end of the month and recorded $500 as COGS, which was calculated by subtracting the value of the unsold inventory from the purchased amount. This adjustment ensures that the company accurately reflects the expense associated with the goods sold during the period.

Liabilities and Cash Flow Management

Liabilities, such as accounts payable and short-term loans, are a normal part of business operations. However, managing liabilities is essential for maintaining a healthy cash flow. For Happy Pets Supplies, the company paid off its supplier promptly, reducing its liability and preserving its cash flow position.

In managing liabilities, the company needs to ensure that it has sufficient liquidity to pay off its short-term obligations while continuing to reinvest in the business. This is particularly important for small businesses that often operate with tight cash flow margins.

By following these transactions and understanding their impact on the financial statements, we see how a pet supplies company applies basic accounting principles to track revenue, expenses, and liabilities. The double-entry accounting system ensures that each transaction is accurately recorded, maintaining the integrity of the company's financial records. Managing inventory, accounts receivable, and liabilities effectively ensures that the business can operate smoothly and remain financially stable.

Equity: Defining Ownership and Value

In financial accounting, equity represents the ownership interest in a company, reflecting the residual value of the business after liabilities have been subtracted from assets. Equity is a key component of the balance sheet, and it plays a significant role in assessing a company's financial health and value. Understanding equity is crucial for investors, business owners, and stakeholders because it helps determine the worth of a business and the distribution of profits and losses.

In this section, we will explore the different types of equity, how it is calculated, and its importance in both financial reporting and business decision-making. We will also discuss how equity is impacted by various business activities and its significance for both internal and external users of financial statements.

What is Equity?

Equity represents the owners' claim on the assets of a company after all liabilities have been paid. Essentially, it is the portion of the business that belongs to the owners or shareholders. In the context of a sole proprietorship or partnership, equity refers to the capital invested by the owner(s) or partners. In the case of a corporation, equity is typically represented by shareholders' equity, which includes common stock, retained earnings, and additional paid-in capital.

The equity section of the balance sheet shows the financial position of the company from the owners' perspective. The basic equation that defines equity is:

$$\text{Equity} = \text{Assets} - \text{Liabilities}$$

This equation is the backbone of the balance sheet, and it emphasizes that the equity value is determined by subtracting what the company owes (liabilities) from what it owns (assets).

Types of Equity

Equity can be divided into different categories depending on the business structure and the way ownership is represented. Here's an overview of the types of equity that are commonly seen in businesses:

Type of Equity	Description	Examples
Owner's Equity	In sole proprietorships and partnerships, this is the capital contributed by the owner(s) plus retained earnings.	Owner's Capital, Partner Contributions, Withdrawals

Type of Equity	Description	Examples
Shareholders' Equity	In corporations, this represents the ownership interest of shareholders, including both invested capital and retained earnings.	Common Stock, Retained Earnings, Additional Paid-In Capital
Paid-In Capital	The amount of money invested by shareholders or owners into the business in exchange for shares or ownership stakes.	Common Stock, Preferred Stock, Additional Paid-In Capital
Retained Earnings	The accumulated net income of a business that is not distributed to shareholders as dividends but is reinvested in the business.	Retained Earnings (Cumulative Profit)

Owner's Equity:

- **Sole Proprietorships**: The owner's equity in a sole proprietorship is the amount invested in the business plus any accumulated profits or losses. This is typically referred to as **owner's capital**. In a sole proprietorship, the owner has full control and responsibility for the business.

Shareholders' Equity:

- **Corporations**: Shareholders' equity represents the total value of a company that is attributable to its shareholders. It includes funds raised through the issuance of stock (both common and preferred) and retained earnings, minus any treasury stock.

Components of Equity in a Corporation

In a corporation, equity is typically composed of several elements. These components can provide insight into how much of the business is financed by ownership and how much is attributed to earnings that have been retained for reinvestment. The main components of shareholders' equity are:

1. **Common Stock**:
   Common stock represents ownership in the company and entitles the shareholder to voting rights and a claim on dividends. The value of common stock is based on the number of shares issued and the par value assigned to those shares. It is the basic unit of ownership in a company.
2. **Preferred Stock**:
   Preferred stockholders have a higher claim on the company's assets and earnings than common stockholders. Preferred stockholders receive dividends before common stockholders, but they typically do not have voting rights. Preferred stock is often issued to raise capital while

providing a steady income stream to investors.

3. **Retained Earnings**:
Retained earnings represent the accumulated net income of the business that has not been distributed to shareholders as dividends. These earnings are reinvested in the business for growth, expansion, or debt reduction. Retained earnings are a key indicator of a company's profitability and ability to generate value over time.

4. **Additional Paid-In Capital**:
Also known as **capital surplus**, this represents the amount paid by shareholders for shares above their nominal or par value. For example, if a share has a par value of $1 but is sold for $10, the additional $9 per share would be recorded as additional paid-in capital.

5. **Treasury Stock**:
Treasury stock refers to shares that were repurchased by the company from the open market. These shares are no longer considered outstanding and are excluded from the calculation of earnings per share. Treasury stock reduces shareholders' equity, as it represents a reduction in the number of shares outstanding.

The Role of Equity in Business Operations

Equity is not just a financial metric but a fundamental aspect of how a business operates. The level and structure of equity in a company have important implications for:

1. **Financial Flexibility**:
Equity provides a source of capital that businesses can use to invest in growth, pay down debt, or weather economic downturns. The higher the equity base, the greater the financial flexibility a company has in making strategic decisions.

2. **Ownership and Control**:
Equity ownership often determines the level of control that individuals or groups have over the company. In a **sole proprietorship**, the owner has complete control, while in a **corporation**, control is divided among shareholders based on the number of shares they own.

3. **Dividend Payments**:
Shareholders receive dividends from the company's profits based on their ownership stake in the business. The decision to distribute dividends is made by the board of directors, and it impacts the level of retained earnings and overall equity in the business.

4. **Investment and Growth**:
Companies with strong equity positions are more likely to attract investors and secure financing. Equity serves as a foundation for raising

capital, whether through the issuance of new shares, private equity investment, or venture capital.

Equity and the Balance Sheet

In the **Balance Sheet**, equity is listed under the "**Shareholders' Equity**" section, typically following assets and liabilities. The equity section reflects the **residual interest** in the company after all liabilities have been deducted from assets.

The basic accounting equation that represents this relationship is:

Assets = Liabilities + Owner's Equity

As liabilities and assets change, equity adjusts accordingly. If a business takes on more debt or increases its liabilities, equity may decrease unless offset by an increase in assets. Conversely, a company can increase its equity by retaining profits (through **retained earnings**) or issuing new stock to investors.

The key components of equity shown on the Balance Sheet include:

- **Common Stock**
- **Retained Earnings**
- **Additional Paid-In Capital**
- **Preferred Stock** (if applicable)
- **Treasury Stock** (if applicable)

Together, these elements provide a complete picture of the ownership structure and the financial health of the business.

Impact of Equity on Company Valuation

Equity is a key component when determining the value of a business. In **business valuations**, equity plays a significant role in assessing the value of the ownership interest and determining the market value of the company. The two most common methods used for equity-based business valuations are:

1. **Market Capitalization**:
   Market capitalization is calculated by multiplying the company's share price by the number of shares outstanding. This method is typically used for publicly traded companies to determine their market value based on the current stock price.
2. **Book Value of Equity**:
   The book value of equity is the difference between total assets and total liabilities as reported on the Balance Sheet. This represents the net value of the company from an accounting perspective. While it may differ from market value, it provides insight into the company's historical investment and retention of earnings.

3. **Discounted Cash Flow (DCF) Analysis**:
   DCF analysis estimates the present value of future cash flows, which is then used to calculate the equity value of the company. This method is commonly used in mergers and acquisitions to determine the value of a company's equity based on projected earnings.

In a corporation, the management of equity—through issuing stock, reinvesting earnings, or paying dividends—has important implications for the company's future growth and profitability. For investors, equity serves as a key indicator of the company's potential for long-term value creation and financial stability. By understanding equity and its components, businesses can make informed decisions that support their strategic goals and ensure their long-term success.

Chapter 4: Recording Transactions

An **invoice** is a formal request for payment issued by a seller to a buyer for goods or services provided. It typically includes detailed information about the products or services sold, the quantity, the agreed-upon price, and the payment terms. An invoice serves as both a legal document and a record of sale for both parties involved in the transaction.

From an accounting perspective, an invoice is crucial because it marks the revenue recognition point for the seller. For the buyer, the invoice serves as proof of purchase and a record of the accounts payable. Invoices are essential in accounts receivable management for businesses, ensuring that payments are collected and recorded properly.

Types of Invoices

Invoices can vary in structure and content depending on the nature of the transaction, the business, and the terms agreed upon. Below is a summary of the most common types of invoices used by businesses:

Type of Invoice	Description	When It's Used
Standard Invoice	The most common type of invoice, listing the products or services provided, their quantities, prices, and payment terms.	Used for regular sales transactions, goods, or services.
Pro Forma Invoice	A preliminary invoice issued before goods or services are delivered, often used to provide a cost estimate.	Used to provide an estimate or quotation to a customer.
Credit Invoice (Credit Memo)	Issued when a buyer returns goods or services, or when there's a need to adjust a previous invoice.	Used for returns, discounts, or price adjustments.
Debit Invoice (Debit Memo)	Used to adjust the original invoice when additional charges are added, such as for late fees or extra services.	Used to correct undercharged amounts or add fees.
Recurring Invoice	An invoice that is sent on a regular schedule (e.g., monthly or annually) for ongoing services or subscriptions.	Used for subscription-based services or regular payments.

Type of Invoice	Description	When It's Used
Timesheet Invoice	An invoice based on the hours worked or services provided over a period, often used by contractors or consultants.	Used by service-based businesses that bill by the hour.

Each of these invoices has its own purpose and application, depending on the nature of the business transaction and the agreed terms.

Key Components of an Invoice

A typical invoice contains several essential elements that provide clarity about the transaction and ensure that both parties understand their rights and obligations. The following table outlines the key components of an invoice:

Component	Description
Invoice Number	A unique identifier for the invoice, ensuring that it can be easily referenced for tracking and payment purposes.
Date of Issue	The date the invoice is issued, which is crucial for determining the payment due date and recording the transaction.
Due Date	The date by which the payment is expected, usually based on the payment terms (e.g., Net 30, due within 30 days).
Seller's Information	The name, address, and contact details of the business issuing the invoice.
Buyer's Information	The name, address, and contact details of the customer or client receiving the invoice.
Description of Goods/ Services	A detailed list of the products or services provided, including quantities, unit prices, and any applicable discounts.
Total Amount Due	The total amount the buyer owes, including taxes, shipping fees, and any discounts applied.
Payment Terms	The terms for payment, such as the method (e.g., wire transfer, check, credit card) and the deadline for payment.
Tax Information	Any applicable sales tax or VAT (Value Added Tax) applied to the transaction, often required by law for businesses.
Additional Notes	Any extra information or instructions, such as late payment fees or specific conditions of sale.

These components ensure that both the seller and buyer have all the necessary information to facilitate payment and keep track of the transaction for accounting purposes.

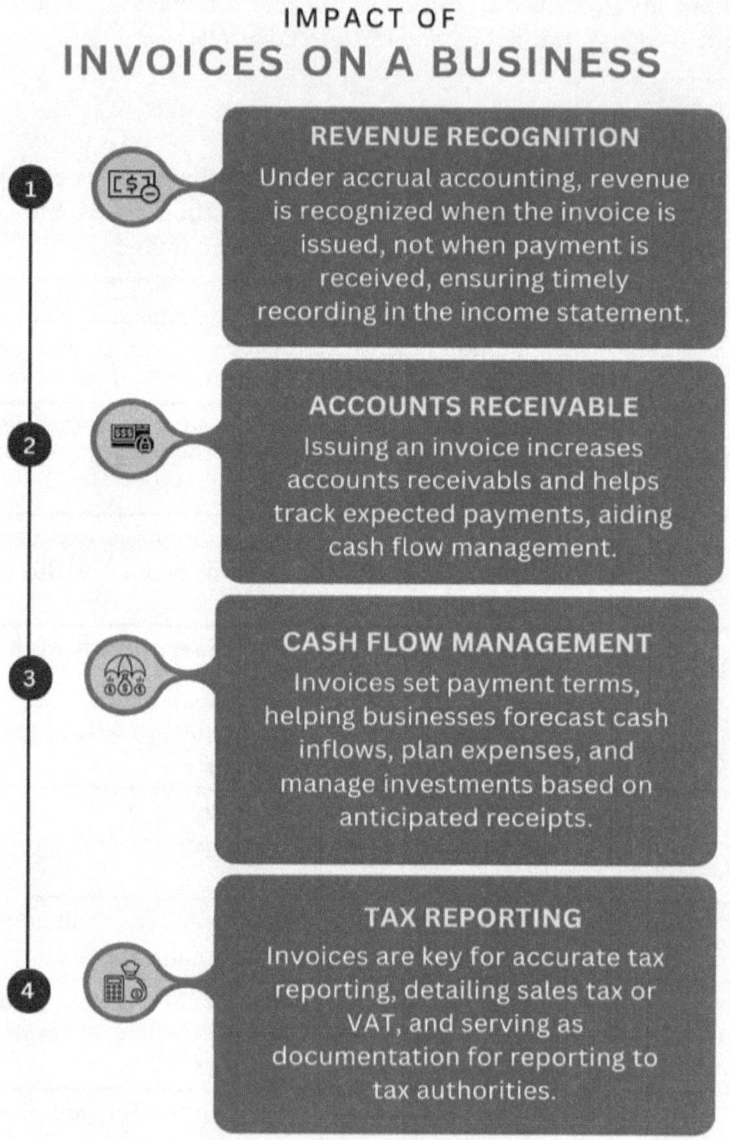

Managing Invoices and Cash Flow

For businesses, effective invoice management is essential for maintaining a healthy cash flow and ensuring that payments are received on time. Poor invoice management can lead to delayed payments, missed revenue, and cash flow problems. The following strategies help businesses manage invoices effectively:

Strategy	Description
Clear Payment Terms	Clearly stating payment terms (e.g., Net 30, due within 30 days) on every invoice helps customers know when and how to pay.
Timely Invoicing	Issuing invoices promptly after goods or services are delivered ensures that payments are collected in a timely manner.
Follow-Up on Unpaid Invoices	Regular follow-ups, such as sending reminders or contacting customers for overdue payments, can help accelerate collections.
Use of Invoice Tracking Software	Accounting or invoicing software can help track issued invoices, payments received, and outstanding balances, making it easier to manage and monitor cash flow.
Offering Early Payment Discounts	Providing discounts for early payment can encourage customers to pay invoices sooner, improving cash flow.

These practices help ensure that businesses maintain adequate liquidity and avoid issues like bad debt or cash shortages, which can disrupt operations.

Invoices have important legal implications, as they serve as evidence of the terms of a transaction and can be used in legal disputes to resolve conflicts between buyers and sellers. An invoice functions as proof of sale, confirming that goods or services were provided and outlining key transaction details such as payment amounts and due dates. The terms included in the invoice, such as payment deadlines and interest on late payments, may also be legally binding if both parties have agreed to them. Additionally, if the invoice includes terms for late payment penalties or interest on overdue amounts, these can be enforced by law, provided they align with applicable regulations. Furthermore, invoices must comply with local tax regulations, serving as crucial documents for businesses to calculate and remit sales tax or VAT to the appropriate tax authorities.

For business owners, accountants, and financial managers, mastering the invoicing process is essential for maintaining healthy financial practices and keeping the company's financial health on track. Whether for small businesses or large corporations, proper invoice management ensures timely payments and helps the company stay financially stable.

The Basics of a T-Account

A T-account is one of the most fundamental tools in accounting, used to visualize the recording of debits and credits in the double-entry accounting system. The T-account provides a simple, clear representation of how transactions affect individual accounts, making it easier for accountants and business owners to track the movement of financial elements. Although more modern accounting systems use general ledger software, understanding the T-account is still essential for grasping the basic principles of accounting.

In this section, we will explore what a T-account is, its components, how to set it up, and how to use it for recording transactions. We'll also cover common mistakes and best practices when using T-accounts.

What is a T-Account?

A T-account is a graphic representation of an individual account in the general ledger, shaped like the letter "T." The account's title is written at the top, and the left side is used to record debits, while the right side is used to record credits. This visual format helps accountants keep track of how each transaction impacts specific accounts and ensures the accounting equation remains balanced.

The T-account is called such because it resembles a "T," with the left side representing debits and the right side representing credits. Each side of the T-account will contain amounts that either increase or decrease the balance of the account depending on the type of account involved.

A T-account is typically set up with the following components:

Component	Description
Account Title	The name of the account being represented (e.g., Cash, Accounts Payable).
Left Side (Debit)	Used to record debits, which are usually increases in asset accounts or decreases in liability and equity accounts.
Right Side (Credit)	Used to record credits, which are usually decreases in asset accounts or increases in liability and equity accounts.

When transactions occur, debits and credits are recorded in the left and right columns, respectively. The balance of the account is calculated by subtracting the total credits from the total debits.

Example 1: Selling Goods for Cash

Let's say a company sells $500 worth of pet food and receives payment in cash. The transaction would involve two accounts: Cash (an asset) and Sales Revenue (a revenue account). To record this in T-accounts:

Cash	Sales Revenue
Debit $500	Credit $500
Total: $500	**Total:** $500
Balance: $500 (Debit Balance)	

In this example:

- The Cash account is debited because cash is an asset, and assets increase with debits.
- The Sales Revenue account is credited because revenue increases with credits.

Example 2: Paying Rent

Now let's say the company pays $200 in rent. The transaction affects **Cash** (an asset) and **Rent Expense** (an expense).

Cash	Rent Expense
Credit $200	Debit $200
Total: $200	**Total:** $200
Balance: $300 (Debit Balance)	

In this case:

- The **Cash** account is credited because cash is an asset, and assets decrease with credits.
- The **Rent Expense** account is debited because expenses increase with debits.

Balancing a T-Account

The purpose of a T-account is to maintain the balance of each account in the general ledger. After recording the debits and credits, the balance of the account is determined by subtracting the total credits from the total debits.

For example, let's look at the Cash account in a scenario where multiple transactions have occurred:

Cash	
Debit $500	Credit $200

Cash	
Total: $500	**Total:** $200
Balance: $300 (Debit Balance)	

This balance reflects the available cash in the company's cash account after the transactions.

Common Mistakes in Using T-Accounts

While T-accounts are simple in concept, they can be prone to errors if not used properly. Some common mistakes include:

1. **Incorrect Placement of Debits and Credits**:
   A common mistake is placing debits and credits on the wrong side of the T-account, which can result in an inaccurate representation of a transaction. For example, debiting a revenue account instead of crediting it can lead to an overstatement of revenue.
2. **Forgetting to Balance Accounts**:
   It's essential to ensure that the total debits equal the total credits. If they don't, there's likely an error in recording the transaction.
3. **Omitting Transactions**:
   Missing entries or transactions can lead to incomplete accounting records. It's important to record every transaction to maintain the accuracy of financial statements.
4. **Incorrectly Categorizing Accounts**:
   Sometimes, accounts are misclassified, which can lead to errors in financial reporting. For instance, recording an asset as an expense can result in an incorrect balance sheet or income statement.

The Role of T-Accounts in the Accounting Process

T-accounts play a critical role in the accounting cycle, helping businesses track financial transactions and prepare financial statements. The accounting process begins with recording each transaction in the journal and then transferring those entries to the general ledger, where T-accounts are maintained.

From the general ledger, accountants can prepare financial statements such as the balance sheet, income statement, and cash flow statement. By ensuring that debits and credits are recorded correctly, T-accounts help maintain the integrity of these financial reports.

Journal Entries and General Ledgers

In accounting, journal entries and general ledgers are the backbone of the double-entry system. They are essential tools for recording and organizing financial transactions. Journal entries ensure that every transaction is documented in detail, while the general ledger aggregates this information to provide a comprehensive view of a company's financial health.

This section will explore the relationship between journal entries and the general ledger, their importance in the accounting cycle, and how they contribute to maintaining accurate financial records. Through examples and explanations, we will demonstrate how these concepts are applied in practice.

What is a Journal Entry?

A journal entry is the initial record of a financial transaction, made in a company's journal, the first step in the accounting cycle. It is a detailed log of every financial activity that affects the business, recorded in chronological order. Journal entries are the raw data that will later be transferred to the general ledger. Each journal entry must contain certain key components, including the date of the transaction, the accounts affected, the debit and credit amounts, and a brief description or narration of the transaction.

Key Components of a Journal Entry:

1. **Date**: The date when the transaction occurred.
2. **Accounts**: The specific accounts impacted by the transaction (e.g., Cash, Revenue, Accounts Payable).
3. **Debit and Credit Amounts**: The amounts being debited and credited for each account.
4. **Narration**: A brief description of the transaction for clarification.

In a journal entry, debits and credits are recorded in a way that ensures the accounting equation (Assets = Liabilities + Equity) remains balanced. Every debit must have a corresponding credit of equal value.

Example of a Journal Entry:

Let's say Happy Pets Supplies sells $500 worth of pet food to a customer on credit:

Date	Account	Debit	Credit	Description
January 1, 2025	Accounts Receivable	$500		Sold pet food on credit to customer.
January 1, 2025	Sales Revenue		$500	

In this example:

- **Accounts Receivable** is debited, increasing the company's receivables (an asset).
- **Sales Revenue** is credited, increasing the company's income (equity).

SAMPLE

JOURNAL ENTRY

Date	Particulars	Debit	Credit
Apr 1, 2025	Cash A/c	$100,000	
	To Common Stock A/c		$100,000
(Being the common stock issued worth $100,000)			
Apr 1, 2025	Rent A/c	$10,000	
	To Cash A/c		$10,000
(Being the rent for the current month paid amounting $10,000)			
Apr 1, 2025	Prepaid Rent A/c	$50,000	
	To Cash A/c		$50,000
(Being the advance rent for the next 5 months paid amounting $50,000)			
Apr 3, 2025	Office Supplies A/c	$12,500	
	To Accounts Payable A/c		$12,500
(Being office supplies purchased on account having cost of $12,500)			

What is a General Ledger?

The general ledger is a comprehensive collection of all the company's accounts, where all the journal entries are ultimately posted. The general ledger provides a detailed view of each account's activity, allowing accountants to track the balances of each account over time. It serves as the foundation for preparing the company's financial statements, such as the balance sheet and income statement.

Unlike the journal, which is organized by date, the general ledger is organized by account. Each account in the general ledger has its own T-account or ledger page, where transactions are recorded.

Account	Debit	Credit	Balance
Cash	$500		$500
Accounts Receivable	$500		$500
Sales Revenue		$500	$500

In the example above, the Sales Revenue account shows the amount earned from the sale of pet food, while Accounts Receivable reflects the amount the company is owed.

How Journal Entries Affect the General Ledger

Every journal entry is posted to the general ledger, which helps provide a complete record of all financial transactions. After journal entries are made, they are transferred to the respective accounts in the general ledger, ensuring that all transactions are accurately recorded. This process is known as **posting**.

Let's break down how this works in practice. Assume a business transaction involves selling goods on credit, and the following journal entry is made:

Date	Account	Debit	Credit	Narration
January 1, 2025	Accounts Receivable	$1,000		Sold goods on credit.
January 1, 2025	Sales Revenue		$1,000	

In this case, both Accounts Receivable and Sales Revenue are affected. The next step is to **post** this journal entry into the general ledger:

Posting to General Ledger:

Account	Debit	Credit	Balance
Accounts Receivable	$1,000		$1,000
Sales Revenue		$1,000	$1,000

By posting the journal entry to the general ledger, the company now has an up-to-date record of its accounts receivable and sales revenue. The balance in each account will reflect the cumulative effect of all transactions recorded.

The Role of Journal Entries and General Ledgers in the Accounting Cycle

Journal entries and the general ledger are integral parts of the **accounting cycle**, which begins when a transaction occurs and ends with the preparation of financial statements. The accounting cycle involves several steps, including:

1. **Identifying and Analyzing Transactions**: Determine the financial impact of business activities.
2. **Journalizing Transactions**: Record transactions in the journal using appropriate debits and credits.
3. **Posting to the General Ledger**: Transfer journal entries to the general ledger, where accounts are updated.
4. **Trial Balance**: Prepare a trial balance to ensure that debits and credits balance.
5. **Adjusting Entries**: Make adjustments for accruals, deferrals, depreciation, etc.
6. **Preparing Financial Statements**: Use the general ledger to prepare the company's financial statements.

Through this cycle, journal entries and the general ledger work together to ensure that financial records are accurate and up-to-date. Proper recording and posting of transactions allow businesses to maintain reliable financial data that is essential for internal decision-making and external reporting.

Common Mistakes and Best Practices in Using Journal Entries and General Ledgers

When working with journal entries and the general ledger, mistakes can easily occur. Here are some common mistakes and best practices to ensure accuracy:

Common Mistakes:

1. **Incorrect Classification of Accounts**:
   Misclassifying an account (e.g., recording a liability as an asset) can lead to errors in the general ledger. Always ensure that accounts are properly classified and follow standard accounting conventions.
2. **Omitting Transactions**:
   Failing to record transactions in the journal or neglecting to post journal entries to the general ledger can lead to incomplete financial records. Keep a detailed record of all transactions.
3. **Unequal Debits and Credits**:
   Double-entry accounting relies on the principle that for every debit, there must be a corresponding credit. Errors in this process can result in imbalances that are hard to detect.

Best Practices:

1. **Regularly Reconcile Accounts**:
   Reconcile accounts periodically to ensure that the balances in the general ledger match the actual financial condition of the business.

2. **Use Accounting Software**:
   Accounting software can help automate the process of recording journal entries and posting them to the general ledger, reducing the risk of human error.

3. **Train Staff**:
   Ensure that employees involved in the accounting process are properly trained to handle journal entries and general ledger updates efficiently and accurately.

The Importance of Journal Entries and General Ledgers for Financial Reporting

The journal and general ledger serve as the foundation for preparing a company's financial statements, including the balance sheet, income statement, and cash flow statement. These statements provide an overview of a company's financial health and performance, helping management, investors, and creditors make informed decisions.

The journal and general ledger are essential tools for ensuring that the financial statements reflect accurate, up-to-date information about a company's financial condition. By properly recording transactions and maintaining accurate ledgers, businesses can produce reliable financial reports that provide transparency and facilitate decision-making.

Understanding how to properly use journal entries and the general ledger is crucial for anyone involved in the accounting process, whether you're a business owner, accountant, or financial analyst. By following best practices and maintaining accurate records, businesses can ensure the integrity of their financial data and support sound decision-making.

Creating and Using a Chart of Accounts

The Chart of Accounts (COA) is a fundamental tool in accounting that helps organize and categorize all the accounts used by a company in its financial transactions. It provides a structured framework for recording and managing financial data, ensuring that every transaction is categorized properly for accurate financial reporting. Whether you're managing a small business or a large corporation, creating and using a well-structured chart of accounts is essential for clarity and efficiency in accounting.

In this section, we will explore the purpose of the Chart of Accounts, its structure, and how businesses can design and implement it to streamline their accounting processes. We will also discuss the relationship between the COA and the company's financial statements, and offer insights into how the chart can evolve as a business grows.

What is a Chart of Accounts?

The Chart of Accounts is a categorized list of all the accounts a company uses in its general ledger. These accounts track every financial transaction made by the business and help ensure that accounting records are organized and classified in a way that supports the preparation of financial statements.

The COA acts as a skeleton structure that defines the company's financial framework, laying the foundation for how financial transactions will be recorded. A well-designed chart enables accountants to accurately track assets, liabilities, equity, revenues, and expenses, and it helps maintain compliance with accounting standards.

Key Features of a Chart of Accounts:

- **Organization**: The chart categorizes accounts into major groups such as assets, liabilities, income, and expenses.
- **Flexibility**: It can be adapted to meet the needs of businesses of all sizes, from small startups to multinational corporations.
- **Scalability**: As the business grows, the COA can be expanded to accommodate new accounts.

Structure of a Chart of Accounts

A typical chart of accounts is divided into five primary categories:

1. **Assets**: Accounts that represent what the company owns, including both current and non-current assets.
2. **Liabilities**: Accounts that represent what the company owes to others, including current and long-term liabilities.
3. **Equity**: Accounts that track the ownership interest in the business, including capital contributions and retained earnings.
4. **Revenue**: Accounts that represent the company's earnings from business activities.
5. **Expenses**: Accounts that represent costs incurred by the company to generate revenue.

Each of these categories is further subdivided into sub-accounts to provide greater detail. For example, under Assets, you might have Cash, Accounts Receivable, and Inventory.

Account Category	Example Accounts
Assets	Cash, Accounts Receivable, Inventory, Prepaid Expenses, Equipment
Liabilities	Accounts Payable, Loans Payable, Accrued Expenses

Account Category	Example Accounts
Equity	Owner's Capital, Retained Earnings, Common Stock, Dividends
Revenue	Sales Revenue, Service Revenue, Interest Income
Expenses	Rent Expense, Utilities Expense, Salaries Expense, Depreciation

Creating a Chart of Accounts

Designing a Chart of Accounts (COA) requires careful consideration of the company's structure, the nature of its business, and the level of detail required for financial reporting. Below are the steps to create an effective COA:

Step 1: Determine the Account Structure

The first step is to define the general structure of the COA. This involves deciding on the main account categories (as shown above) and the numbering system used to identify accounts. Businesses often use a numbering system for accounts, where each category is assigned a range of numbers to help organize accounts and make it easier to locate them in the general ledger.

- **Assets**: Accounts starting with "1" (e.g., 1000 for Cash, 1010 for Accounts Receivable).
- **Liabilities**: Accounts starting with "2" (e.g., 2000 for Accounts Payable, 2100 for Long-Term Debt).
- **Equity**: Accounts starting with "3" (e.g., 3000 for Common Stock, 3100 for Retained Earnings).
- **Revenue**: Accounts starting with "4" (e.g., 4000 for Sales Revenue, 4100 for Service Revenue).
- **Expenses**: Accounts starting with "5" (e.g., 5000 for Rent Expense, 5100 for Utilities Expense).

Step 2: Identify the Necessary Sub-Accounts

Once the main categories are defined, break them down further into sub-accounts. Sub-accounts provide a more detailed level of tracking and ensure that transactions are recorded accurately. For instance:

- **Assets**: You might break down Cash into separate accounts for Petty Cash, Checking Account, and Savings Account.
- **Revenue**: Instead of just a generic Sales Revenue account, you might have sub-accounts for Pet Food Sales, Toys Sales, and Grooming Services Revenue.

This level of detail helps track financial activity more precisely and allows for better reporting when generating financial statements.

Step 3: Align the COA with Business Needs

The chart should reflect the company's operations, industry, and accounting needs. A retail company may need more detailed inventory accounts, while a service-based business may have more revenue accounts. Consider the future growth of the company—having flexibility to add new accounts as the business evolves is crucial.

For example, a small pet supplies store might start with a basic COA for inventory and sales. As the company grows, it may add accounts for employee benefits, loan repayments, and marketing expenses.

Using the Chart of Accounts for Financial Reporting

Once the COA is established and transactions are recorded, businesses can use it to generate financial statements. The COA acts as the foundation for the general ledger, where all transactions are posted.

The general ledger aggregates all account balances, and these balances are used to create the trial balance. The trial balance is a summary of all debit and credit balances, ensuring that debits and credits are equal. From the trial balance, companies can prepare the balance sheet, income statement, and cash flow statement.

Example of How Accounts Feed into Financial Statements:

Account	**Balance**
Assets	
Cash	$10,000
Accounts Receivable	$5,000
Inventory	$3,000
Liabilities	
Accounts Payable	$4,000
Loans Payable	$2,000
Equity	
Owner's Capital	$10,000
Revenue	
Sales Revenue	$20,000
Expenses	
Rent Expense	$3,000
Salaries Expense	$5,000

From this COA structure, the company can calculate the net income (Sales Revenue - Expenses) and determine its financial position (Assets - Liabilities = Equity).

ETSY - USING A CHART OF ACCOUNTS

Central to Etsy's financial management is the creation and use of an effective Chart of Accounts (COA).

CHALLENGES

- Ensuring Scalability as the Business Grows
- Streamlining Financial Reporting Across Multiple Product Lines

OBJECTIVES

DESIGN CLEAR CHART OF ACCOUNTS

The primary goal was to ensure clarity and ease of use.

BUILD A SCALABLE ACCOUNTING SYSTEM

Etsy's objective was to design a COA that could accommodate many product lines, currencies, and regional operations, all while being consistent.

RESULT AND BENEFITS

- Etsy's Chart of Accounts is divided into five primary categories.
- By using a clear numbering system, Etsy can easily classify and track each transaction.

Best Practices for Using the Chart of Accounts

Creating a functional COA is only part of the process. To make it truly effective, businesses should adhere to certain best practices to ensure that the chart is easy to use and scalable:

1. **Keep It Simple and Organized**: Avoid overcomplicating the COA with unnecessary sub-accounts. The COA should be detailed enough to track necessary financial activities but not so complex that it becomes difficult to maintain.
2. **Consistency**: Use consistent naming conventions and account numbers across the company. This makes it easier to track accounts, especially when reviewing financial records or training new employees.
3. **Review and Adjust Regularly**: As the company grows and evolves, the COA should be reviewed and updated to reflect new business activities or changes in the accounting requirements.
4. **Ensure Alignment with Tax Requirements**: Make sure the COA aligns with the tax reporting needs of the business. Certain accounts, such as taxes payable, may need to be categorized in a way that supports accurate tax filing.
5. **Use Software Tools**: Many accounting software programs offer pre-designed charts of accounts tailored to various industries. These tools can simplify the setup and maintenance of your COA, while ensuring compliance with accounting standards.

By carefully designing and maintaining a COA, businesses can simplify their accounting processes, improve financial reporting accuracy, and ensure compliance with tax and regulatory standards. A well-organized COA not only helps in generating accurate financial statements but also facilitates decision-making, budgeting, and growth planning.

Subsidiary Ledgers and Their Role in Accounting

In accounting, subsidiary ledgers are essential tools used to manage and organize the details of certain financial accounts. A subsidiary ledger is a detailed record that supports a control account in the general ledger. For example, the accounts receivable subsidiary ledger provides detailed information about individual customer balances, while the accounts payable subsidiary ledger tracks the amounts owed to individual creditors. Rather than recording all transactions directly in the general ledger, which can become cumbersome for large businesses, subsidiary ledgers allow businesses to group similar types of transactions together.

In essence, a subsidiary ledger helps businesses track and manage specific accounts that require detailed information. The totals of all individual accounts in a subsidiary ledger are then summarized and reported in a corresponding control account in the general ledger.

The Structure of a Subsidiary Ledger

Subsidiary ledgers typically have the same structure as the general ledger but are designed to provide more granular detail. Each subsidiary ledger is organized by account type (e.g., accounts receivable or accounts payable), and each account is further categorized by individual customers or suppliers.

For instance, in an accounts receivable subsidiary ledger, each entry corresponds to an individual customer. When a sale is made to a customer on credit, a new entry is added to that customer's account in the subsidiary ledger, reflecting the amount owed.

Here is an example of how individual entries in a subsidiary ledger might look for Accounts Receivable:

Customer	Date	Debit	Credit	Balance
Customer X	Feb 2	$12,000		$12,000
Customer Y	Feb 12	$6,000		$6,000
Customer Z	Feb 20	$6,000		$6,000

At the end of the period, the totals from the individual customer accounts in the subsidiary ledger are summed up to determine the total balance in the Accounts Receivable Control Account in the general ledger.

General Ledger - Accounts Receivable	Debit	Credit	Balance
Total	$24,000		$8,000

The balance in the general ledger should always match the sum of the individual customer balances in the subsidiary ledger. If these amounts do not match, an error has occurred in the accounting records.

Why Use Subsidiary Ledgers?

There are several reasons why businesses use subsidiary ledgers, rather than relying solely on the general ledger:

1. **Organization and Clarity**:
   In businesses with numerous transactions, particularly those with many customers or vendors, keeping detailed records in the general ledger can be overwhelming. Subsidiary ledgers help businesses keep track of

individual transactions more clearly by separating them by category (e.g., customer, vendor, or expense type).

2. **Efficiency**:
   With subsidiary ledgers, accountants can quickly locate specific transactions related to particular customers or suppliers without having to search through a lengthy general ledger. This increases efficiency in the day-to-day management of financial transactions.

3. **Separation of Duties**:
   By using subsidiary ledgers, businesses can assign different employees to manage various aspects of the accounting process. For example, one employee may be responsible for managing accounts receivable, while another focuses on accounts payable. This division of labor speeds up the accounting process and introduces internal checks and balances.

4. **Detailed Information for Decision-Making**:
   Subsidiary ledgers provide more detailed information than the general ledger, which helps businesses make better-informed decisions. For instance, an accounts payable subsidiary ledger can help a company identify which vendors are most frequently used, while an accounts receivable subsidiary ledger can show patterns of customer payments and potential cash flow problems.

How Subsidiary Ledgers Interact with the General Ledger

While subsidiary ledgers provide detailed information, the general ledger provides the summary of that data. The control accounts in the general ledger (e.g., Accounts Receivable, Accounts Payable) are used to summarize the totals of all the individual accounts found in the subsidiary ledgers.

Each month, the balances in the subsidiary ledgers are transferred to the general ledger. For instance, the Accounts Receivable Control Account in the general ledger will reflect the total amount of money owed to the company by all customers, as calculated from the accounts receivable subsidiary ledger. This ensures that the total for accounts receivable is reflected accurately in the company's financial statements.

Example: Balancing Subsidiary Ledgers with the General Ledger

Let's consider the following scenario:

- The total balance of accounts receivable from individual customers in the subsidiary ledger is $8,000.
- The corresponding Accounts Receivable Control Account in the general ledger should also show $8,000.

Subsidiary Ledger – Accounts Receivable	Amount
Customer X	$12,000
Customer Y	$6,000
Customer Z	$6,000
Total	**$24,000**

General Ledger – Accounts Receivable	Amount
Accounts Receivable	$8,000

By matching the control account with the subsidiary ledger, businesses can verify that all transactions have been recorded correctly. If the amounts don't match, an error can be traced and corrected in the individual subsidiary ledgers.

Common Types of Subsidiary Ledgers

While accounts receivable and accounts payable are the most common subsidiary ledgers, there are other types that businesses may use, depending on the nature of their operations:

Type of Subsidiary Ledger	Description	Example Accounts
Accounts Receivable Subsidiary Ledger	Tracks amounts owed by individual customers.	Customer Accounts
Accounts Payable Subsidiary Ledger	Tracks amounts owed to individual suppliers or creditors.	Supplier Accounts
Inventory Subsidiary Ledger	Tracks the quantity and value of inventory items.	Inventory by Item
Fixed Assets Subsidiary Ledger	Tracks individual fixed assets, such as buildings and equipment.	Equipment, Vehicles, Property

Benefits of Using Subsidiary Ledgers

1. **Improved Accuracy**:
   By separating and categorizing transactions, subsidiary ledgers help ensure that all transactions are properly recorded, reducing the likelihood of errors.
2. **Better Cash Flow Management**:
   An accounts receivable subsidiary ledger helps businesses track customer payments and aging balances, which is critical for managing cash flow. The accounts payable subsidiary ledger helps businesses keep track of

outstanding debts and payment due dates.

3. **Detailed Reporting**:

   Subsidiary ledgers provide businesses with detailed insights into specific accounts, making it easier to monitor performance and make strategic decisions.

4. **Efficient Audit and Reconciliation**:

   Having detailed subsidiary ledgers allows businesses to perform regular audits and reconciliations. By comparing subsidiary ledger totals with control account balances, businesses can identify discrepancies quickly and ensure the integrity of their financial records.

Subsidiary ledgers play a crucial role in the accounting process by organizing detailed information about accounts receivable, accounts payable, and other business transactions. They enable businesses to manage financial data more efficiently, improve accuracy in record-keeping, and support better decision-making. By using subsidiary ledgers in conjunction with control accounts in the general ledger, businesses can maintain a clear, accurate, and well-organized accounting system.

Prepaid Expenses & Unearned Revenues

In accounting, prepaid expenses and unearned revenues are two critical concepts related to the timing of revenue and expense recognition. These concepts are essential for businesses that operate on an **accrual basis** of accounting, where transactions are recorded when they occur, regardless of when cash is exchanged.

Prepaid expenses represent payments made in advance for goods or services that will be used in the future, while unearned revenues refer to payments received in advance for goods or services that have not yet been delivered. Understanding how to account for both is crucial for accurate financial reporting and ensuring that the balance sheet correctly reflects the company's financial position.

In this section, we will explore what prepaid expenses and unearned revenues are, how they are accounted for, and their impact on financial statements. We will also delve into examples and explain how these items are adjusted over time as the benefits are received or obligations are fulfilled.

What Are Prepaid Expenses?

Prepaid expenses are payments made in advance for goods or services that will be consumed in future periods. These payments represent assets because they provide future economic benefits. However, until the benefit is actually received, these payments are recorded as an asset on the balance sheet.

The most common examples of prepaid expenses include:

- **Insurance premiums**: Businesses often pay insurance premiums upfront for coverage over a specific period, such as one year.
- **Rent**: Companies may prepay rent for office space or equipment for several months or even years.
- **Subscriptions**: Payments for magazines, software services, or other recurring subscriptions are often paid in advance.

Recording Prepaid Expenses

At the time of payment, prepaid expenses are recorded as assets. Over time, as the benefit of the prepaid item is realized, the expense is gradually amortized and transferred to the income statement.

Example: Prepaid Insurance

Let's assume a company pays $12,000 for a one-year insurance policy on January 1st. The initial journal entry will look like this:

Date	Account	Debit	Credit	Description
January 1	Prepaid Insurance	$12,000		Payment for one-year policy
January 1	Cash		$12,000	Payment made for insurance

In the balance sheet, Prepaid Insurance is classified as an asset because it represents a future benefit. Each month, as the insurance coverage is used, the company will recognize part of the payment as an expense:

Date	Account	Debit	Credit	Description
January 31	Insurance Expense	$1,000		One-month insurance expense
January 31	Prepaid Insurance		$1,000	Adjust prepaid insurance

The balance in Prepaid Insurance decreases over time, while the Insurance Expense increases to reflect the usage of the policy.

What Are Unearned Revenues?

Unearned revenue, also called deferred revenue, occurs when a business receives payment in advance for goods or services that have not yet been delivered or performed. Unearned revenue represents an obligation for the company, as it must fulfill the terms of the agreement (e.g., deliver the product or perform the service) before recognizing the revenue as earned.

Unearned revenue is initially recorded as a liability on the balance sheet because the company has an obligation to provide goods or services in the future. Once the goods or services are provided, the revenue is recognized and moved to the income statement.

Example of Unearned Revenue: Subscription Service

A company that provides an online subscription service might receive $120 for a 12-month subscription. When the company receives the $120, it has not yet earned the revenue because the service will be provided over the next year. Therefore, the company records the payment as **unearned revenue**.

Date	Account	Debit	Credit	Description
January 1	Cash	$120		Payment received for subscription
January 1	Unearned Revenue		$120	Liability for unearned revenue

Each month, as the company delivers the subscription service, a portion of the unearned revenue is recognized as earned revenue. The company records this as follows:

Date	Account	Debit	Credit	Description
January 31	Unearned Revenue	$10		Recognized earned revenue
January 31	Revenue		$10	Earned revenue from subscription

Over the next 12 months, $10 is recognized each month as earned revenue, while the liability decreases.

Adjusting for Prepaid Expenses and Unearned Revenues

At the end of each accounting period, businesses need to make adjusting entries to account for the portion of prepaid expenses used up and unearned revenue earned during that period. These adjustments ensure that accrual accounting is properly applied, reflecting expenses and revenues in the correct period.

For prepaid expenses, the amount used during the period is moved from the asset side of the balance sheet to the expense section of the income statement. For unearned revenues, as the business delivers goods or services, the amount earned is transferred from the liability section of the balance sheet to the revenue section of the income statement.

Example of Adjusting Entries for Prepaid Expenses

Let's assume a business paid $3,600 for a two-year insurance policy. At the end of each month, the business will recognize one month of insurance expense:

Date	Account	Debit	Credit	Description
January 31	Insurance Expense	$150		Recognized one-month expense
January 31	Prepaid Insurance		$150	Reduced prepaid insurance

The adjusting entry reflects that the prepaid insurance asset is being gradually consumed and that the expense is being recognized.

Example of Adjusting Entries for Unearned Revenues

For a business that receives $1,200 for an annual service, the business needs to adjust the unearned revenue liability to recognize the revenue as it provides the service. At the end of each month, $100 is earned:

Date	Account	Debit	Credit	Description
January 31	Unearned Revenue	$100		Recognized earned revenue
January 31	Revenue		$100	Earned revenue from service

This ensures that the financial statements accurately reflect the business's actual revenue and liabilities.

Impact on Financial Statements

Prepaid Expenses and Unearned Revenues have direct effects on the balance sheet and the income statement.

1. **Balance Sheet**:
   - **Prepaid Expenses** are initially recorded as assets but gradually move to expenses on the income statement.
   - **Unearned Revenues** are recorded as liabilities but move to revenues once the associated goods or services are delivered.
2. **Income Statement**:
   - **Prepaid Expenses**: As prepaid expenses are recognized, they are recorded as an expense on the income statement, reducing the company's net income for that period.
   - **Unearned Revenues**: As the company earns revenue by providing goods or services, it is recognized as income, increasing the company's net income.

Why Accurate Accounting for Prepaid Expenses and Unearned Revenues is Important

Accurate accounting for prepaid expenses and unearned revenues ensures that a business's financial statements are in line with **accrual accounting principles**. This provides a clearer picture of the company's financial position and performance, allowing for better decision-making and financial planning.

For example:

Prepaid expenses affect a company's liquidity. Overstating prepaid expenses can give the illusion of more cash available than is actually the case.

Unearned revenue represents an obligation. If it's not adjusted correctly, a company might appear to have more income than it actually earned, leading to misleading profit figures.

Properly managing these concepts helps businesses maintain accurate records, comply with accounting standards, and avoid issues during audits.

Incorporating appropriate adjustments for prepaid expenses and unearned revenues ensures compliance with accounting standards and provides valuable insights into a company's operations, helping business owners, accountants, and investors make informed decisions.

Trial Balance: Ensuring the Books Are Balanced

The trial balance is one of the most important tools in accounting, used to ensure that a company's books are balanced and that the debits and credits recorded in the general ledger are equal. It serves as a preliminary check for errors before the preparation of the final financial statements. Although modern accounting software has automated many aspects of this process, understanding how and why a trial balance is prepared remains a crucial step in the accounting cycle.

A trial balance is a report that lists the balances of all accounts from the general ledger at a particular point in time. The purpose of this report is to ensure that the total debits equal the total credits, as the double-entry accounting system requires each transaction to be recorded with an equal debit and credit.

The trial balance is divided into two main columns:

1. **Debit column**: Records the total of all debits for each account.
2. **Credit column**: Records the total of all credits for each account.

These balances are summed at the bottom of each column, and the totals should be equal. If they are, it indicates that the books are "in balance," meaning the general ledger accounts have been recorded correctly according to double-entry accounting principles.

ADOBE SYSTEMS - MANAGING PREPAID EXPENSES AND UNEARNED REVENUES

CHALLENGES

- Managing Large-Scale Subscription Revenue
- Prepaid Expenses and Subscription Costs

OBJECTIVES

ENSURE ACCURATE REVENUE RECOGNITION

This is crucial for internal reporting and meeting compliance requirements.

TRACK PREPAID EXPENSES CORRECTLY

The company needed a streamlined process to track prepaid expenses.

MAINTAIN ACCURATE FINANCIAL STATEMENTS

RESULT AND BENEFITS

- Adobe implemented a system for tracking revenues, which ensured that revenue from subscriptions was recognized systematically over the subscription period.
- Adobe uses prepaid expenses to manage costs, which are paid upfront.

Example of a Trial Balance Format

Account Title	Debit	Credit
Cash	$5,000	
Accounts Receivable	$3,000	
Accounts Payable		$1,500
Sales Revenue		$3,500
Rent Expense	$1,000	
Total	**$9,000**	**$9,000**

In this example, the debit and credit columns are equal, indicating that the trial balance is correctly balanced.

The Purpose of a Trial Balance

The trial balance serves several important functions in accounting:

1. **Checking for Errors**:
   The most basic function of a trial balance is to ensure that debits equal credits. This helps accountants detect any arithmetical mistakes in the ledger entries, such as incorrect amounts or posting to the wrong side of the account. If the trial balance does not balance, it signals that there is an error somewhere in the journal entries or ledger.
2. **Preliminary Financial Reporting**:
   While a trial balance is not a financial statement in itself, it is a useful tool for preparing the company's financial statements—such as the income statement, balance sheet, and cash flow statement. It provides a snapshot of all account balances at a specific point in time, making it easier to compile these statements.
3. **Verification of Posting**:
   The trial balance confirms that all transactions from the journal have been properly posted to the correct accounts in the general ledger. This verification ensures that the company's financial records are complete and accurate before moving on to the final preparation of financial statements.
4. **Internal Control**:
   Preparing a trial balance helps reinforce internal control measures by regularly checking the accuracy of the company's records. It reduces the likelihood of errors and misstatements, contributing to a more reliable and transparent financial reporting process.

How to Prepare a Trial Balance

The process of preparing a trial balance is fairly straightforward, but it requires careful attention to detail to ensure accuracy. Here are the steps involved:

1. Prepare the General Ledger Accounts

The first step is to ensure that all transactions have been correctly recorded in the general ledger. The general ledger is where all accounts, such as assets, liabilities, equity, revenues, and expenses, are listed. Each account should contain its running balance, with all debits and credits properly recorded.

2. List All Accounts and Their Balances

Once the general ledger is updated, all the account balances are transferred to the trial balance. This includes both balance sheet accounts (such as Cash, Accounts Payable, and Retained Earnings) and income statement accounts (such as Sales Revenue, Rent Expense, and Salaries Expense).

3. Record Debit and Credit Balances

For each account, the balance is placed in either the debit or credit column. Generally:

- Asset accounts (like Cash and Accounts Receivable) have debit balances.
- Liability accounts (like Accounts Payable) and equity accounts (like Capital or Owner's Equity) have credit balances.
- Revenue accounts (like Sales Revenue) typically have credit balances, while expense accounts (like Rent Expense) have debit balances.

4. Calculate Totals

Once all the accounts have been listed, the totals for the debit and credit columns are calculated. The trial balance is considered balanced if the total of the debit column equals the total of the credit column.

Ensuring the Trial Balance is Balanced

If the trial balance does not balance, it indicates an error in the accounting records. Here are some common reasons why the trial balance might not balance:

1. **Arithmetic Mistakes**:
   Errors can occur during the summation of the debit and credit columns. Double-checking the calculations can often resolve this.
2. **Double Posting**:
   If a transaction has been recorded twice, once in the debit column and once in the credit column, it will result in an imbalance.
3. **Transposition Errors**:
   If numbers are transposed when posting (e.g., entering $1,200 as $2,100), the trial balance will not balance.

4. **Omitted Entries**:
   If a transaction was not recorded at all in the journal or ledger, it will lead to an imbalance in the trial balance.
5. **Incorrect Posting**:
   Sometimes, amounts may be posted to the wrong side of the account. For example, crediting an expense account instead of debiting it.

Limitations of a Trial Balance

Although the trial balance is a useful tool for detecting errors, it has limitations. A balanced trial balance does not guarantee that the financial statements are free of errors. Some errors may remain undetected, even if the trial balance is correct. For example:

1. **Errors of Omission**:
   If a transaction is completely omitted from the accounting records, it won't appear in the trial balance, but the books will still balance.
2. **Compensating Errors**:
   If two errors offset each other, the trial balance will still balance. For instance, if one account is under-debited and another is over-credited by the same amount, the total debits and credits will still match.
3. **Errors of Principle**:
   Mistakes involving the application of accounting principles (such as misclassifying an expense as an asset) may not be detected by the trial balance.

AX CARS, INC.

TRIAL BALANCE

Account	Debit	Credit
Cash	$32,800	
Accounts Receivable	$300	
Inventory	$39,800	
Leasehold Improvements	$100,000	
Accounts Payable		$49,000
Long-term Liabilities		$99,500
Common Stock		$10,000
Dividends	$1,000	
Revenues		$27,800
Cost of Goods Sold	$10,200	
Rent Expense	$500	
Supplies Expense	$500	
Utilities Expense	$200	
Wages Expense	$500	
Interest Expense	$500	
Totals	$186,300	$186,300

Chapter 5: Financial Statements

The income statement is one of the primary financial statements that companies use to assess their financial performance over a specific period. It is sometimes referred to as the profit and loss statement or the statement of operations. This statement provides a detailed breakdown of a company's revenues, expenses, gains, and losses, and ultimately calculates the net income or net loss for the period.

In this section, we will dissect the key components of the income statement, explain how they are calculated, and explore their significance. By understanding the structure and purpose of the income statement, we can gain valuable insights into a company's profitability and financial health.

Earnings Per Share (EPS): How It's Calculated and Interpreted

Earnings Per Share (EPS) is a critical financial metric that provides insight into a company's profitability on a per-share basis. It is widely used by investors, analysts, and stakeholders to assess a company's financial performance, particularly its ability to generate profit relative to its number of outstanding shares. EPS is also a key indicator used to determine a company's profitability and financial health over a specific period, typically reported quarterly or annually.

In this section, we will explore what EPS is, how it is calculated, the different types of EPS, and how to interpret this metric. By understanding EPS, you will be better equipped to analyze financial statements and make informed investment decisions.

What Is Earnings Per Share (EPS)?

Earnings Per Share (EPS) represents the portion of a company's profit allocated to each outstanding share of common stock. It serves as a useful tool for evaluating how well a company is generating profits for its shareholders. EPS is often considered a key indicator of a company's financial performance and is closely watched by investors, as it provides a clear view of the company's profitability on a per-share basis.

EPS is usually calculated for a specific period, such as a quarter or a fiscal year. By comparing EPS over time, investors can gauge whether a company is improving its profitability or facing challenges. It is also a critical metric when comparing companies within the same industry, as it provides a common ground for evaluating performance.

How Is Earnings Per Share (EPS) Calculated?

EPS is calculated by dividing the net income (or earnings) of the company by the weighted average number of shares outstanding during the period. The formula

for basic EPS is:

Net Income is the total profit of the company after all expenses, taxes, and interest have been deducted.

- **Preferred Dividends** are dividends paid to preferred shareholders, which must be subtracted because EPS is concerned with the earnings available to common shareholders.
- **Weighted Average Shares Outstanding** represents the average number of shares outstanding during the reporting period, adjusted for stock splits, stock dividends, and other equity-related changes.

Example Calculation of Basic EPS:

Let's assume that a company, XYZ Corp, reports the following:

Net Income	$5,000,000
Preferred Dividends	$500,000
Weighted Average Shares Outstanding	1,000,000 shares

Using the basic EPS formula:

In this case, the EPS is $4.50, meaning that for each share of common stock, XYZ Corp earned $4.50 during the period.

Diluted EPS: A More Conservative Measure

While basic EPS provides valuable insight, it doesn't account for potential dilution of shares. Diluted EPS is a more conservative measure that takes into account the impact of stock options, convertible securities (such as bonds or preferred stock), and other potential sources of dilution. Diluted EPS reflects the worst-case scenario, assuming all potential shares are converted into common stock.

The formula for diluted EPS is:

Where:

- **Dilutive Shares** are the additional shares that would be created from the conversion of convertible securities and stock options.

Example Calculation of Diluted EPS:

Let's assume XYZ Corp has the following:

- **Net Income**: $5,000,000
- **Preferred Dividends**: $500,000
- **Weighted Average Shares Outstanding**: 1,000,000 shares
- **Dilutive Shares from Stock Options**: 100,000 shares

Using the diluted EPS formula:

Here, the **diluted EPS** is $4.09, which is slightly lower than the basic EPS due to the potential dilution of shares from stock options.

Why Is EPS Important?

EPS is one of the most commonly used metrics for assessing a company's profitability and financial health. Here are a few reasons why EPS is so important:

1. **Investor Sentiment**:
   EPS is a key indicator of a company's ability to generate profit for its shareholders. A higher EPS typically suggests that the company is effectively managing its operations and generating substantial profit, which can lead to increased investor confidence and potentially higher stock prices.
2. **Valuation Metric**:
   EPS is often used in conjunction with the **Price-to-Earnings (P/E) ratio** to value a company's stock. The P/E ratio compares the company's stock price to its earnings per share, providing insight into how much investors are willing to pay for each dollar of earnings. A higher P/E ratio may indicate that investors expect future growth in EPS.
3. **Performance Comparison**:
   EPS allows for the comparison of profitability across companies in the same industry, regardless of their size. By comparing EPS, investors can evaluate how effectively companies are generating profit relative to their number of shares outstanding.
4. **Profitability Indicator**:
   EPS provides a clear measure of how profitable a company is on a per-share basis. This helps stakeholders assess whether the company is efficiently utilizing its resources to generate income and whether it is managing its costs effectively.

Interpreting EPS: What Does It Tell Us?

While EPS provides valuable information about a company's profitability, it is essential to interpret this number in context. Here are several ways to interpret EPS:

1. **Trends in EPS**:
   A rising EPS over time generally indicates that a company is growing its profitability. Investors may see this as a sign of a strong and well-managed company. Conversely, a declining EPS might signal problems, such as declining revenue, increasing costs, or operational inefficiencies.
2. **Comparison with Industry Peers**:
   Comparing a company's EPS with that of its competitors in the same

industry can provide insights into how the company is performing relative to its peers. A company with a higher EPS than its competitors may indicate a competitive advantage in terms of profitability.

3. **EPS and Dividend Policy**:
   A company with a high EPS may be more likely to pay out higher dividends to shareholders, although this depends on its dividend policy. Some companies choose to reinvest their earnings to fuel future growth, while others distribute a portion of profits as dividends.
4. **Effect of Stock Buybacks**:
   Companies can increase their EPS by repurchasing their own shares, thereby reducing the number of outstanding shares. This can make the company's earnings per share appear stronger without any actual increase in profitability. Investors should be cautious and evaluate whether an increase in EPS is due to real growth or simply the result of share buybacks.

Limitations of EPS

While EPS is a valuable metric, it does have certain limitations:

1. **Does Not Reflect Cash Flow**:
   EPS is calculated based on **net income**, which may include non-cash items such as depreciation, amortization, and gains or losses from the sale of assets. As a result, EPS does not directly reflect the company's **cash flow**, which is also an important indicator of financial health.
2. **Manipulation Risk**:
   EPS can be influenced by accounting practices, such as choosing when to recognize revenue or expense, or by non-recurring items like asset sales or tax adjustments. This can lead to fluctuations in EPS that do not necessarily reflect the company's ongoing operations.
3. **Does Not Account for Capital Structure**:
   EPS does not take into account the company's **capital structure**, such as the mix of debt and equity financing. A company with high debt might have a lower EPS due to higher interest expenses, even though its operations are profitable.

Analyzing Liquidity Through Liquidity Ratios

Liquidity is a critical aspect of a company's financial health, indicating its ability to meet short-term obligations without compromising operational efficiency. Liquidity ratios provide a quantitative measure of this ability by comparing different components of a company's balance sheet. These ratios play a pivotal role in assessing a company's short-term financial health, ensuring that it can continue to operate smoothly without the risk of financial distress due to cash shortages.

Liquidity refers to a company's ability to quickly convert assets into cash without significant loss of value. For businesses, liquidity is crucial because it enables them to meet short-term obligations, such as paying suppliers, covering operational costs, and servicing debt. In simple terms, liquidity reflects the company's financial flexibility—how quickly it can access cash to handle unforeseen expenses or capitalize on opportunities.

A company with sufficient liquidity is less likely to experience disruptions in its operations or have difficulty securing additional financing. On the other hand, a company with poor liquidity might struggle to cover immediate obligations, potentially leading to solvency issues or even bankruptcy. This makes liquidity ratios an important tool for investors, creditors, and management to evaluate a company's financial position.

Liquidity Ratios: Key Indicators of Short-Term Financial Health

Liquidity ratios are designed to measure a company's ability to convert its assets into cash to meet its short-term liabilities. Several key liquidity ratios provide insights into different aspects of a company's financial flexibility.

Current Ratio: A Measure of Short-Term Solvency

The **current ratio** is one of the most commonly used liquidity ratios. It compares a company's current assets to its current liabilities to assess its ability to pay off short-term obligations with short-term assets. The formula for the current ratio is:

"Current Ratio"="Current Assets" /"Current Liabilities"

Where:

- **Current Assets** include cash, accounts receivable, inventory, and other assets expected to be converted into cash within one year.
- **Current Liabilities** are obligations that the company must settle within a year, such as accounts payable, short-term debt, and accrued expenses.

Interpretation of the Current Ratio

A **current ratio** greater than **1.0** generally indicates that the company has enough current assets to cover its current liabilities. For example, a current ratio of 2.0 means that for every dollar of liability, the company has two dollars in assets, suggesting strong short-term financial health.

However, a ratio that is too high (e.g., above 3.0) may indicate inefficiency, where the company might be holding excessive cash or inventory that could be better utilized to generate returns. Conversely, a current ratio significantly below 1.0 could be a red flag, suggesting potential liquidity problems.

Example: Current Ratio Calculation

Let's say Company A has the following data:

- **Current Assets**: \$500,000
- **Current Liabilities**: \$250,000

The current ratio would be:

$$\text{"Current Ratio"}=500{,}000/250{,}000=2.0$$

This indicates that Company A has twice as many assets as liabilities, which suggests a healthy liquidity position.

Quick Ratio: A Stricter Measure of Liquidity

The **quick ratio**, also known as the **acid-test ratio**, provides a more stringent measure of liquidity than the current ratio by excluding inventory from current assets. Inventory is excluded because it may not be as easily converted into cash as other current assets, such as receivables. The formula for the quick ratio is:

$$\text{"Quick Ratio"}=(\text{"Current Assets"} - \text{"Inventory"})/\text{"Current Liabilities"}$$

Where:

- **Inventory** is subtracted from current assets, reflecting the idea that inventory may not be as liquid as other assets like cash or receivables.

Interpretation of the Quick Ratio

A quick ratio greater than **1.0** is considered acceptable, indicating that the company can cover its short-term obligations without relying on inventory sales. A quick ratio of 2.0, for example, means that the company has two dollars in liquid assets for every dollar of short-term liabilities.

However, if the quick ratio is less than 1.0, it might signal potential liquidity issues, as the company may not have enough easily liquidated assets to meet its obligations.

Let's say Company B has the following:

Current Assets: \$400,000

Inventory: \$100,000

Current Liabilities: \$250,000

The quick ratio would be:

$$\text{"Quick Ratio"}=(400{,}000-100{,}000)/250{,}000=300{,}000/250{,}000=1.2$$

This indicates that Company B has enough liquid assets to cover its liabilities, even without relying on inventory.

Cash Ratio: The Ultimate Liquidity Test

The **cash ratio** is the most conservative liquidity ratio, measuring the company's ability to pay off short-term obligations using only its most liquid assets—**cash and cash equivalents**. This ratio excludes receivables and inventory, focusing solely on the company's immediate liquidity. The formula for the cash ratio is:

"Cash Ratio"="Cash + Cash Equivalents" /"Current Liabilities"

Interpretation of the Cash Ratio

A cash ratio greater than 1.0 indicates that the company has sufficient cash to cover all of its short-term liabilities. While a higher cash ratio provides a strong cushion, it could also indicate that the company is holding too much cash and not investing it efficiently. A cash ratio of less than 1.0 could signal potential liquidity problems, especially if the company is relying too much on other current assets like receivables or inventory.

Let's assume Company C has the following:

Cash and Cash Equivalents: $150,000

Current Liabilities: $250,000

The cash ratio would be:

"Cash Ratio"=150,000/250,000=0.6

This indicates that Company C has only 60 cents in cash for every dollar of current liabilities, suggesting a weaker liquidity position compared to the other ratios.

Receivables Turnover Ratio

The receivables turnover ratio measures how efficiently a company is collecting its accounts receivable. It reflects the number of times, on average, that receivables are collected during a given period. The formula is:

"Receivables Turnover Ratio"="Net Credit Sales" /"Average Accounts Receivable"

Where:

- **Net Credit Sales** is the total revenue generated from sales made on credit.
- **Average Accounts Receivable** is the average of beginning and ending accounts receivable for the period.

A higher receivables turnover ratio generally indicates that the company is efficiently collecting its debts, improving its liquidity by converting receivables into cash quickly.

LIQUIDITY RATIOS

AT A GLANCE

$$\textbf{Current Ratio} = \frac{\text{Current Assets}}{\text{Current Liabilities}}$$

$$\textbf{Quick Ratio} = \frac{\text{Current Assets - Inventory}}{\text{Current Liabilities}}$$

$$\textbf{Cash Ratio} = \frac{\text{Cash + Cash Equivalents}}{\text{Current Liabilities}}$$

$$\textbf{Receivables Turnover Ratio} = \frac{\text{Net Credit Sales}}{\text{Average Accounts Receivable}}$$

LIQUIDITY RATIO

COMPANY X

Key Metrics	Units	FY 20	FY 21	FY 22
Total Debt	$ M	7,500	7,200	7,400
Net Debt	$ M	5,300	5,150	5,200
Common Shareholders' Equity	$ M	2,750	3,150	3,000
Total Capital	$ M	10,250	10,350	10,400
Net Capital	$ M	7,600	8,000	8,200
Current Liabilities	$ M	2,300	2,450	2,600
Current Assets	$ M	6,400	6,550	6,200
Cash + Cash-Equivalents	$ M	2,300	1,950	1,800
Accounts Receivable	$ M	2,100	2,400	2,500
Working Capital	$ M	4,100	4,100	3,600
Change in Working Capital	$ M	80	-100	-500
Revenue	$ M	11,500	12,800	13,200

LIQUIDITY RATIOS AND CREDIT RATIOS

Ratio	FY 20	FY 21	FY 22
Current Ratio	2.78	3	2
Quick Ratio	2.78	3	2
Cash Ratio	1	1	1

Interpreting Liquidity Ratios

Liquidity ratios provide valuable insights into a company's financial health, but they must be interpreted within the context of the company's industry, business model, and economic environment. For example, a company with a high inventory turnover might not need as much cash or receivables to meet its obligations. Similarly, companies in industries like technology or consulting, which have less inventory, may show stronger quick or cash ratios.

1. **High Liquidity Ratios**: A higher liquidity ratio (especially current and quick ratios) generally indicates that the company has more than enough short-term assets to cover its liabilities. While this may seem positive, excessively high liquidity can also suggest that the company is not using its assets efficiently. For example, holding too much cash may lead to missed investment opportunities.
2. **Low Liquidity Ratios**: A lower liquidity ratio (especially below 1.0) indicates that the company might struggle to meet its short-term obligations, which can lead to cash flow problems, reliance on credit, or even insolvency if the situation worsens. This signals the need for immediate attention to improve the company's cash position or working capital management.
3. **Industry Benchmarks**: Comparing liquidity ratios across companies within the same industry helps assess whether a company's liquidity is above or below the industry average. Each industry has different norms and requirements for liquidity based on the nature of its operations and capital structure.

Liquidity ratios are essential tools for assessing a company's ability to meet its short-term obligations and ensuring that it can continue to operate without financial stress. Key ratios like the current ratio, quick ratio, cash ratio, and receivables turnover ratio provide deep insights into a company's liquidity management. By understanding and interpreting these ratios, investors, creditors, and business owners can evaluate financial health, make informed decisions, and implement strategies to maintain financial stability.

While liquidity ratios offer valuable data, they should be analyzed alongside other financial metrics and within the context of the company's specific circumstances to provide a holistic view of its financial well-being.

Solvency Ratios

Solvency ratios are financial metrics used to evaluate a company's long-term financial health and its ability to meet its long-term debt obligations. Unlike liquidity ratios, which focus on short-term obligations, solvency ratios provide insights into whether a company can stay financially viable over the long term, ensuring its operations can continue without facing bankruptcy or insolvency. These ratios help investors, creditors, and management assess the overall financial structure of the business and the risk associated with its debt.

Solvency ratios measure a company's ability to sustain its operations over the long term by comparing its total assets to its total liabilities. These ratios evaluate the extent to which a company can cover its long-term obligations using its assets, and they are key to understanding the company's capital structure and financial stability.

Companies that rely heavily on debt financing may face higher financial risks because they are obligated to make debt repayments regardless of their financial performance. Solvency ratios, therefore, provide insight into whether a company can handle its debt load without compromising its operational stability. High solvency generally indicates that a company is less reliant on debt and has more flexibility to weather financial downturns, while low solvency may indicate high levels of financial risk.

Key Solvency Ratios

Several solvency ratios are commonly used to assess the long-term financial health of a business. These ratios give different perspectives on the company's ability to handle debt and manage financial obligations.

1. Debt-to-Equity Ratio

The debt-to-equity ratio is one of the most commonly used solvency ratios. It compares a company's total debt to its total equity, reflecting the proportion of debt financing relative to equity financing. This ratio indicates how much debt the company is using to finance its operations compared to the capital provided by shareholders.

The formula for the debt-to-equity ratio is:

"Debt-to-Equity Ratio"="Total Liabilities" /"Owner's Equity"

Where:

- **Total Debt** includes both short-term and long-term debt.
- **Total Equity** refers to the shareholders' equity, which represents the owners' claim on the company's assets after all liabilities have been paid.

Interpretation of the Debt-to-Equity Ratio

A high debt-to-equity ratio indicates that a company relies heavily on debt to finance its operations, which could be a sign of increased financial risk. This is especially concerning if the company's cash flow is insufficient to cover its debt obligations. Conversely, a low debt-to-equity ratio suggests that the company relies more on equity financing, which typically indicates lower financial risk.

For example:

A debt-to-equity ratio of 1.5 means the company has $1.50 in debt for every dollar of equity, suggesting a higher reliance on debt.

A debt-to-equity ratio of 0.5 indicates that the company has only 50 cents in debt for every dollar of equity, suggesting a more conservative capital structure.

2. Debt Ratio

This measures the proportion of a company's total assets that is financed by debt. It provides insight into the company's overall leverage and financial risk. The formula for the **debt ratio** is:

"Debt Ratio"="Total Debt" /"Total Assets"

Where:

- **Total Debt** includes both short-term and long-term liabilities.
- **Total Assets** represents the company's total resources, including both tangible and intangible assets.

Interpretation of the Debt Ratio

A **higher debt ratio** indicates that a larger proportion of the company's assets is financed through debt, which increases the risk of financial instability. A **lower debt ratio** suggests that the company is more conservatively financed, with a larger portion of its assets funded by equity.

For example:

A debt ratio of 0.6 means that 60% of the company's assets are financed by debt, leaving 40% to be financed by equity.

A debt ratio of 0.3 indicates that only 30% of the company's assets are financed by debt, with the rest funded by equity.

In general, a lower debt ratio is preferred as it indicates lower financial leverage and less risk. However, the appropriate level of debt varies across industries and business models.

3. Interest Coverage Ratio

The interest coverage ratio is a solvency ratio that measures a company's ability to meet its interest payments on outstanding debt. It reflects how many times a company can cover its interest expenses with its earnings before interest and taxes (EBIT). The formula for the interest coverage ratio is:

"Interest Coverage Ratio"="EBIT" /"Interest Expense"

Where:

- EBIT is the company's earnings before interest and taxes.

- Interest Expense is the total interest payable on debt during the period.

Interpretation of the Interest Coverage Ratio

A higher interest coverage ratio indicates that the company has a strong ability to meet its interest obligations, which signals financial stability. On the other hand, a lower ratio suggests that the company may struggle to cover its interest payments, raising concerns about its ability to manage its debt load.

An interest coverage ratio of 5.0 means that the company's EBIT is five times its interest expense, suggesting that it can comfortably cover its interest payments.

An interest coverage ratio of 1.5 means that the company's EBIT is only 1.5 times its interest expense, indicating potential difficulty in meeting interest obligations if there is a downturn in earnings.

In general, an interest coverage ratio above 3.0 is considered healthy, indicating that the company can comfortably meet its interest payments.

4. Equity Ratio

The equity ratio is a solvency ratio that compares a company's total equity to its total assets. It indicates the proportion of the company's assets that are financed by the owners' equity rather than debt. The formula for the equity ratio is:

"Equity Ratio"="Total Equity" /"Total Assets"

Interpretation of the Equity Ratio

A higher equity ratio suggests that a company is less reliant on debt to finance its assets, which is generally considered a lower-risk financial structure. Conversely, a lower equity ratio indicates that the company relies more on debt financing, which could increase its financial risk.

For example:

An equity ratio of 0.7 means that 70% of the company's assets are financed by equity, suggesting a conservative and stable capital structure.

An equity ratio of 0.4 means that only 40% of the company's assets are financed by equity, indicating higher leverage and potentially higher risk.

5. Capitalization Ratio

The capitalization ratio is another solvency ratio that measures the proportion of a company's capital structure that is financed by debt. It focuses on long-term debt as a percentage of the company's total long-term capital. The formula for the capitalization ratio is:

"Capitalization Ratio"="Long-Term Debt" /"Long-Term Debt + Equity"

Interpretation of the Capitalization Ratio

A high capitalization ratio suggests that a large portion of the company's long-term capital is financed through debt, which can increase the company's financial risk. A low capitalization ratio indicates that the company is less dependent on debt financing, which may provide more financial flexibility.

Interpreting Solvency Ratios: A Holistic Approach

While each solvency ratio provides valuable insight into a company's financial health, it is important to interpret them together to get a complete picture of a company's solvency. For example:

A high debt-to-equity ratio combined with a low interest coverage ratio could indicate that the company is highly leveraged and may struggle to meet its debt obligations.

A low debt ratio and a high equity ratio generally suggest a financially stable company with less reliance on debt.

Solvency ratios should also be analyzed in the context of the industry norms and the company's historical performance. Different industries have varying capital structures, and comparing a company's solvency ratios to its competitors can provide a better understanding of its financial risk.

Equity Differences

Equity is a crucial component in both corporations and small businesses as it represents ownership in the company. While the basic concept remains the same, there are notable differences in how equity is structured and managed between these two business types. These differences can have significant implications for decision-making, access to capital, and the rights of owners.

Equity in Corporations

Corporations are legally recognized entities that are distinct from their owners. In corporations, equity is divided into shares of stock, which can be bought, sold, and traded. The ownership percentage of shareholders is determined by the number of shares they hold. Corporations typically issue common stock and preferred stock. Common shareholders have voting rights and a claim on dividends, but they are last in line in the event of liquidation. Preferred shareholders, on the other hand, receive dividends before common shareholders but usually do not have voting rights.

Corporations have better access to capital since they can issue additional shares or go public through an Initial Public Offering (IPO). This enables them to raise substantial funds for business expansion or acquisitions. The profits in corporations are often retained within the business to fund future growth rather than being fully distributed as dividends. Corporations are subject to strict regulatory oversight, including rules from government agencies such as the Securities and Exchange Commission (SEC), which regulate how shares are issued, how profits are distributed, and how financial information is disclosed.

Equity in Small Businesses

In small businesses, equity is typically based on the owners' contributions. In sole proprietorships, the owner has full ownership of the business. In partnerships, ownership is usually divided according to the terms agreed upon by the partners, such as their initial investment. Limited Liability Companies (LLCs) combine features of partnerships and corporations, with owners called members. Here, equity is typically represented through capital accounts, and ownership is more flexible than in corporations. There are no shares issued in small businesses, and ownership is not publicly traded.

Small businesses usually rely on personal savings, bank loans, or private investors for funding, and they do not have the ability to raise large amounts of capital like corporations. Profit-sharing in small businesses is more informal, and the distribution is based on the ownership stake or the agreement between the owners. The business structure in small businesses is more flexible, with fewer regulatory requirements, making it simpler to manage and control. However, owners may face greater personal financial risk, especially in sole proprietorships, where the owner is personally liable for the business's debts.

Key Differences Between Equity in Corporations and Small Businesses

Feature	Corporations	Small Businesses
Ownership Structure	Divided into shares of stock	Based on owner contributions (capital accounts or personal ownership)
Issuance of Shares	Can issue shares publicly or privately	No shares issued; ownership based on capital contribution
Access to Capital	Can raise large amounts through stock issuance or IPO	Limited to personal investment, bank loans, or private investors
Profit Distribution	Dividends based on shares; profits may be reinvested	Profits distributed based on ownership or agreement between owners
Legal and Regulatory Oversight	Heavily regulated by government agencies like SEC	Minimal regulatory oversight, mainly local or state laws

Feature	Corporations	Small Businesses
Flexibility	More rigid; governed by corporate laws and bylaws	Highly flexible; governed by owner agreements (e.g., partnership agreements, LLC operating agreements)
Transferability of Ownership	Shares can be bought/sold publicly or privately	Ownership transfers are more complex and may require an agreement
Financial Statements	Must adhere to formal reporting standards (GAAP or IFRS)	Less formal, though LLCs and partnerships may prepare financial statements for tax purposes

Considerations for Business Owners

When deciding between forming a corporation or a small business like a sole proprietorship or LLC, the equity structure is a critical factor. Corporations offer greater access to capital and the ability to scale through shares. However, this comes with greater regulatory oversight, complexity in ownership structure, and formal financial reporting requirements.

On the other hand, small businesses offer more flexibility with fewer regulations and a simpler ownership structure. However, small businesses may struggle with raising large amounts of capital, and owners may face more personal risk depending on the business type. For example, in a sole proprietorship, the owner is personally liable for business debts.

In conclusion, the choice between incorporating or running a small business depends on various factors, including the need for capital, control, regulatory considerations, and the level of personal financial risk an owner is willing to take. Each structure has its own advantages and challenges, and understanding the implications of equity in each can help owners make informed decisions about their business's future.

Depreciation and Asset Valuation

Depreciation and asset valuation are two fundamental concepts in accounting that affect a company's financial statements, tax obligations, and overall financial health. Understanding how depreciation works and how assets are valued is crucial for businesses, accountants, investors, and other stakeholders involved in financial analysis.

Depreciation refers to the process of allocating the cost of a long-term tangible asset over its useful life. Over time, physical assets such as machinery, buildings, vehicles, and equipment lose value due to wear and tear, aging, or obsolescence. Instead of expensing the entire cost of an asset in the year it was purchased, depreciation spreads the cost over several years, matching the asset's expense with the revenue it helps generate.

Depreciation is essential for businesses to accurately reflect the declining value of assets over time and allocate costs appropriately in their financial statements. By doing so, companies can avoid overstating their profits in the years they make a significant capital purchase.

Why Is Depreciation Important?

Depreciation plays several critical roles in business and financial reporting:

1. **Accurate Financial Reporting**:
   Depreciation ensures that the company's income statement reflects the ongoing cost of using assets over time, rather than reporting an immediate and large expense. This provides a more accurate view of profitability.
2. **Tax Deductions**:
   In many countries, businesses can deduct depreciation expenses from their taxable income, which reduces their overall tax liability. Depreciation, therefore, has a direct impact on the company's cash flow.
3. **Asset Management**:
   Depreciation allows businesses to track the diminishing value of assets and plan for replacements or upgrades. By understanding how assets lose value over time, businesses can make better long-term investment decisions.

How is Depreciation Calculated?

The **calculation of depreciation** involves determining the initial cost of an asset, its useful life, and its residual value (also called salvage value or scrap value). The basic formula for calculating depreciation is:

$$\text{Depreciation Expense} = \frac{\text{Cost of Asset} - \text{Residual Value}}{\text{Useful Life}}$$

Where:

- **Cost of Asset** is the amount paid to acquire the asset.
- **Residual Value** is the estimated value of the asset at the end of its useful life (the amount the company expects to sell the asset for).
- **Useful Life** is the period over which the asset is expected to be used, often measured in years.

The key challenge in depreciation is selecting the appropriate method to allocate the depreciation expense across the asset's useful life.

Depreciation Methods

There are several methods used to calculate depreciation, each of which allocates the expense in a different way. The choice of method depends on the asset's nature, usage pattern, and how the company prefers to report its financials. Below are the most commonly used depreciation methods:

1. Straight-Line Depreciation

Straight-line depreciation is the simplest and most commonly used method. It allocates an equal amount of depreciation expense each year over the asset's useful life. The formula for straight-line depreciation is:

$$\text{"Annual Depreciation Expense"} = (\text{"Cost of Asset"} - \text{"Residual Value"})/\text{"Useful Life"}$$

For example, if a company purchases an asset for $10,000, expects it to have a residual value of $1,000, and a useful life of 5 years, the annual depreciation expense would be:

Thus, the asset would depreciate by $1,800 each year for 5 years.

2. Declining Balance Depreciation

The **declining balance method** allocates a higher depreciation expense in the earlier years of the asset's useful life, and progressively lower amounts as time goes on. This method is often used for assets that lose their value more quickly in the initial years. The most common type is the **double declining balance (DDB)** method, which doubles the straight-line depreciation rate.

The formula for the declining balance method is:

$$\text{"Depreciation Expense"} = 2 \times 1/\text{"Useful Life"} \times \text{"Book Value at Beginning of Year"}$$

For example, if an asset costs $10,000, has a useful life of 5 years, and no residual value, the depreciation expense for the first year would be:

$$\text{"Depreciation Expense Year 1"} = 2 \times 1/5 \times 10{,}000 = 4{,}000$$

In subsequent years, the depreciation expense will be calculated based on the book value (cost minus accumulated depreciation), which decreases over time.

3. Units of Production Depreciation

The **units of production method** ties depreciation directly to the asset's usage, making it ideal for assets that are used unevenly over time. With this method, depreciation is calculated based on the number of units the asset produces or the hours it operates.

The formula is:

$$\text{"Depreciation Expense"} = ((\text{"Cost of Asset"} - \text{"Residual Value"})/\text{"Total Units Expected to be Produced"}) \times \text{"Units Produced in the Period"}$$

For example, if a machine costs $10,000, has a residual value of $1,000, and is expected to produce 100,000 units over its life, the depreciation expense per unit would be:

$$(10{,}000-1{,}000)/100{,}000=0.09\text{" per unit"}$$

If the machine produces 10,000 units in a given year, the depreciation expense for that year would be:

$$0.09\times 10{,}000=900$$

This method reflects actual asset usage, making it more accurate for some types of equipment.

Impact of Depreciation on Financial Statements

Depreciation affects both the income statement and the balance sheet.

Income Statement:

Depreciation is recorded as an expense on the income statement, reducing the company's taxable income. While depreciation does not affect cash flow directly, it does reduce the net income reported. This is especially important for tax purposes, as businesses can deduct depreciation from their income, thereby lowering their tax liability.

Balance Sheet:

On the balance sheet, depreciation reduces the book value of assets over time. The accumulated depreciation is subtracted from the asset's original cost, showing the net book value of the asset. For example, if an asset with an original cost of $10,000 has accumulated depreciation of $3,000, its book value would be:

$$\text{Book Value} = 10{,}000 - 3{,}000 = 7{,}000$$

Over time, this will continue until the asset's book value reaches its residual value.

Analyzing Cash Flow Statements

The cash flow statement—officially known as the statement of cash flows—is a fundamental financial statement that reports how cash enters and leaves a business during a specific period. Unlike the income statement, which is based on accrual accounting and reflects revenues and expenses when they are incurred, the cash flow statement provides a clear picture of the actual cash position, showing how a company generates and uses cash through its core activities, investments, and financing efforts.

The cash flow statement is an essential tool for investors, creditors, and business owners to assess the liquidity, solvency, and overall financial health of a company. It is particularly useful because it allows stakeholders to see how well a company can generate cash to meet its obligations and fund its operations.

What Does the Cash Flow Statement Tell Us?

The cash flow statement helps answer some critical questions about a company's financial operations:

- How much cash did the company generate from its core business operations?
- How did the company invest its funds, and were there any significant purchases or sales of assets?
- How did the company raise capital or repay debt?
- Has the company generated sufficient cash to meet its short-term obligations and finance future growth?

By analyzing these aspects, the cash flow statement complements the income statement and balance sheet, offering a more complete view of the company's financial position.

Key Components of the Cash Flow Statement

The cash flow statement is divided into three main sections that categorize cash flows based on the activity from which they originate:

1. **Operating Activities**
2. **Investing Activities**
3. **Financing Activities**

There is also a fourth section that provides supplemental information, detailing significant non-cash transactions and items like interest and tax payments. Let's break down each of these components to understand their significance.

1. Cash Flow from Operating Activities

The operating activities section reports the cash flows related to the core operations of the business. This section adjusts the net income (from the income statement) to reflect the cash that was actually received and paid during the period. Since the income statement is prepared on an accrual basis, it includes non-cash items such as depreciation, unrealized gains, or losses. The operating section of the cash flow statement removes these non-cash items to provide a true picture of the company's cash flow from its everyday business activities.

Key Adjustments in Operating Activities

The adjustments made in this section typically include:

- **Changes in Current Assets and Liabilities**: This involves adjustments for changes in accounts like **accounts receivable**, **accounts payable**, **inventory**, and **accrued expenses**. For example, an increase in accounts payable means the company has more cash available, as it has delayed payments to suppliers.

- **Depreciation and Amortization**: These non-cash charges are added back to net income because they were deducted when calculating profit but didn't actually involve an outflow of cash.
- **Gains and Losses from Sales of Assets**: Any gains or losses from selling long-term assets (such as equipment or property) are adjusted because they are included in net income but are not part of operating activities.

The formula for calculating cash flow from operating activities (using the indirect method) is:

$$\text{"Cash Flow from Operating Activities"}=$$
$$\text{"Net Income"}+\text{"Non-Cash Expenses"}+\text{"Changes in Working Capital"}$$

For example, a company might start with net income of $50,000, add back $10,000 of depreciation, and adjust for a $5,000 increase in accounts payable. This section reflects the true cash generated from the business's operations.

2. Cash Flow from Investing Activities

The investing activities section of the cash flow statement reports cash flows related to the company's purchases and sales of long-term assets, such as property, plant, and equipment (PPE), intangible assets, and investments. This section provides insight into how the company is investing its capital and whether it is expanding or divesting assets.

Types of Transactions Included in Investing Activities

- **Purchases of Fixed Assets**: When a company buys new equipment or property, it uses cash, which will be shown as an outflow in this section.
- **Sales of Assets**: When a company sells long-term assets, such as machinery or real estate, the proceeds from these sales are recorded as an inflow of cash.
- **Investments in Securities**: Cash used to purchase securities or other long-term investments, such as stocks or bonds, is also reported in this section.
- **Proceeds from Investments**: When the company sells investments, such as stocks or bonds, the cash received from these sales is an inflow.

This section reveals the company's investment strategy and whether it is spending its resources on growth or selling off assets to generate cash.

3. Cash Flow from Financing Activities

The financing activities section of the cash flow statement shows how the company raises and repays capital. This section includes transactions related to debt and equity financing, providing insight into the company's capital structure.

Key Transactions in Financing Activities

- **Issuance of Debt**: Cash inflows from borrowing money, such as issuing bonds or obtaining bank loans, are shown in this section.
- **Repayment of Debt**: Cash outflows related to the repayment of loans, bond payments, and other forms of debt.
- **Issuance of Equity**: When the company raises funds by issuing stock, the cash received from investors is recorded as an inflow.
- **Repurchase of Shares**: If the company buys back its own stock, this is recorded as a cash outflow.
- **Dividend Payments**: Cash payments made to shareholders as dividends are also included in this section.

This section helps investors understand the company's approach to funding its operations, whether through borrowing or equity financing, and how it is managing its debt obligations.

4. Supplemental Information

The supplemental information section of the cash flow statement includes details about significant non-cash transactions, such as the issuance of stock in exchange for assets, the conversion of debt into equity, or the acquisition of assets through leasing.

Additionally, the section reports cash paid for interest and income taxes. While these amounts might be included in the operating section in some cases, they are often disclosed separately for transparency.

Importance of the Cash Flow Statement

While the income statement and balance sheet provide valuable financial information, the cash flow statement offers a more direct insight into the company's liquidity and cash management. Here are some reasons why the cash flow statement is so important:

1. **Liquidity Assessment**:
   The cash flow statement provides a clear view of the company's ability to generate enough cash to meet its short-term obligations. A company might show profitability on its income statement but still face liquidity problems if it cannot convert profits into cash.
2. **Evaluating Business Operations**:
   By analyzing cash flow from operating activities, investors can assess how well the company's core operations are generating cash. If cash flow from operations is consistently negative, it could signal operational

inefficiencies or potential financial distress.

3. **Capital Management**:
   The investing and financing sections help stakeholders understand how the company is managing its capital. Is the company reinvesting profits into new assets? Is it over-relying on debt to fund growth? These questions can be answered by analyzing the cash flow from investing and financing activities.

4. **Cash Flow as a Performance Indicator**:
   A strong and consistent positive cash flow, particularly from operations, is often viewed as a sign of business strength. Conversely, negative cash flow over an extended period could be a warning sign of financial instability.

The cash flow statement is a powerful tool for understanding the financial health of a company. It provides insights that cannot be gleaned from the income statement or balance sheet alone. By analyzing the cash flow from operating, investing, and financing activities, businesses, investors, and creditors can assess the company's ability to meet its obligations, invest in growth, and maintain long-term financial stability. While profitability is important, cash flow reveals whether the company is truly in control of its financial situation and can sustain its operations in the future.

HOME DEPOT - ANALYZING CASH FLOW STATEMENTS

As a publicly traded company, Home Depot must provide financial reports, including its cash flow statement.

CHALLENGES

- Managing High Operating Cash Flow
- Large-Scale Capital Investments
- Financing to Support Growth

OBJECTIVES

MAINTAIN STRONG CASH FLOW FROM OPERATIONS

This ensured the company could fund its day-to-day operations, meet financial obligations, and reinvest.

OPTIMIZE FINANCING ACTIVITIES

Home Depot's strategy involved balancing debt issuance with equity financing.

RESULT AND BENEFITS

- In fiscal year 2020, Home Depot reported a net income of $12.9 billion and generated $14.2 billion in cash flow.
- The company reported $3.4 billion in cash outflows for investing activities, driven by store openings and upgrades.

Capital Expenditure vs. Revenue Expenditure

Understanding the distinction between capital expenditure (CapEx) and revenue expenditure (RevEx) is essential for accurate financial reporting and decision-making. These expenditures play a crucial role in how a company allocates resources and reports its financial performance. While both types of expenditure are related to the operations of a business, they are treated differently on the financial statements, with significant implications for tax, profitability, and long-term financial strategy.

In this section, we will explore the key differences between capital and revenue expenditures, their impact on financial statements, and why it's important to correctly categorize these expenses.

What is Capital Expenditure (CapEx)?

Capital expenditure (CapEx) refers to funds used by a business to acquire, improve, or maintain fixed assets, such as property, plant, equipment (PPE), and intangible assets like patents or trademarks. CapEx typically involves large, one-time purchases or investments that will benefit the company over an extended period.

Key Characteristics of Capital Expenditure:

- **Long-Term Investment**: Capital expenditure is made to enhance the long-term operational capacity of the business. The asset purchased will be used for many years and contribute to the company's revenue generation over that time.
- **Increase in Asset Value**: Capital expenditures increase the value of the company's fixed assets, either through the acquisition of new assets or by improving existing ones. For example, purchasing a new machine or upgrading an office building are capital expenditures.
- **Depreciation**: Since capital expenditures result in long-term assets, they are not fully expensed in the year they occur. Instead, they are capitalized on the balance sheet and then depreciated (or amortized for intangible assets) over the asset's useful life.
- **Non-Recurring**: Capital expenditures are generally non-recurring and often involve substantial amounts of money. They are usually planned and budgeted in advance.

Examples of Capital Expenditure:

- Purchasing land, buildings, or machinery
- Upgrading existing machinery or equipment to improve efficiency or capacity
- Installing a new production line or factory expansion
- Purchasing patents or intellectual property that will be used long-term

- Building or renovating an office building

Capital Expenditure in the Financial Statements

On the balance sheet, capital expenditures are classified as assets. Over time, the cost of these assets is depreciated and deducted from the asset's value on the balance sheet. For example, if a company purchases a machine for $100,000, the asset will appear on the balance sheet as a long-term asset. Each year, depreciation will reduce the book value of the asset and appear as an expense on the income statement, without affecting the company's immediate cash flow.

What is Revenue Expenditure (RevEx)?

Revenue expenditure refers to the costs incurred by a business for its day-to-day operations. These expenditures are necessary for maintaining the company's existing operations and do not result in the acquisition or enhancement of long-term assets. Unlike capital expenditures, revenue expenditures are fully expensed in the year they occur, meaning they reduce the company's profit for that period.

Key Characteristics of Revenue Expenditure:

- **Short-Term Expense**: Revenue expenditure relates to costs that are typically incurred within a single financial year. These expenses are part of normal business operations and are vital for generating revenue.
- **Maintenance Costs**: Revenue expenditures usually maintain existing assets in working order, rather than enhancing or extending their value. For example, repairs, utilities, and wages are revenue expenditures.
- **Impact on Profit**: Since these expenditures are fully deducted from income in the period they are incurred, they directly reduce the company's net profit for that year.
- **Recurring**: Unlike capital expenditures, revenue expenditures are recurrent and necessary for the regular functioning of the business.

Examples of Revenue Expenditure:

- Routine repairs and maintenance of equipment
- Salaries and wages of employees
- Office supplies and utilities (e.g., electricity, water, rent)
- Advertising and marketing expenses
- Insurance premiums
- Depreciation of assets

Revenue Expenditure in the Financial Statements

Revenue expenditures are recorded on the income statement as expenses. Since these costs are necessary to maintain the company's day-to-day operations, they are deducted from the company's revenue to determine its net income for the period. For instance, if a business spends $10,000 on repairs to a machine, that amount is fully expensed in the year it occurs and reduces the company's net profit for the period.

CAPITAL EXPENDITURE
VS.
REVENUE EXPENDITURE

KEY DIFFERENCES

Feature	Capital Expenditure	Revenue Expenditure
Definition	Expenditure for acquiring or improving long-term assets.	Expenditure for daily operational costs.
Purpose	Increases the value of fixed assets and contributes long-term value.	Maintains operations and does not extend the useful life of assets.
Impact on Financial Statements	Capitalized as an asset on the balance sheet and depreciated over time.	Expensed in full on the income statement in the year incurred.
Example	Purchase of machinery, real estate, patents.	Salaries, utility bills, repairs, office supplies.
Duration of Benefit	Benefits the company for many years.	Benefits are immediate, used within the same year.
Accounting Treatment	Depreciated or amortized over the asset's useful life.	Fully expensed in the period they occur.

Deferred Revenue Expenditure: A Special Case

A deferred revenue expenditure is a type of revenue expenditure that benefits the business over multiple years but is accounted for as an expense. These expenses are typically large in nature but cannot be fully written off in one year due to their size. Therefore, they are deferred and written off over time.

Common Examples of Deferred Revenue Expenditure:

- **Preliminary Expenses**: Costs incurred to set up a business, such as legal fees and marketing research, which will be amortized over several years.
- **Brokerage Fees**: Fees paid for the issuance of shares or bonds that provide long-term benefits.
- **Business Relocation Costs**: Expenses incurred in moving a business from one location to another.
- **Major Repairs**: Exceptional repairs that significantly extend the life of an asset.

These expenses are initially recorded on the balance sheet as an asset and then written off over several periods, often using a systematic allocation, such as the straight-line method.

Capital Receipts vs. Revenue Receipts

While capital expenditure and revenue expenditure deal with how money is spent, capital receipts and revenue receipts refer to the nature of the money received by the business.

- **Capital Receipts**: Funds obtained through activities that provide long-term value, such as issuing shares, borrowing money, or selling long-term assets. These are recorded on the balance sheet.
- **Revenue Receipts**: Income generated from day-to-day business operations, such as sales revenue, interest income, or dividends. These are recorded on the income statement.

Understanding the difference between capital expenditure and revenue expenditure is essential for accurate financial reporting, tax planning, and business strategy. Capital expenditures are long-term investments in assets that will contribute to the business over several years, while revenue expenditures are the day-to-day costs necessary to keep the business running. The classification of these expenditures determines how they are reported in financial statements and can affect a company's tax obligations, profitability, and overall financial health.

By correctly categorizing expenditures, businesses ensure that their financial statements reflect the true cost of operations, enabling better decision-making for management, investors, and other stakeholders. The distinction between these types of expenditure is fundamental in preparing accurate financial accounts and ensuring long-term financial sustainability.

What Is the Income Statement?

The income statement provides a summary of a company's financial performance over a specific period, typically a fiscal quarter or year. It answers a crucial question: is the company profitable? Unlike the balance sheet, which shows assets, liabilities, and equity at a specific point in time, the income statement focuses on revenues, expenses, and the resulting profit or loss.

Key Components:

1. **Revenue**: Represents total earnings from the company's core activities, like sales of products or services.
2. **Expenses**: Costs incurred to generate revenue, including cost of goods sold (COGS), operating expenses, and non-operating expenses like interest.
3. **Gains and Losses**: Non-recurring items, such as profits from asset sales or losses from legal settlements.
4. **Net Income**: The final result after accounting for revenues, expenses, gains, and losses. This indicates overall profitability.

Formats:

- **Single-Step Income Statement**: Simple format, subtracts total expenses from total revenues to find net income.
- **Multi-Step Income Statement**: Offers more detail, separating operating and non-operating activities and providing subtotals like gross profit and operating income.

Understanding the Balance Sheet

The **balance sheet** is one of the core financial statements that provide a snapshot of a company's financial position at a specific point in time. It serves as a critical tool for business owners, investors, creditors, and analysts to assess the company's health, evaluate its capacity to meet financial obligations, and understand its overall financial structure. The balance sheet reflects the company's assets, liabilities, and equity, encapsulating the accounting equation: Assets = Liabilities + Equity.

This section will break down the components of the balance sheet, how it is structured, and its role in financial reporting. We will explore the types of assets and liabilities, the significance of shareholder equity, and how the balance sheet contributes to decision-making and strategic planning.

What is the Balance Sheet?

The balance sheet, also known as the statement of financial position, is prepared to reflect the financial status of a company at a particular date, typically at the end of a financial period, such as a fiscal quarter or year. Unlike the income statement, which tracks performance over a period of time, the balance sheet provides a snapshot of what a company owns and owes at a specific moment.

It is divided into three main sections:

1. **Assets**: What the company owns.
2. **Liabilities**: What the company owes.
3. **Equity**: The owners' residual interest in the assets after liabilities are deducted.

The balance sheet follows the **accounting equation**:

$$\text{Assets} = \text{Liabilities} + \text{Equity}$$

This equation is the foundation of the balance sheet and reflects the relationship between a company's resources (assets) and the claims against those resources (liabilities and equity).

Assets: What the Company Owns

Assets are the resources that a company owns and expects to provide future economic benefits. These are typically classified into two categories: current assets and non-current (or fixed) assets.

Current Assets

Current assets are assets that are expected to be consumed, sold, or converted into cash within one year or within the company's operating cycle, whichever is longer. These assets are critical for the day-to-day operations of the business. Some of the common examples include:

- **Cash and Cash Equivalents**: The most liquid assets, such as cash in hand or cash in the bank, that are used to meet short-term obligations.
- **Accounts Receivable**: Money owed to the company by customers for goods or services delivered on credit.
- **Inventory**: Goods that are held for sale in the normal course of business, including raw materials, work-in-progress, and finished goods.
- **Prepaid Expenses**: Payments made in advance for services or goods that will be received in the future, such as prepaid insurance or rent.

These assets are crucial for ensuring that the company has enough liquidity to meet its short-term obligations and continue operations smoothly.

Non-Current (Fixed) Assets

Non-current assets, also called **fixed assets**, are resources that a company holds for long-term use. These assets are not intended to be converted into cash within one year and are typically used to support business operations over an extended period. Examples include:

- **Property, Plant, and Equipment (PPE)**: Tangible assets like buildings, machinery, and equipment that are used in the production of goods and services.
- **Intangible Assets**: Non-physical assets, such as patents, trademarks, and goodwill, that provide long-term value to the company.
- **Investments**: Long-term investments that the company expects to hold for more than one year, such as stocks, bonds, or real estate.

Non-current assets play a crucial role in helping the company generate future revenues and are usually depreciated over their useful life to reflect their declining value.

Liabilities: What the Company Owes

Liabilities represent the company's financial obligations or debts, which must be settled over time through the transfer of money, goods, or services. Liabilities are classified into **current liabilities** and **non-current liabilities**.

Current Liabilities

Current liabilities are obligations that the company expects to settle within one year or within the operating cycle, whichever is longer. These are short-term debts that must be paid off to ensure the company maintains liquidity. Common examples include:

- **Accounts Payable**: Money owed to suppliers for goods and services purchased on credit.
- **Short-Term Debt**: Loans or lines of credit that are due within the next 12 months.
- **Accrued Expenses**: Expenses that have been incurred but not yet paid, such as wages, taxes, and utilities.

These liabilities represent the company's short-term financial commitments and are critical in assessing its ability to meet immediate obligations.

Non-Current Liabilities

Non-current liabilities, also known as long-term liabilities, are debts that are due beyond one year. These obligations are typically used to finance long-term investments or business growth. Examples include:

- **Long-Term Debt**: Loans or bonds payable over more than one year, often used to finance the company's long-term projects or capital expenditures.

- **Deferred Tax Liabilities**: Taxes that are owed but not yet paid, typically arising due to differences between accounting and tax treatments of certain transactions.
- **Pension Liabilities**: Obligations to pay retirement benefits to employees in the future.

Non-current liabilities are important for assessing the company's long-term financial stability and its ability to manage long-term debt.

Equity: The Owners' Residual Interest

Equity represents the ownership interest in the company, or the residual value of assets after all liabilities have been deducted. In simple terms, equity reflects the amount that would be returned to the owners if the company were liquidated and all its debts were paid.

Key Components of Equity

1. **Owner's Equity (or Shareholders' Equity)**: In a corporation, this includes common stock, retained earnings, and other forms of equity. For sole proprietorships, it is simply the owner's equity in the business.
2. **Retained Earnings**: The portion of net income that is retained in the company rather than paid out as dividends. Retained earnings reflect the company's cumulative profits or losses over time.
3. **Additional Paid-In Capital**: The amount of capital that shareholders have invested in the company above the par value of the stock.
4. **Treasury Stock**: Shares that the company has repurchased from shareholders but has not yet retired.

Equity provides insights into the ownership structure of the business and is a key indicator of financial health. Positive equity indicates that the company has more assets than liabilities, while negative equity suggests financial distress.

The Accounting Equation and the Balance Sheet

The **accounting equation** is the fundamental equation that governs the balance sheet:

$$\text{Assets} = \text{Liabilities} + \text{Equity}$$

This equation shows the relationship between the resources owned by the company (assets) and the claims against those resources (liabilities and equity). The balance sheet must always balance, meaning that the total value of the company's assets must equal the sum of its liabilities and equity. This ensures that the books are correctly maintained and that the company's financial position is accurately reflected.

For example, if a company has $1,000,000 in assets, it could have $400,000 in liabilities and $600,000 in equity. This balance reflects that the company's assets have been financed by both external creditors and the company's shareholders.

The Balance Sheet in Financial Decision Making

The balance sheet provides essential information for a variety of stakeholders, including investors, creditors, and management. Here's how it is used in decision-making:

1. **Investors**: Investors use the balance sheet to assess the company's financial health, liquidity, and long-term viability. By examining the balance sheet, they can determine if the company is in a strong position to generate future profits.
2. **Creditors**: Creditors analyze the balance sheet to evaluate the company's ability to repay its debts. Key indicators like the current ratio (current assets/current liabilities) help creditors assess liquidity and short-term solvency.
3. **Management**: Company management uses the balance sheet to track the company's financial performance, manage resources, and plan for future growth. It helps them make strategic decisions about financing, investment, and cost management.

Chapter 6: Managerial Accounting

The Purpose of Managerial Accounting

Managerial accounting serves a very different purpose from financial accounting, even though both rely on the same underlying financial information. While financial accounting focuses on creating standardized reports for external users such as investors, creditors, and regulatory agencies, managerial accounting exists entirely to support internal decision-making. It provides managers with the data, analysis, and forecasts they need to plan operations, control costs, evaluate performance, set strategies, and make informed choices in real time.

At its core, managerial accounting translates raw financial data into practical insights. These insights help managers understand how the business is performing today and what decisions must be made to improve tomorrow. The goal is not compliance or record-keeping, but clarity. Managerial accounting gives meaning to numbers so that leaders can operate with confidence and precision.

A Forward-Looking Approach

Unlike financial accounting, which records and reports what has already happened, managerial accounting is concerned with what will happen. This future-oriented focus distinguishes it from all other areas of accounting. Managers cannot rely solely on historical results to shape decisions about pricing, production levels, hiring, or expansion. They need forecasts, projections, and scenario analyses.

Managerial accounting provides tools such as cost-volume-profit analysis, budgeting, and variance reports to help managers anticipate outcomes. These tools allow leaders to ask questions like:

What will happen to profit if production volume changes?

How would a price increase affect demand?

What level of sales is required to break even?

Are we using resources efficiently, or are costs rising unnecessarily?

By addressing questions like these, managerial accounting becomes a roadmap for planning the future of the business.

Supporting Daily Operational Decisions

Managerial accounting is deeply connected to daily operations. A company's managers make dozens of small decisions every day, and each decision carries financial implications. Whether a supervisor adjusts staffing for a shift, approves overtime, orders raw materials, or reviews departmental performance, financial insight is essential.

For instance, a production manager might use cost data to determine whether it is more economical to produce a component in-house or outsource it. A retail store manager might use inventory turnover rates to decide how to allocate shelf space. A sales manager might analyze contribution margins to determine which product lines deserve more marketing resources.

The usefulness of managerial accounting lies in its ability to provide detailed, relevant data at the exact level where decisions are made. Reports can be customized to track specific departments, product lines, regions, or even individual employees. This fine-grained level of analysis is rarely found in financial accounting.

Emphasis on Relevance Over Precision

Financial accounting must adhere to strict standards, such as GAAP or IFRS, to ensure accuracy and comparability across companies. Managerial accounting, however, prioritizes relevance over strict precision. Managers need information that is timely, flexible, and specific to the questions they are trying to answer.

If a manager is deciding whether to discontinue a product line, the important data is not perfectly reconciled numbers from audited statements, but rather the product's variable costs, manufacturing time, contribution margin, marketing expenses, and potential savings from reallocation. Managerial accounting may use estimates, projections, and cost behavior patterns rather than exact historical numbers because the goal is to support a decision, not meet external reporting standards.

This flexibility makes managerial accounting adaptable. The reports produced can change depending on the industry, business size, department, or nature of the problem being solved. A small business may rely heavily on simple spreadsheets and estimates, while a large manufacturing company may use sophisticated software to track cost drivers and inventory flows.

Cost Management and Efficiency

One of the most important purposes of managerial accounting is helping businesses control costs. Costs have a direct impact on profitability, and understanding them allows managers to improve efficiency. Managerial accounting breaks costs down into meaningful categories such as fixed, variable, direct, indirect, product, and period costs.

By doing so, it helps managers evaluate:

- Which costs change with production volume
- Which costs can be reduced without harming product quality
- Whether resources are being used effectively
- Whether certain functions are operating above or below expected cost levels

Common managerial tools such as standard costing, variance analysis, and activity-based costing help managers identify inefficiencies before they become serious problems. For example, if actual labor costs exceed the standard labor cost for a period, variance analysis will highlight the difference and guide managers toward solutions such as retraining workers, adjusting schedules, or improving workflows.

Budgeting and Planning

Managerial accounting plays a central role in the budgeting process. A budget is essentially a financial plan that outlines expected revenues, expenses, and resource needs for a future period. Well-prepared budgets help managers set goals, allocate resources, and monitor performance.

Different types of budgets serve different purposes:

- **Operating budgets** outline expected sales, production levels, and expenses.
- **Cash budgets** ensure the business has enough liquidity to meet obligations.
- **Capital budgets** evaluate long-term investments and asset purchases.

Budgeting is not simply a calculation exercise. It forces managers to articulate goals, coordinate across departments, and anticipate challenges. Managerial accounting organizes this process, providing estimates, historical data, and projections that shape the final budget. Once the period begins, actual performance is compared to the budget, and any variances are investigated.

This continuous cycle of planning and evaluation supports better decision-making and keeps the business aligned with its strategic goals.

Performance Measurement and Responsibility Accounting

Managerial accounting also helps evaluate the performance of departments, teams, and managers. This process is known as **responsibility accounting**, where responsibility centers are created to assign financial accountability to different areas.

A responsibility center may be classified as:

- A **cost center**, responsible for controlling costs
- A **revenue center**, responsible for generating sales
- A **profit center**, responsible for both revenues and expenses
- An **investment center**, responsible for return on invested assets

By assigning responsibility and measuring the results, businesses encourage accountability and improvement. Performance reports can show, for example, whether a division met its sales targets, kept within its budget, or improved its profit margin. These evaluations help upper management reward strong performance and address areas needing support or correction.

Strategic Decision-Making

Finally, managerial accounting supports high-level strategic decisions. Decisions such as entering a new market, discontinuing a product line, automating a production process, or restructuring operations require detailed financial projections and an understanding of long-term consequences.

Managerial accounting provides tools such as:

- **Cost-benefit analysis**
- **Sensitivity analysis**
- **Capital budgeting**
- **Break-even analysis**
- **Make-or-buy analysis**

These tools allow managers to evaluate alternatives, predict outcomes under different scenarios, and choose the path that aligns best with the company's goals.

The purpose of managerial accounting is to empower managers with the information they need to plan, control, and make informed decisions. Its value lies not in formal compliance or strict reporting rules, but in its ability to turn raw financial data into insights that guide action. Through forecasting, cost analysis, budgeting, performance evaluation, and strategic planning, managerial accounting becomes an essential framework for building a more efficient, profitable, and forward-thinking business.

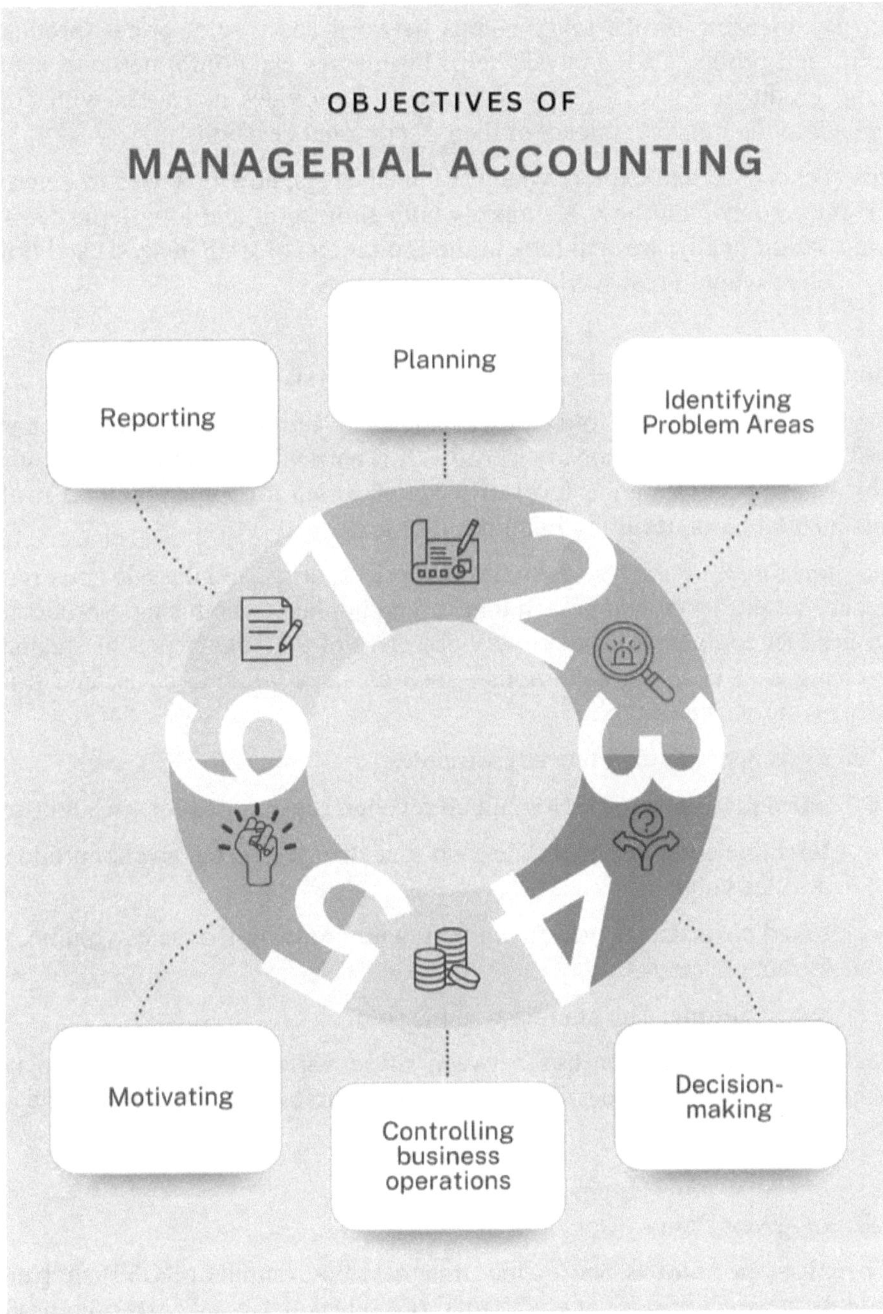
OBJECTIVES OF
MANAGERIAL ACCOUNTING
Planning
Reporting
Identifying Problem Areas
1
2
3
4
5
6
Motivating
Controlling business operations
Decision-making

Cost-Volume-Profit (CVP) Analysis

Cost-Volume-Profit (CVP) analysis is a powerful tool for understanding how various factors such as sales volume, costs, and pricing influence a company's profit. By focusing on the relationships between costs, sales prices, production volume, and profits, CVP analysis helps businesses make informed decisions on pricing, production levels, and cost control. It provides managers with critical insights into the financial impact of their operational decisions.

In this section, we will explore what CVP analysis is, how it is used to determine break-even points, and how it supports both short-term and long-term decision-making. Additionally, we will look at the limitations of CVP analysis and how to apply it effectively in real-world business scenarios.

Understanding Cost-Volume-Profit (CVP) Analysis

At its core, Cost-Volume-Profit (CVP) analysis investigates the effects of changes in cost and volume on a company's profits. It is particularly useful for determining the break-even point, or the level of sales at which a company's total revenue equals its total costs, resulting in no profit or loss.

In the short run, CVP analysis assumes that prices, costs, and the sales mix remain constant. It is a dynamic approach that can be applied to both single-product and multi-product companies. The primary objective of CVP analysis is to understand how changes in business conditions—such as sales volume, costs, and pricing strategies—impact profitability.

CVP analysis operates on a few key variables:

- **Sales price per unit**: How much revenue is generated for each unit sold.
- **Variable costs per unit**: The costs that change with the level of production or sales volume.
- **Fixed costs**: Costs that do not vary with production or sales volume, such as rent or salaries.
- **Sales volume**: The number of units sold.

By calculating the relationship between these variables, CVP analysis helps managers answer critical questions about pricing strategies, cost control, and sales targets.

The Break-Even Point

The **break-even point** is one of the most essential outputs of CVP analysis. It represents the level of sales at which total revenue equals total costs—no profit or loss is made. Understanding the break-even point helps businesses set sales targets and identify how much of a product needs to be sold to cover all fixed and variable costs.

The formula for the **break-even point in units** is:

"Break-even point (in units)"="Fixed Costs" /"Contribution per Unit"

Where:

- **Fixed Costs** are the costs that remain constant regardless of the number of units produced or sold (e.g., rent, salaries).
- **Contribution per Unit** is the amount each unit contributes to covering fixed costs, calculated as:

For example, if a company has fixed costs of $100,000, a selling price of $50 per unit, and variable costs of $30 per unit, the contribution per unit would be:

$$\text{Contribution per Unit} = 50 - 30 = 20$$

The break-even point would be:

"Break-even point"=100,000/20=5,000" units"

This means that the company must sell 5,000 units to cover all its fixed and variable costs. Any sales beyond this point will contribute to profit.

Methods for Calculating the Break-even Point

There are several methods for calculating the break-even point, each offering unique advantages depending on the level of detail and precision required.

1. The Equation Method

The equation method is a simple way of determining the break-even point using basic algebra. The equation is based on the relationship between total revenue, total variable costs, and total fixed costs:

"Total Revenue"-"Total Variable Costs"-"Total Fixed Costs"="Profit"

For a business to break even, the profit must equal zero. So, the equation becomes:

"Selling Price per Unit"×"Quantity"-"Variable Cost per Unit"×"Quantity"-"Fixed Costs"=0

Simplifying this equation, we can solve for the quantity (Q) at which the company breaks even.

2. The Contribution Margin Method

The **contribution margin** method focuses on the contribution that each unit makes toward covering fixed costs. The formula is:

"Contribution Margin"="Selling Price"-"Variable Costs"

Using this method, we divide fixed costs by the contribution margin per unit to find the break-even point in units:

"Break-even point (in units)"="Fixed Costs" /"Contribution Margin per Unit"

This method is often easier to use when you have a clear understanding of the contribution margin.

3. The Graphical Method

The graphical method provides a visual representation of the break-even point. The total cost line (which includes both fixed and variable costs) and the total revenue line are plotted on a graph. The point where the two lines intersect is the break-even point.

While this method is not often used in financial reporting, it can be helpful for visualizing the relationship between costs, sales, and profits. The space between the total revenue line and total cost line beyond the break-even point represents profits, while the area below the break-even point represents losses.

Target Profit and CVP Analysis

While the break-even point shows where total revenue equals total costs, businesses are often more concerned with achieving a specific target profit. CVP analysis can be adjusted to calculate the sales volume required to reach a desired level of profit.

The formula for target profit is:

"Required Sales (units)"=("Fixed Costs" +"Target Profit")/"Contribution per Unit"

For example, if a company wants to achieve a profit of $50,000, with fixed costs of $100,000 and a contribution per unit of $20, the required sales volume would be:

"Required Sales"=(100,000+50,000)/20=7,500" units"

This calculation shows that the company would need to sell 7,500 units to cover both its fixed costs and achieve a profit of $50,000.

Margin of Safety

The margin of safety is a measure of risk. It indicates how much sales can drop before the company reaches its break-even point and begins to incur losses. A larger margin of safety indicates a greater cushion against risk.

The margin of safety can be calculated in units, as follows:

"Margin of Safety (in units)"="Budgeted Sales"-"Break-even Sales"

Alternatively, it can be expressed as a percentage of sales:

"Margin of Safety (in %)"=("Budgeted Sales" -"Break-even Sales")/"Budgeted Sales" ×100

Limitations of CVP Analysis

While CVP analysis is a valuable tool for decision-making, it is based on several assumptions that may not hold true in real-world scenarios:

1. **Constant Selling Price**: CVP assumes that the selling price per unit remains constant. In reality, prices may change due to market conditions, competition, or customer demand.
2. **Linear Cost Behavior**: CVP assumes that costs are linear, meaning variable costs increase at a constant rate with production volume, and fixed costs remain constant within the relevant range. However, some costs may be semi-variable or may change non-linearly as production levels change.
3. **Constant Sales Mix**: In multi-product businesses, CVP assumes that the sales mix remains constant. This may not be the case if consumer preferences shift or if a company changes its product offerings.
4. **Short-Term Focus**: CVP analysis typically applies to the short term, and may not account for long-term factors such as changes in capacity or strategic decisions.

Cost-Volume-Profit (CVP) analysis is an essential tool for managers to assess the impact of changes in costs, sales volume, and pricing on a company's profitability. By calculating the break-even point, understanding target profit, and evaluating the margin of safety, businesses can make informed decisions that help ensure profitability. While CVP analysis is a powerful tool, its assumptions must be considered when applying it to real-world scenarios. Nevertheless, when used correctly, CVP analysis provides valuable insights for both operational and strategic decision-making.

Setting Target Income Goals

Setting **target income goals** is a critical step in business planning and financial management. Whether for an individual or an organization, clearly defined income goals provide a roadmap for achieving financial success. These goals offer a way to measure progress, motivate stakeholders, and make informed decisions. For businesses, target income goals serve as both a benchmark and a performance guide, helping executives and managers track how well the company is doing in terms of profitability.

In this section, we'll explore the process of setting target income goals, the factors that influence them, and how to effectively use them to drive business decisions and growth.

Why Set Target Income Goals?

Income goals serve several important purposes for individuals and businesses. They help define success and provide a basis for decision-making. Specifically, target income goals:

1. **Provide Focus and Direction**: Clear income goals help prioritize resources and efforts toward achieving specific financial outcomes.

2. **Drive Motivation**: Setting goals creates a sense of urgency and purpose. It helps to align the organization toward achieving the desired income target.
3. **Measure Performance**: Income goals provide a quantifiable measure of success. Managers can track their progress by comparing actual performance with their target.
4. **Enhance Strategic Decision-Making**: Knowing the income goal allows businesses to make informed decisions about pricing, marketing, investments, and operational adjustments.
5. **Manage Cash Flow and Capital**: Setting income targets helps businesses predict their cash inflows, enabling better management of working capital and long-term financial sustainability.

Types of Target Income Goals

There are various types of income goals businesses might set, depending on their specific needs, objectives, and stage of development. These can be broadly categorized as:

1. Profit-Oriented Goals

These income goals are primarily focused on achieving a specific level of net profit after all expenses. They are typically set as:

- **Fixed Profit Goals**: A company aims for a particular profit amount, such as $500,000 by the end of the fiscal year.
- **Profit Margin Goals**: These targets are expressed as a percentage of revenue, such as aiming for a 10% profit margin. The business focuses on increasing the profitability of each sale.

Profit-oriented goals are common for businesses that are looking to improve their overall financial health, expand operations, or meet investor expectations.

2. Revenue-Oriented Goals

Revenue goals are more focused on the top line, meaning the total sales or income generated before any expenses are deducted. This type of goal is often set by businesses looking to increase their market share or expand into new markets. For example:

- **Revenue Growth Goals**: A company might set a target to increase revenue by 15% over the next year.
- **Sales Volume Goals**: A company may aim to sell a certain number of units within a specific period.

Revenue goals are especially useful for companies in growth stages or in competitive industries where increasing sales is crucial.

3. Break-Even Goals

Break-even goals focus on achieving a level of income that covers all fixed and variable costs, ensuring that the business neither makes a profit nor incurs a loss. This is a crucial milestone for businesses, especially startups or those with fluctuating income.

- **Break-even Point Analysis**: A company may set a target to reach a break-even point in a certain time frame. This allows them to focus on covering their costs before aiming for profits.

Setting break-even goals is critical for businesses that are new or going through tough financial periods.

4. Cash Flow Goals

Cash flow is the lifeblood of any business. While profit-oriented goals focus on overall profitability, **cash flow goals** focus on the liquidity of the business. Businesses may set targets for:

- **Positive Net Cash Flow**: Ensuring that the cash inflow exceeds outflows for a particular period.
- **Cash Reserves**: Setting a target for maintaining a certain level of cash reserves to meet operational needs or investments.

Cash flow goals help businesses ensure they have enough liquidity to fund their operations and avoid financial crises.

How to Set Realistic Income Goals

Setting realistic income goals is vital for the success and sustainability of a business. Unrealistic targets can lead to disappointment and poor decision-making, while achievable goals provide a solid foundation for growth. Here's how to set realistic income goals:

1. Understand Your Current Financial Situation

Before setting any income goal, it is crucial to analyze the business's current financial standing. This includes understanding:

- **Current Profitability**: Is your business already profitable? If not, what are the key challenges?
- **Revenue Streams**: Which products, services, or markets generate the most income?
- **Cost Structure**: Understand both fixed and variable costs and identify areas for improvement.
- **Cash Flow**: Assess whether there's enough liquidity to support operations and expansion.

By understanding these aspects, you can set a goal that aligns with your business's current capacity and growth trajectory.

2. Analyze Market Conditions

Market conditions significantly impact a company's ability to reach its income targets. Analyze:

- **Industry Trends**: Are there emerging opportunities or challenges in your industry?
- **Competitive Landscape**: What are your competitors doing, and how can you position your business differently to gain a market edge?
- **Economic Factors**: Broader economic conditions, such as inflation rates, consumer confidence, and spending power, can influence your income potential.

By understanding external factors, you can adjust your targets to reflect the realities of the market.

3. Align Goals with Business Objectives

Your income goals should align with your long-term business objectives. If you aim to expand into new markets, for example, your revenue goals may need to be more aggressive. On the other hand, if your goal is to focus on improving profitability, you might set profit margin or cost control goals instead.

For example:

- **Growth-focused businesses** may set higher revenue goals.
- **Profit-focused businesses** may set targets based on increasing profitability and reducing expenses.

Aligning your goals with the broader vision will ensure that your efforts are directed toward the right areas.

4. Break Goals into Smaller, Achievable Milestones

Income goals should be broken down into smaller, short-term milestones. For instance, a business aiming for $1 million in annual revenue might set quarterly revenue targets and track progress closely.

This approach allows businesses to stay focused, make adjustments if necessary, and celebrate small successes along the way, creating a sense of progress.

Tools for Setting and Tracking Income Goals

Effective tracking is crucial to ensuring that target income goals are met. Here are some common tools and methods for tracking income goals:

1. Budgeting and Forecasting Tools

Budgets and forecasts help to outline expected income, expenses, and profits over a specific period. These tools are useful for setting realistic income goals and identifying the key drivers of business performance. Some common tools include:

- **Excel Spreadsheets**: Customizable and flexible for creating forecasts and tracking performance.
- **Accounting Software**: Tools like QuickBooks, Xero, and FreshBooks can track income and expenses in real-time, helping businesses adjust to changing conditions.

2. Key Performance Indicators (KPIs)

KPIs are metrics that track specific aspects of business performance, such as:

- **Sales Growth**: Measures the rate at which sales are increasing or decreasing.
- **Profit Margin**: Tracks the percentage of profit compared to revenue.
- **Customer Acquisition Cost**: Helps assess how much it costs to acquire new customers and whether it's sustainable.
- **Cash Flow Ratios**: Measures liquidity and operational efficiency.

By focusing on KPIs, businesses can monitor progress toward income goals and identify areas for improvement.

3. Financial Dashboards

Financial dashboards visually display key metrics in real-time, allowing businesses to track their income goals on a daily or weekly basis. These tools offer a snapshot of financial performance and help businesses stay on course to meet their targets.

Adjusting Goals Based on Performance

Even the best-laid plans may require adjustments. Regularly reviewing progress against your target income goals helps identify whether the business is on track or if modifications are needed.

- **If performance is behind schedule**, analyze the causes. Are expenses higher than expected? Are sales underperforming? Is the business facing unforeseen external challenges?
- **If the business is exceeding expectations**, determine whether it's sustainable or if changes need to be made to scale up efforts.

Setting target income goals is a crucial part of business planning that allows managers and business owners to focus efforts, measure progress, and make informed decisions. Whether the goal is related to profit, revenue, cash flow, or break-even analysis, having clear, realistic targets provides the framework for making strategic choices. By analyzing market conditions, understanding internal resources, and breaking goals into achievable milestones, businesses can stay on track to reach their financial objectives. Ultimately, the key to successful income goal-setting is adaptability and continual monitoring, ensuring that the company

TARGET CORP – SETTING TARGET INCOME GOALS

Target sets clear income goals to guide its financial performance, strategic decisions, and long-term growth objectives.

CHALLENGES

- Revenue Growth Amidst Intense Competition
- Profitability and Cost Management

OBJECTIVES

ACHIEVE CONSISTENT REVENUE GROWTH

The company aims for a year-over-year revenue increase of 5–7%, driven by both brick-and-mortar and online channels.

IMPROVE PROFIT MARGINS

The company aims for a target profit margin of 25%, without compromising on quality.

RESULT AND BENEFITS

- In 2020, Target reported a revenue of $93.56 billion, a 19.8% increase compared to the previous year.
- The company's gross profit margin improved to 30% in 2020, from 28.6% in 2019.

remains responsive to changes in both the internal and external environment.

Marginal Cost vs. Absorption Costing

Costing methods play a critical role in business decision-making, providing essential insights into profitability, pricing, and cost management. Two commonly used costing methods in managerial accounting are marginal costing and absorption costing. Both methods have their own merits and applications, but understanding the differences between them is key to selecting the right approach for different business situations.

In this section, we will explore marginal costing and absorption costing, their differences, advantages, and how each method can be applied effectively in various scenarios.

What is Marginal Costing?

Marginal costing is a method that focuses on the costs that vary directly with production volume, known as variable costs. Under this approach, only variable costs—such as direct materials, direct labor, and variable overhead—are considered when calculating the cost of a product. Fixed costs, such as rent, salaries, and utilities, are excluded from the product cost and treated as period costs, expensed in the period in which they are incurred.

Key Features of Marginal Costing:

- **Focus on Variable Costs**: Only variable costs are included in product cost calculations.
- **Fixed Costs Treated as Period Expenses**: Fixed costs are not allocated to products but are expensed in full in the period incurred.
- **Contribution Margin**: Marginal costing highlights the contribution margin, which is the sales revenue minus variable costs. This margin represents the amount available to cover fixed costs and generate profit.

Advantages of Marginal Costing:

- **Simpler Decision Making**: By isolating variable costs, marginal costing simplifies decision-making for pricing, product discontinuation, and make-or-buy decisions.
- **Helps in Break-even Analysis**: It provides a clear picture of the break-even point, helping businesses understand how many units they need to sell to cover fixed costs.
- **Easier for Short-Term Decision Making**: This method is particularly useful in the short-term, especially for decisions like special pricing offers, handling fluctuating demand, and managing variable costs.

Example:

A company produces a product with the following costs:

Selling Price per Unit: $100

Variable Costs per Unit: $60

Fixed Costs: $50,000 (not considered in product costing under marginal costing)

In this case, the contribution margin per unit is:

Contribution Margin = Selling Price - Variable Costs = 100 - 60 = 40

If the company wants to break even, it would need to sell:
"Break-even Units"="Fixed Costs" /"Contribution Margin" =50,000/40=1,250" units"

Thus, 1,250 units need to be sold to cover the fixed costs and break even.

What is Absorption Costing?

Absorption costing, also known as full costing, is a method where both variable costs and fixed costs are included in the cost of a product. Under this method, fixed costs are allocated to products based on a predetermined allocation rate, such as labor hours or machine hours. As a result, each product absorbs a portion of the fixed costs in addition to its variable costs.

Key Features of Absorption Costing:

- **Inclusion of Fixed Costs**: Both variable and fixed costs are included in the cost of production.
- **Fixed Costs Allocated to Products**: Fixed costs are allocated to each unit produced based on an allocation base (e.g., labor or machine hours).
- **Full Cost Calculation**: Absorption costing is used to calculate the total cost of a product, which includes all costs, both variable and fixed, associated with its production.

Advantages of Absorption Costing:

- **More Accurate for Financial Reporting**: Since absorption costing includes all costs associated with production, it is required for external financial reporting and tax purposes under GAAP and IFRS.
- **Better for Long-Term Profitability Analysis**: Absorption costing is useful for long-term decision-making, especially when considering the full cost of producing goods.
- **Helps in Pricing Strategy**: It provides a comprehensive view of product costs, which is useful for setting prices that cover both variable and fixed costs, ensuring profitability.

Example:

Using the same figures as in the marginal costing example, assume that fixed costs are $50,000 and the company produced 5,000 units. The fixed cost per unit would be: "Fixed Cost per Unit"="Fixed Costs" /"Units Produced" =50,000/5,000=10" per unit"

Thus, the total cost per unit under absorption costing would be:
"Total Cost per Unit"="Variable Cost per Unit"+"Fixed Cost per Unit"=60+10=70

In this case, the total cost per unit is $70, which is higher than the variable cost of $60 under marginal costing. The company would need to sell more units to cover its fixed costs and break even.

Marginal Costing vs. Absorption Costing

The primary difference between marginal costing and absorption costing lies in how fixed costs are treated and allocated. Here's a comparison to help clarify the differences:

Feature	Marginal Costing	Absorption Costing
Treatment of Fixed Costs	Fixed costs are treated as period costs and are not allocated to products.	Fixed costs are absorbed into product costs and allocated based on an allocation rate.
Cost of Goods Sold (COGS)	Includes only variable costs.	Includes both variable and allocated fixed costs.
Profit Calculation	Profit is calculated based on contribution margin.	Profit is calculated after full product cost, including fixed costs.
Use in Decision Making	Primarily used for short-term decisions and break-even analysis.	Used for long-term decisions, financial reporting, and tax purposes.
External Reporting	Not suitable for external financial reporting.	Required for external financial reporting under GAAP or IFRS.
Complexity	Simpler and focuses on variable costs and profitability.	More complex due to the allocation of fixed costs.

When to Use Marginal Costing vs. Absorption Costing

Both costing methods have their advantages and specific use cases:

Use Marginal Costing When:

- You are making short-term decisions (e.g., pricing strategies, special orders).
- You want to focus on contribution margins to analyze profitability.
- You are concerned with cost control and variable costs that change with production levels.
- You need to understand how changes in volume (such as sales fluctuations) impact profits.

Use Absorption Costing When:

- You need to comply with external financial reporting standards (e.g., GAAP, IFRS).
- You are making long-term profitability analyses, including pricing strategies that need to consider all production costs.
- You need a complete understanding of the full cost of producing a product, including fixed costs.
- You are analyzing inventory valuation, as absorption costing includes all costs in the value of inventory.

Limitations of Both Methods

While both marginal costing and absorption costing offer valuable insights, each has limitations:

Limitations of Marginal Costing:

- It excludes fixed costs from product costing, which can lead to inaccurate profitability analysis when fixed costs are significant.
- It does not provide a complete picture for businesses that need to track the full cost of producing goods, especially for long-term planning.
- It may be less useful for businesses with complex production processes or those that need to track the value of inventory accurately.

Limitations of Absorption Costing:

- It can be more complex to implement due to the need for allocating fixed costs, especially in multi-product businesses.
- Absorption costing can mask inefficiencies, as it spreads fixed costs across products, potentially leading to distorted cost information for decision-making.
- It may lead to over- or under-costing products if the allocation base is not

accurate.

Understanding the strengths and limitations of each method is key to choosing the appropriate approach for your business's needs. By selecting the right costing method, businesses can better manage costs, set pricing strategies, and make informed decisions that enhance profitability and long-term success.

Go Further

FORD MOTOR COMPANY – COSTING

The Company applies both costing methods to evaluate the profitability of its vehicles, make pricing decisions, and comply with financial reporting standards.

CHALLENGES

- Cost Structure Complexity
- Pricing Decisions
- Financial Reporting Compliance

OBJECTIVES

EVALUATE PRODUCT PROFITABILITY

The company wanted to understand how variable and fixed costs were impacting profitability.

OPTIMIZE PRICING STRATEGY

Ford wanted to use costing methods to set competitive pricing strategies.

RESULT AND BENEFITS

- Ford isolated the costs that directly change with production volume.
- Ford uses absorption costing to generate its financial statements.
- Ford also uses both marginal and absorption costing to conduct break-even analysis.

Variance Analysis: Identifying and Managing Discrepancies

Variance analysis is a critical tool in managerial accounting that helps businesses measure performance against budgets or standards. By identifying the differences, or variances, between expected and actual financial results, businesses can pinpoint areas of strength and weakness, enabling them to take corrective action where necessary. This process is essential for cost control, performance evaluation, and strategic decision-making.

In this section, we will dive into what variance analysis is, the types of variances, how to interpret them, and the best practices for managing discrepancies effectively.

What is Variance Analysis?

Variance analysis involves comparing actual financial outcomes with budgeted or standard costs, then analyzing the reasons for any discrepancies. It is used to assess the performance of various departments or functions within an organization and helps in identifying areas that need attention.

The main purpose of variance analysis is to understand why actual costs deviate from the expected budget or standards, whether those deviations are favorable or unfavorable, and what actions can be taken to manage these discrepancies.

Variance analysis typically involves comparing actual results with budgeted or standard costs for several key areas, including:

Revenue: How much revenue the company expected versus what was actually earned.

Costs: Comparison of budgeted costs (both fixed and variable) with actual costs.

Profits: Analyzing profit variances based on revenue and costs.

Types of Variances

There are two main categories of variances: cost variances and revenue variances. Each of these can be further broken down into favorable or unfavorable variances, depending on the impact on the company's financial performance.

1. Cost Variance

Cost variance refers to the difference between the actual cost incurred and the expected (budgeted) cost for a given activity or operation. It is a measure of how efficiently a company is using its resources, and it is essential for managing expenses.

There are two main types of cost variances:

- **Direct Material Cost Variance**: This variance measures the difference between the expected cost of materials used in production and the actual cost.

- **Direct Labor Cost Variance**: This variance focuses on the difference between the expected and actual labor costs associated with production.

Each cost variance can be further broken down into:

- **Price Variance**: The difference between the actual cost per unit of an input (e.g., labor or materials) and the expected cost.
- **Quantity Variance**: The difference between the actual quantity of inputs used and the expected (standard) quantity.

For example:

- If the **price variance** for materials shows an unfavorable result, it means that the company paid more for materials than expected.
- A **quantity variance** for materials that is unfavorable indicates that more materials were used than planned.

2. Revenue Variance

Revenue variances compare the actual revenue generated to the expected (budgeted) revenue. These variances help determine if the business is performing better or worse than anticipated, primarily due to factors like pricing or sales volume.

- **Sales Volume Variance**: This measures the impact of the actual number of units sold versus the expected sales volume.
- **Sales Price Variance**: This reflects the difference between the actual selling price and the budgeted selling price per unit.

For example:

- A **favorable sales volume variance** occurs when more units are sold than anticipated, leading to higher-than-expected revenue.
- An **unfavorable sales price variance** arises when the actual selling price is lower than expected, which reduces revenue.

Calculating and Interpreting Variances

Variance analysis involves a set of simple calculations, but its interpretation requires a deep understanding of the business's operations. Let's go over the formulae used to calculate common variances:

1. Direct Material Cost Variance

"Direct Material Cost Variance"=("Actual Quantity"×"Actual Price")-("Standard Quantity"×"Standard Price")

This variance can be broken into:

- **Material Price Variance**: (Actual Price - Standard Price) Actual Quantity

- **Material Quantity Variance**: (Actual Quantity - Standard Quantity) Standard Price

2. Direct Labor Cost Variance

"Direct Labor Cost Variance "=

("Actual Hours"×"Actual Rate")-("Standard Hours"×"Standard Rate")

This variance can be broken into:

Labor Rate Variance: ("Actual Rate"-"Standard Rate")×"Actual Hours"

Labor Efficiency Variance: ("Actual Hours"-"Standard Hours")×"Standard Rate"

3. Sales Variance

Sales Variance = (Actual Sales - Budgeted Sales)

This variance can be broken down into:

Sales Volume Variance: ("Actual Units Sold"-"Budgeted Units Sold")×"Standard Price"

Sales Price Variance: ("Actual Price"-"Budgeted Price")×"Actual Units Sold"

These variances provide valuable insights into the reasons behind discrepancies in revenue generation and help in adjusting strategies accordingly.

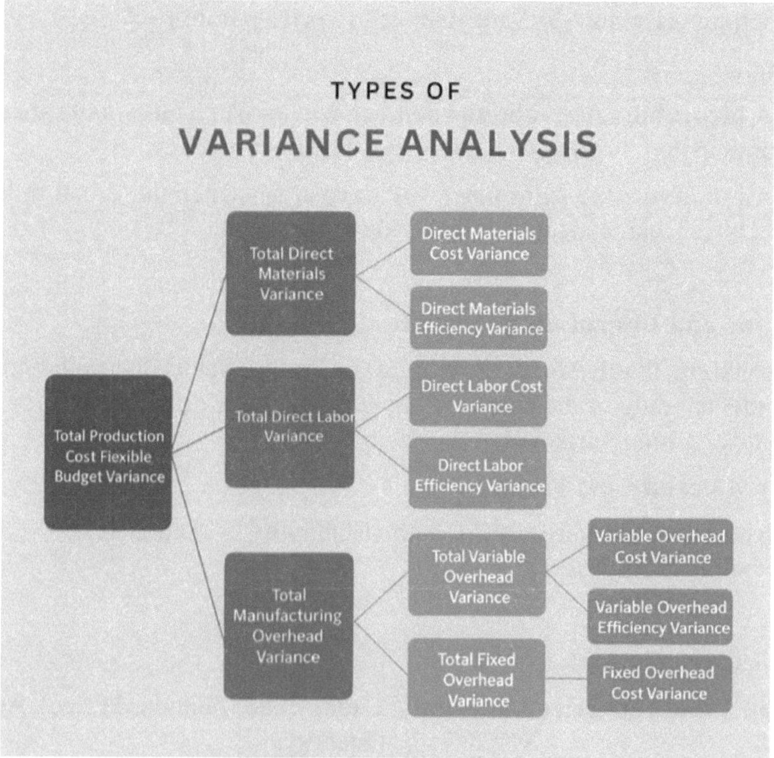

How to Use Variance Analysis for Performance Management

Variance analysis is primarily used to assess performance, particularly in areas of cost control, pricing, and operational efficiency. The process allows management to pinpoint specific areas where discrepancies occur and then address the root causes. Here's how to manage and use variance analysis effectively:

1. Identifying Operational Problems

Variance analysis often reveals inefficiencies or discrepancies in operations. For instance, an unfavorable direct labor variance may point to issues like poor employee performance or excessive overtime. An unfavorable direct material variance might indicate issues with suppliers or wasteful production practices.

2. Corrective Action

Once discrepancies are identified, the next step is to take corrective actions:

- **Investigate the Causes**: Ask questions like: Why did material costs exceed expectations? Did the company overestimate the number of hours needed for production? Did the sales price decrease unexpectedly?
- **Adjust Budgets and Forecasts**: If variances are caused by factors like changing market conditions, it may be necessary to revise future budgets and forecasts.
- **Improve Operational Efficiency**: Unfavorable variances, particularly in labor or material usage, can be reduced through training, more efficient processes, or renegotiating with suppliers.

3. Monitoring Performance

Variance analysis should not be a one-time exercise. It needs to be part of an ongoing process where actual results are continuously compared to budgets, and corrective actions are taken promptly. By monitoring these variances regularly, businesses can ensure they are on track to meet their financial goals and can make adjustments before problems escalate.

4. Decision-Making Support

Variance analysis provides actionable insights that support decision-making. For example, if a company is noticing consistent unfavorable variances in raw material costs, it may decide to:

- Switch suppliers
- Re-engineer the production process to use less material
- Adjust the pricing strategy to offset cost increases

Limitations of Variance Analysis

While variance analysis is an effective tool, it comes with certain limitations:

- **Overemphasis on Short-Term Issues**: Variance analysis tends to focus on the short-term, especially in areas like operating costs and sales performance, which can sometimes divert attention from long-term strategic planning.

- **Difficulty in Accurate Forecasting**: Variance analysis depends on accurate budgeting and forecasting. If initial projections are inaccurate, the analysis can lead to misleading conclusions.
- **Inability to Address All Factors**: Variance analysis focuses primarily on **quantitative data** and may overlook qualitative factors such as customer satisfaction, employee morale, or brand perception.
- **Complexity in Multi-Product Situations**: For businesses with multiple products, analyzing variances can become more complex, especially when determining which factors are responsible for discrepancies.

Variance analysis is a powerful tool for businesses to monitor and manage financial performance. By identifying discrepancies between actual and expected results, companies can make more informed decisions and take corrective actions to improve profitability. However, it is important to recognize the limitations of variance analysis and ensure it is used in conjunction with other tools for long-term strategic planning and decision-making.

By effectively using variance analysis, businesses can stay on top of their costs, pricing, and operations, ultimately improving performance and achieving their financial goals.

Inventory Accounting: How to Track and Evaluate Stock

Effective inventory accounting is essential for businesses to manage their materials, work-in-process goods, and finished products efficiently. Accurate tracking and evaluation of stock not only ensure that companies can meet demand, but also help in minimizing costs and optimizing operations. There are various methods and systems available for inventory accounting, and selecting the right one can make a significant impact on a business's financial performance.

In this section, we will delve into the fundamentals of inventory accounting, the different approaches for tracking and evaluating stock, and how companies can leverage these methods to maintain accurate records and make informed financial decisions.

What is Inventory Accounting?

Inventory accounting involves tracking the cost and value of a company's inventory, which typically includes raw materials, work-in-process, and finished goods. The objective of inventory accounting is to ensure that businesses can accurately value their inventory and control associated costs, which directly affect the cost of goods sold (COGS) and, ultimately, profit margins.

Proper inventory accounting is crucial for:

- **Financial reporting**: Inventory is an important asset on the balance sheet, and accurate inventory values are required for compliance with accounting standards.
- **Tax calculations**: Different inventory methods can impact a company's taxable income.
- **Operational decisions**: Knowing the value and quantity of stock on hand helps businesses make better purchasing and sales decisions.

Inventory can be valued using different methods, and each method has its implications for financial reporting and profitability. The two primary methods for tracking inventory are perpetual inventory systems and periodic inventory systems.

Perpetual vs. Periodic Inventory Systems

1. Perpetual Inventory System

A **perpetual inventory system** continuously updates inventory levels in real time, with each purchase and sale of goods recorded immediately. This method provides the most accurate reflection of inventory levels at any given time and is often used by businesses with high-volume inventory turnover.

- **Advantages**:
  - **Real-time tracking**: Offers up-to-date information on stock levels, helping businesses avoid stockouts and excess inventory.
  - **More accurate financial reporting**: Since the inventory is constantly updated, businesses have a clearer picture of their financial position.
  - **Better decision-making**: Real-time data allows for quicker adjustments to purchasing and pricing strategies.
- **Methods of Valuation in Perpetual Systems**:
  - **Standard Costing**: This method uses a fixed cost per unit, regardless of actual fluctuations in material or labor costs. The company uses predetermined costs for each unit of inventory, simplifying record-keeping and pricing.
  - **Moving Average Cost**: Under this method, the cost of each unit of inventory is recalculated each time a new purchase is made. The average cost per unit is adjusted, reflecting changes in prices over time.
  - **Manual Adjustments**: Even in automated systems, manual adjustments may be necessary to account for issues like spoilage,

shrinkage, or errors in tracking.

2. Periodic Inventory System

The **periodic inventory system** involves updating inventory values at specific intervals (e.g., monthly or annually) rather than continuously. At the end of each period, a physical count of inventory is taken, and the value is adjusted to match the actual count.

- **Advantages**:
    - **Lower costs**: This system requires fewer resources to maintain, making it more suitable for businesses with lower inventory turnover or limited stock.
    - **Simplicity**: The periodic system is easier to implement and maintain, especially for small businesses or those with less complex inventory.
- **Methods of Valuation in Periodic Systems**:
    - **FIFO (First In, First Out)**: This method assumes that the first units purchased are the first ones sold. As a result, older inventory is sold first, and the remaining stock reflects the most recent purchases.
    - **LIFO (Last In, First Out)**: In contrast, LIFO assumes that the most recent purchases are sold first. This method can help reduce taxes in times of inflation, as newer, more expensive inventory is used to calculate COGS.
    - **Weighted Average Cost**: This method averages the cost of all units available for sale, and each unit is assigned this average cost. It's useful in industries where inventory items are indistinguishable from one another.

Valuing Inventory in Multiple Currencies

In businesses that operate internationally or deal with suppliers and customers in different countries, inventory valuation in multiple currencies becomes important. Parallel valuation functions allow companies to track the value of their inventory in various currencies while keeping different accounting standards in mind.

- **Parallel Accounting**: This method uses parallel value management, allowing inventory to be valued in multiple currencies at the same time. It helps businesses monitor their assets across different accounting principles or legal requirements, ensuring compliance with both local and international financial reporting standards.
- **Historical Currency Translation**: Companies operating in high-inflation environments can benefit from using historical currency translation for

their inventory valuations. This method applies the exchange rate at the time of the transaction, rather than the current rate, providing a more stable view of inventory values and mitigating the effects of currency fluctuations.

Adjusting Inventory for Inflation and Market Changes

In some cases, companies may need to account for changes in market conditions or inflation that affect the value of their inventory. There are two primary ways in which these factors are addressed:

1. Inflationary Adjustments

In inflationary environments, the cost of acquiring raw materials and products may rise over time. Adjustments to inventory values are necessary to reflect these changes. Businesses might consider using methods like FIFO, where older, lower-cost inventory is sold first, or moving average costing, which updates inventory prices regularly.

2. Market Value Adjustments

If inventory items are obsolete or damaged, they may need to be written down to their market value. This ensures that the inventory is not overvalued on the balance sheet, and it provides a more accurate representation of the company's assets.

Inventory Valuation Reports and Analysis

Regular **inventory reports** are critical for monitoring stock levels, identifying discrepancies, and making data-driven decisions. Key reports include:

- **Inventory Turnover Ratio**: This ratio shows how efficiently inventory is being managed and sold. It is calculated by dividing COGS by the average inventory for a period. A high turnover ratio suggests efficient inventory management, while a low ratio may indicate overstocking or slow-moving products.
- **Stock Valuation Report**: This report provides a snapshot of the current value of inventory based on the chosen valuation method. It helps businesses determine the cost of inventory that remains unsold and its impact on the balance sheet.
- **Aging Report**: This report categorizes inventory based on how long it has been held. Older inventory may need to be written off or discounted, helping businesses identify slow-moving stock that could impact profitability.

Best Practices for Effective Inventory Accounting

To ensure accurate inventory tracking and valuation, businesses should follow these best practices:

- **Implement Real-Time Tracking**: For businesses with large or fast-moving inventories, real-time tracking through a perpetual inventory system ensures that stock levels are always up-to-date, reducing the chances of stockouts or overstocking.
- **Perform Regular Audits**: Even with perpetual systems, regular physical counts are essential for verifying that the system's records match actual inventory. Periodic audits can help identify discrepancies such as theft, spoilage, or errors.
- **Optimize Inventory Levels**: Businesses should strive to maintain optimal inventory levels, balancing the need to meet customer demand without tying up excessive capital in unsold goods.
- **Utilize Inventory Valuation Software**: Automated systems can simplify the inventory accounting process by ensuring consistent application of valuation methods and generating real-time reports for better decision-making.

Effective inventory accounting is essential for businesses to maintain accurate financial records, optimize stock levels, and make informed decisions. Whether using a perpetual or periodic system, or managing inventory in multiple currencies, choosing the right approach can significantly impact profitability and financial reporting.

By carefully tracking and evaluating stock, businesses can avoid overstocking, reduce waste, improve cash flow, and ensure that financial statements accurately reflect the true value of assets. Implementing the right methods and best practices for inventory accounting will help companies improve operational efficiency, manage costs, and ultimately drive better business outcomes.

TYPES OF

INVENTORY SYSTEMS

Point	Perpetual Inventory System	Periodic Inventory System
Definition	Continuously updates inventory levels in real time with each transaction.	Updates inventory at specific intervals (e.g., monthly, annually).
Advantages	Provides real-time tracking, accurate financial reporting, and better decision-making.	Lower costs and easier to implement for small businesses with less inventory.
Valuation Methods	1. Standard Costing 2. Moving Average Cost 3. Manual Adjustments	1. FIFO (First In, First Out) 2. LIFO (Last In, First Out) 3. Weighted Average Cost
Real-time Updates	Constantly updates stock levels with each sale or purchase.	Inventory is updated only at specific periods after a physical count.
Suitability	Ideal for businesses with high-volume turnover or fast-moving inventory.	Best suited for businesses with low inventory turnover or simpler operations.
Cost and Complexity	Requires more resources to maintain due to continuous tracking and updates.	Lower cost and simpler to manage, with fewer resources needed.

Budgeting: How to Forecast and Plan

Budgeting is one of the most crucial aspects of financial management for any business, regardless of its size or industry. It serves as a road map for a company's financial performance, helping to guide decisions about spending, investments, and growth strategies. Proper budgeting ensures that resources are allocated effectively and that the company can meet its goals within its financial capacity.

In this section, we will explore the fundamentals of budgeting, various budgeting methods, and the importance of forecasting to ensure that businesses stay on track financially.

What is Budgeting?

Budgeting is the process of planning and managing a company's finances by estimating future revenues, expenses, and profits over a specific period. The goal of budgeting is to establish a financial plan that allows the business to allocate resources effectively, manage cash flow, and meet its strategic objectives.

A well-constructed budget helps businesses:

- **Plan for the future**: By estimating future income and expenses, a business can forecast its financial health and plan for growth.
- **Control spending**: Budgets help keep spending within limits and prevent overspending on unnecessary expenses.
- **Evaluate performance**: By comparing actual performance to the budgeted amounts, businesses can track how well they are meeting their financial goals.
- **Make informed decisions**: Having a clear understanding of available resources enables better decision-making regarding investments, hiring, and cost-cutting.

Types of Budgets

There are several types of budgets, each serving a different purpose within an organization. The most common types include:

1. Operating Budget

The operating budget outlines the expected revenues and expenses for a business over a specific period, typically a year. It includes sales forecasts, cost of goods sold, operating expenses (such as salaries, rent, and utilities), and other recurring costs. The operating budget is essential for managing day-to-day operations and ensuring that the company stays within its financial limits.

2. Capital Budget

A capital budget is used for planning significant investments, such as the purchase of new equipment, building expansions, or research and development (R&D) projects. This budget helps determine which large expenditures will be made in the future and how the company will finance them. The capital budget typically spans multiple years and is more focused on long-term goals and growth.

3. Cash Flow Budget

This budget focuses on managing the inflows and outflows of cash to ensure that a business has sufficient liquidity to meet its obligations. Unlike the operating budget, which deals with revenue and expenses, the cash flow budget tracks actual cash transactions, including collections from customers, payments to suppliers, and capital investments.

4. Zero-Based Budgeting

In zero-based budgeting, each budget cycle starts from zero, with no prior year's budget as a baseline. Every expense must be justified for the new period, regardless of whether it was approved in the previous budget. This method ensures that resources are allocated based on current priorities rather than historical trends and helps avoid unnecessary expenditures.

5. Flexible Budget

A flexible budget adjusts for variations in actual activity levels. This type of budget is particularly useful in businesses with fluctuating sales or production volumes. It allows for the modification of budget figures based on the actual output, making it a more dynamic tool for financial planning.

Budgeting Process

The budgeting process involves several key steps to ensure that financial goals are met and resources are allocated appropriately. Below is an outline of the typical process involved in budgeting:

1. **Setting Financial Goals**:
   The first step in budgeting is defining clear financial goals. These goals should align with the company's strategic objectives and may include increasing profitability, reducing costs, or expanding into new markets.
2. **Estimating Revenues**:
   Estimating revenues is essential for understanding how much income the company expects to generate. This estimate is often based on historical data, market trends, and sales forecasts. Revenue projections should be as realistic as possible to avoid underestimating or overestimating income.
3. **Identifying Fixed and Variable Costs**:
   Costs need to be broken down into fixed and variable categories. Fixed costs, such as rent and salaries, remain constant regardless of production levels, while variable costs, such as raw materials and direct labor, change with production or sales volume. Understanding the nature of

these costs helps with cost control and pricing decisions.

4. **Allocating Resources**:
Once the revenue and cost estimates are in place, resources are allocated to different areas of the business. This may include funding for marketing, operations, R&D, and employee compensation. Resource allocation should be done based on the company's strategic priorities and objectives.

5. **Monitoring and Adjusting the Budget**:
A budget is not a static document; it needs to be reviewed regularly and adjusted based on actual performance. Monitoring variance (the difference between budgeted and actual results) is crucial for identifying potential problems and making timely adjustments.

Forecasting in Budgeting

Forecasting is the process of predicting future financial outcomes based on historical data, market trends, and other relevant factors. In budgeting, forecasting helps provide more accurate estimates of revenues, expenses, and cash flows, allowing businesses to make more informed decisions.

Forecasting Methods:

- **Historical Data**: Businesses often use past performance as the basis for forecasting future revenues and expenses. Historical trends can help predict demand, seasonal fluctuations, and market changes.
- **Market Research**: Forecasting can be improved with external data, such as industry trends, customer behavior, and economic indicators.
- **Econometric Models**: These models use statistical methods to predict future trends based on historical data and other variables. They are especially useful for long-term forecasting.
- **Qualitative Forecasting**: In situations where historical data is scarce or unreliable, qualitative methods like expert opinion or focus groups can provide valuable insights.

Benefits of Budgeting

1. **Financial Control**:
Budgeting gives a business a clear picture of its financial health and helps prevent overspending. By closely monitoring income and expenses, companies can identify areas where they may be deviating from their budget and take corrective action.

2. **Strategic Planning**:
A well-prepared budget serves as a financial blueprint for the company's

growth. It helps prioritize investments and resource allocation in line with the company's strategic objectives, ensuring that funds are directed toward high-impact initiatives.

3. **Performance Measurement**:
   Budgets provide a standard for measuring actual performance. By comparing actual results with budgeted amounts, businesses can evaluate their financial performance and identify areas for improvement.

4. **Improved Decision Making**:
   Budgets provide valuable insights into the company's ability to meet its financial goals. This helps managers make better decisions regarding expansion, staffing, marketing, and investments.

Challenges in Budgeting

While budgeting is a powerful tool, it is not without its challenges. Some common issues businesses face in budgeting include:

- **Inaccurate Forecasting**: Incorrect estimates of revenue or costs can lead to unrealistic budgets, making it difficult to achieve financial goals.
- **Changes in Market Conditions**: Unforeseen market shifts, such as economic downturns or changes in consumer demand, can render a budget ineffective.
- **Lack of Flexibility**: Strict adherence to budgets can be detrimental if market conditions or business priorities change. Businesses need flexibility to adjust budgets as needed.
- **Data Overload**: Having too much data or overly detailed budget breakdowns can make it difficult to focus on the most important financial metrics.

Budgeting is an essential tool for businesses of all sizes, enabling them to plan, track, and manage their finances effectively. By forecasting revenues, controlling costs, and allocating resources strategically, companies can ensure that they meet their financial goals and remain financially healthy. The budgeting process, while challenging, provides businesses with the necessary framework to make informed decisions, maximize profitability, and sustain long-term growth.

Adopting a systematic approach to budgeting—along with appropriate forecasting methods and regular adjustments—helps businesses stay agile in a dynamic market environment and secure a stable financial future.

Top Budgeting Software for Small and Medium Businesses

For small and medium-sized businesses (SMBs), effective budgeting is crucial for managing finances, optimizing resources, and achieving long-term growth. The right budgeting software can simplify the process, provide real-time insights into cash flow, and help businesses plan for future expenses with ease. In this section, we will review some of the top budgeting software options available to SMBs, highlighting their features, benefits, and suitability for various business needs.

1. QuickBooks Online

Overview: QuickBooks Online is one of the most popular accounting and budgeting tools for small businesses. It offers an easy-to-use interface with a range of features, including expense tracking, financial reporting, and budgeting tools.

Key Features:

Budgeting and Forecasting: QuickBooks helps businesses create custom budgets based on actual financial data and forecasts for future periods.

Real-Time Tracking: Businesses can track income and expenses in real time, with automatic syncing of bank transactions.

Reports: Provides detailed reports, including Profit and Loss, Balance Sheets, and Cash Flow Statements, to keep track of financial health.

Best For: SMBs looking for a comprehensive accounting and budgeting solution with the flexibility to scale as the business grows.

2. Xero

Overview: Xero is a cloud-based accounting software that allows businesses to track and manage their finances efficiently. It includes tools for budgeting, invoicing, payroll, and expense tracking, making it a one-stop solution for SMBs.

Key Features:

Budgeting Tools: Xero provides budgeting tools that allow businesses to compare actual spending against budgeted amounts, helping to keep expenses in check.

Cash Flow Management: Real-time cash flow tracking ensures that businesses can manage their financial obligations without risk of overspending.

Integration: Xero integrates with over 800 apps, including project management tools, inventory management systems, and payroll services.

Best For: SMBs that need an intuitive, cloud-based platform for both accounting and budgeting, with strong reporting capabilities.

3. FreshBooks

Overview: FreshBooks is an accounting software primarily designed for small businesses and freelancers. It offers a range of budgeting tools alongside its core functions of invoicing, time tracking, and expense management.

Key Features:

Simple Budgeting: Allows users to create and manage custom budgets with ease, tracking project costs and comparing them against budgeted amounts.

Expense Tracking: Syncs bank accounts and credit cards to automatically import and categorize transactions for accurate financial tracking.

Financial Reports: FreshBooks provides detailed reports on profitability, expenses, and cash flow to help businesses stay on top of their budgets.

Best For: Freelancers and small businesses that need a simple, user-friendly solution for budgeting and financial management.

4. Wave

Overview: Wave is a free, cloud-based accounting software that offers a suite of tools for managing finances, including invoicing, expense tracking, and budgeting. It's a great option for SMBs that need basic budgeting features without the cost.

Key Features:

- **Free Budgeting Tools**: Wave offers a free budget tracking feature that allows businesses to set budgets, track actual spending, and view financial reports.
- **Expense Management**: Automatic bank syncing and transaction categorization make it easy to keep track of spending.
- **Financial Reports**: Businesses can generate key reports like profit and loss, balance sheet, and cash flow to monitor financial health.

Best For: Small businesses and startups that are looking for a cost-effective budgeting solution with basic features.

5. PlanGuru

Overview: PlanGuru is a budgeting and forecasting software that provides SMBs with advanced tools for financial planning. It is designed for businesses that need more in-depth budgeting and forecasting capabilities, including scenario planning and long-term projections.

Key Features:

- **Advanced Budgeting**: PlanGuru allows users to create complex, multi-year budgets, complete with detailed forecasting.
- **Financial Projections**: The software can generate projections for P&L, balance

sheets, and cash flows, which is useful for planning and funding purposes.

Scenario Analysis: Businesses can test various financial scenarios to see how different factors (such as sales or expenses) impact their bottom line.

Best For: SMBs that require more advanced budgeting and forecasting tools, particularly those with longer-term financial planning needs.

6. Zoho Books

Overview: Zoho Books is a comprehensive accounting software for small businesses that also includes strong budgeting tools. It offers features such as expense tracking, invoicing, and financial reporting, making it a complete financial management solution.

Key Features:

Budgeting and Expense Tracking: Zoho Books allows businesses to create and monitor budgets, track spending, and set up alerts when they're nearing budget limits.

Project Costing: SMBs can track project-specific budgets to ensure they stay within financial limits.

Real-Time Insights: Businesses receive real-time financial reports to help make timely decisions.

Best For: SMBs looking for a well-rounded accounting tool with strong budgeting and project management features.

7. Adaptive Insights (Workday Adaptive Planning)

Overview: Adaptive Insights, now part of **Workday**, is a more advanced budgeting and planning tool designed for growing SMBs and larger companies. It helps businesses streamline financial planning, budgeting, and forecasting processes.

Key Features:

Collaborative Budgeting: Allows teams to collaborate on creating and managing budgets, making it ideal for businesses with multiple departments or locations.

Scenario Planning: Helps businesses model different financial scenarios to assess how changes in key assumptions will impact their budget.

Real-Time Data: Provides real-time access to financial data, helping businesses make more informed decisions.

Best For: Mid-sized businesses with complex budgeting needs that require a more powerful, scalable solution.

Whatever the choice, investing in the right budgeting software can provide clarity, improve financial planning, and help businesses achieve their long-term goals.

Chapter 7: Income Tax Accounting

Marginal Tax Rate vs. Average Tax Rate

Understanding the differences between the marginal tax rate and the average tax rate is essential for both individuals and businesses as they navigate the complexities of income tax accounting. These two terms are often used interchangeably, but they have distinct meanings and implications for tax planning and financial decision-making.

In this section, we will explore the definitions of both tax rates, how they are calculated, and their relevance in the context of income taxation. We will also discuss how these rates impact the financial planning strategies for individuals and businesses.

What is the Marginal Tax Rate?

The **marginal tax rate** refers to the rate at which the last dollar of income is taxed. In other words, it is the tax rate that applies to the next dollar of taxable income earned. The marginal tax rate is a crucial concept for understanding how progressive tax systems work, particularly in countries like the United States, where the tax system is structured with multiple tax brackets.

In progressive tax systems, the more income you earn, the higher your marginal tax rate becomes. However, it is important to note that the marginal tax rate applies only to the portion of income that falls within the specific tax bracket, not the entire income. For example, if an individual's income falls within the 22% tax bracket, only the income within that bracket is taxed at 22%, while income below that bracket is taxed at lower rates.

The marginal tax rate is important because it influences decisions related to earning additional income. For instance, if you are considering taking on a side job or earning a bonus, the marginal tax rate helps you determine how much of your additional income will actually be kept after taxes. Knowing your marginal tax rate can help you make more informed financial decisions regarding savings, investments, and career moves.

What is the Average Tax Rate?

The average tax rate is a broader measure, reflecting the percentage of total income that is paid in taxes. It is calculated by dividing the total taxes paid by the total taxable income. Unlike the marginal tax rate, which is concerned only with the last dollar earned, the average tax rate provides an overall picture of the effective tax burden on an individual or business.

For example, if an individual earns $100,000 and pays $15,000 in taxes, the average tax rate would be 15% ($15,000 ÷ $100,000). The average tax rate is useful in understanding the total proportion of income that is subject to taxation, especially for those looking to assess the overall tax impact on their earnings.

Unlike the marginal tax rate, the average tax rate tends to be lower in progressive tax systems. This is because, in these systems, only income above certain thresholds is taxed at higher rates, while income below those thresholds is taxed at lower rates. Thus, the average tax rate reflects the weighted average of all tax rates applied across the various income brackets.

The Relationship Between Marginal and Average Tax Rates

The marginal and average tax rates are related but reflect different aspects of the tax burden. For individuals and businesses in a progressive tax system, the marginal tax rate will always be higher than the average tax rate, unless the individual or business falls entirely within a single tax bracket.

As income increases, the marginal tax rate typically increases, while the average tax rate rises more slowly because the lower portions of income are taxed at lower rates. This means that individuals with higher incomes may feel a greater financial burden due to their marginal tax rate, but their average tax rate is still lower because a significant portion of their income is taxed at lower rates.

This difference can be illustrated by considering a hypothetical individual who earns $50,000 in taxable income. If their income falls into two tax brackets—say, 10% for the first $20,000 and 20% for the next $30,000—the marginal tax rate would be 20%, reflecting the tax rate on the last dollar of income. However, their average tax rate would be lower because they are paying 10% on the first $20,000 and 20% on the remaining $30,000. Their average tax rate would be a weighted average of the two rates, resulting in a tax rate somewhere between 10% and 20%.

How Do Marginal and Average Tax Rates Affect Tax Planning?

Both the marginal and average tax rates play significant roles in **tax planning**, a process that involves organizing income, investments, and other financial factors to minimize tax liabilities. Understanding the difference between these rates is essential for making decisions about income recognition, deductions, and tax credits.

- **Income Timing**: The marginal tax rate is especially important for timing income. Since the marginal tax rate increases as income rises, tax planning strategies often aim to **defer income** to future periods, particularly if an individual or business expects to be in a lower tax bracket in the future. Conversely, if an individual is in a lower marginal tax bracket, it may make sense to accelerate income to take advantage of the lower tax rate.
- **Deductions and Tax Credits**: The average tax rate provides insight into the overall tax burden and can help determine the effectiveness of deductions

and tax credits. For example, high-income earners in a higher marginal tax bracket may benefit more from deductions because the value of the deduction is tied to the tax rate. If an individual is in a 35% marginal tax bracket, a $1,000 deduction reduces their tax liability by $350. In contrast, an individual in a 15% marginal tax bracket would save only $150 with the same deduction.

- **Investment Decisions**: Understanding the marginal tax rate is important for investment decisions, especially in relation to capital gains, interest income, and tax-advantaged accounts like IRAs and 401(k)s. Investments that generate capital gains are generally taxed at lower rates than ordinary income. By managing the timing of investments and understanding how taxes impact different types of income, individuals can reduce their tax liability over time.

Real-World Examples

Let's consider a simple example to illustrate the difference between marginal and average tax rates:

Suppose an individual has a taxable income of $100,000. Based on current tax brackets, the first $50,000 is taxed at 10%, and the remaining $50,000 is taxed at 20%. Their marginal tax rate is 20%, reflecting the tax rate on the last dollar of income. However, their average tax rate would be lower because the first $50,000 is taxed at a lower rate.

In this case, the total taxes paid would be:

- 10% on $50,000 = $5,000
- 20% on the remaining $50,000 = $10,000
- Total Taxes Paid = $15,000

The average tax rate would then be calculated as:

$$\text{"Average Tax Rate"} = \text{"Total Taxes Paid"} / \text{"Total Taxable Income"} = 15{,}000/100{,}000 = 15\%$$

Even though the marginal tax rate is 20%, the average tax rate is only 15%. This reflects the progressive nature of the tax system.

The marginal tax rate and the average tax rate are both essential concepts in income tax accounting, and understanding their differences is key to making informed financial decisions. While the marginal tax rate applies to the last dollar earned, the average tax rate provides a broader perspective on the overall tax burden. In progressive tax systems, these rates help businesses and individuals plan their finances, manage their tax liabilities, and make strategic decisions about income, deductions, and investments. Proper tax planning, based on these rates, can lead to significant tax savings and more efficient financial management.

Accrual vs. Cash Accounting for Tax Purposes

In the world of accounting, businesses often face a decision about which method to use for recording their revenues and expenses: cash basis accounting or accrual basis accounting. While both methods aim to track financial transactions, the way they recognize income and expenses differs significantly, especially when it comes to tax reporting. Understanding these differences is crucial for making informed decisions about financial planning, cash flow management, and tax obligations.

In cash basis accounting, transactions are recorded only when cash changes hands—i.e., when payment is received or made. Revenue is recognized when it is received in the form of cash, and expenses are recorded when they are paid. This method is commonly used by small businesses, freelancers, and individuals who want a simple and straightforward way to track their income and expenses.

For instance, if a business completes a service in December but does not receive payment until January, under cash basis accounting, the income would not be recognized until January, the month in which the payment is actually received. Similarly, if the business incurs an expense in December but doesn't pay for it until January, the expense would not be recorded until January as well.

One of the key advantages of cash basis accounting is its simplicity. Since it only accounts for actual cash transactions, it is easier to track and understand. There is no need to deal with accounts receivable or payable, which can be complex for businesses with numerous transactions. It also provides an accurate reflection of cash flow since it directly shows the movement of cash in and out of the business.

From a tax perspective, cash basis accounting can be beneficial for businesses with fluctuating income or those seeking to defer taxes. Since income is only reported when received, businesses can control the timing of their taxable income by managing when they invoice customers or make payments. For example, a business can delay invoicing until the new year to push income into the next tax period, potentially lowering the current year's tax liability.

What is Accrual Basis Accounting?

In accrual basis accounting, revenue is recognized when earned, and expenses are recorded when incurred, regardless of when the actual payment is received or made. This means that even if a business completes a project or sells a product in one period but receives payment in the next, the revenue is recognized in the period when the service or product was provided, not when the money changes hands. Similarly, if the business incurs an expense, it is recorded as soon as the liability is incurred, even if payment is made in a later period.

Accrual accounting provides a more accurate picture of a business's financial health because it matches revenues with the expenses incurred to generate them. For instance, if a business sells $10,000 worth of goods in December but doesn't receive payment until January, the revenue would still be recognized in December, along with the related cost of goods sold. This method is typically used by larger businesses or those that require a more detailed view of their financial position, as it provides a clearer understanding of profitability and financial performance.

From a tax perspective, accrual accounting can lead to different tax implications compared to cash basis accounting. Since income is recognized when earned, businesses are required to report it as taxable income, even if they haven't yet received the payment. Similarly, expenses are recognized when incurred, which can result in tax deductions being reported before the actual cash payment is made.

Key Differences in Tax Reporting

The primary difference between cash and accrual accounting for tax purposes lies in the timing of income and expense recognition. These differences can have significant implications for tax liabilities, depending on the timing of transactions.

Timing of Income: Under cash basis accounting, income is recognized when it is received in cash. This means businesses can defer reporting income to a later period by delaying invoicing or payment receipt. In contrast, under accrual accounting, income is recognized as soon as it is earned, regardless of when the cash is received. This can lead to businesses paying taxes on income they have not yet received.

Timing of Expenses: Similarly, expenses under cash basis accounting are only recognized when paid. This can allow businesses to delay expenses and thus reduce their taxable income in the short term. In contrast, under accrual accounting, expenses are recognized when they are incurred, not when paid. This means businesses may be able to deduct expenses in the current period, even if payment is made in a future period.

For example, let's consider a business that earns $7,000 in December by completing a project but does not receive the payment until January. If the business uses cash basis accounting, the $7,000 will be recorded as income in January. However, if the business uses accrual accounting, the $7,000 will be recognized in December, even though the cash is not received until the next period.

This distinction is particularly important for businesses that experience significant fluctuations in income or expenses during the year. By understanding how each accounting method impacts the timing of tax reporting, businesses can make strategic decisions regarding when to recognize income and expenses in order to optimize their tax positions.

ADVANTAGES AND DISADVANTAGES

OF ACCOUNTING METHODS

Point	Cash Basis Accounting	Accrual Basis Accounting
Advantages	Clearer view of cash flow; allows deferring income to delay taxes.	More accurate financial picture; matches revenues and expenses.
Disadvantages	May not reflect true profitability due to ignoring receivables and payables.	Taxes on income not yet received; requires complex record-keeping.
Tax Reporting Impact	Easier tax reporting as income and expenses are recognized when cash is received or paid.	Can result in taxes being due on income not yet received, making cash flow harder to manage.
Record-Keeping	Simpler, with less tracking of accounts receivable and payable.	More complex, requiring tracking of both accounts receivable and payable.
Suitability for Small Businesses	Ideal for businesses with tight cash flow or smaller operations.	Better for larger businesses or those that carry inventory, offering a more accurate financial picture.
Cash Flow Management	Provides a clearer picture of cash flow, helping businesses manage cash more effectively.	Less effective for cash flow management, as it doesn't reflect actual cash movement.

Tax Deductions vs. Tax Credits

Tax planning is a crucial aspect of managing personal and business finances, and understanding the difference between **tax deductions** and **tax credits** is essential for optimizing your tax situation. Both tax deductions and tax credits serve to reduce the amount of tax you owe, but they do so in very different ways. Knowing how each works and when to use them can lead to significant tax savings.

In this section, we will explore the key differences between tax deductions and tax credits, how they affect your tax return, and some common examples of each. We'll also address how businesses and individuals can strategically use these tools to maximize tax savings.

What is a Tax Deduction?

A **tax deduction** is an expense that you can subtract from your total income, effectively lowering the amount of your income that is subject to tax. This reduction in taxable income reduces the overall amount of tax you owe based on your income tax rate.

For instance, if you are a self-employed individual, business expenses like office supplies, business-related travel, and professional fees can all be deducted from your gross income. Similarly, if you're an employee, certain deductions, like mortgage interest or charitable contributions, may apply. After applying deductions, your income is "lowered," and your tax is calculated on this new, lower amount.

There are two primary types of tax deductions: **standard deductions** and **itemized deductions**.

- **Standard Deduction**: The IRS allows taxpayers to deduct a fixed amount from their taxable income. For the tax year 2025, the standard deduction for single filers is $13,850, and for married couples filing jointly, it is $27,700. This deduction automatically applies if you do not itemize deductions. The amount of the standard deduction is adjusted for inflation annually.
- **Itemized Deductions**: If your deductible expenses exceed the standard deduction, you can opt to itemize deductions. This includes things like state and local taxes, mortgage interest, medical expenses (above a certain threshold), and charitable donations. Itemizing allows taxpayers to deduct specific expenses rather than taking the standard deduction, but it requires more documentation and tracking of expenses.

One important thing to note is that tax deductions only reduce the amount of taxable income. The reduction in tax depends on your **marginal tax rate**. For example, if you are in a 22% tax bracket, a $1,000 deduction reduces your taxes by $220 (22% of $1,000). The greater your tax bracket, the larger your savings from a deduction.

What is a Tax Credit?

A **tax credit**, on the other hand, directly reduces the amount of tax you owe, dollar for dollar. Unlike a deduction, which lowers taxable income, a credit reduces the final tax liability directly. Tax credits are often seen as more valuable than tax deductions because they directly lower the tax amount owed.

There are two types of tax credits: **nonrefundable credits** and **refundable credits**.

- **Nonrefundable Credits**: These credits reduce the amount of tax you owe but cannot result in a refund if they exceed the taxes due. In other words, if the tax credit is higher than your tax liability, you lose the excess amount. For example, if you owe $500 in taxes and have a $700 nonrefundable tax credit, your tax liability would be reduced to $0, but you would not receive the $200 balance.
- **Refundable Credits**: These credits can reduce your tax liability below $0, resulting in a refund from the government. Refundable credits are highly beneficial because they can provide a tax refund even if you owe no taxes. For instance, the **Earned Income Tax Credit (EITC)** and the **Child Tax Credit** are refundable. If you qualify, these credits can not only reduce your tax liability to zero but also result in a refund, often benefiting lower-income individuals and families.

How Tax Deductions and Credits Work Together

While both tax deductions and credits help reduce your tax burden, they work in different ways. A **tax deduction** reduces your taxable income, meaning your overall tax liability decreases based on your tax rate. A **tax credit** directly reduces your tax liability, making it a more powerful tool for lowering your taxes.

For example, let's assume you have a taxable income of $50,000, and you qualify for a $1,000 tax deduction and a $1,000 tax credit.

- With the **tax deduction**, you subtract the $1,000 from your taxable income, reducing it to $49,000. If you're in the 22% tax bracket, this results in a $220 reduction in your tax liability (22% of $1,000).
- With the **tax credit**, you directly subtract the $1,000 from your tax liability, reducing your tax owed by $1,000, regardless of your tax bracket.

In this case, the tax credit offers a far greater reduction in taxes owed than the tax deduction.

Common Examples of Tax Deductions and Tax Credits

Tax Deductions:

- **Mortgage Interest Deduction**: Homeowners can deduct the interest paid on their mortgage, subject to certain limits.
- **Charitable Donations**: Contributions made to qualifying charitable

organizations can be deducted from taxable income.

- **Medical Expenses**: If you itemize deductions, medical expenses exceeding 7.5% of your adjusted gross income (AGI) can be deducted.
- **State and Local Taxes (SALT)**: You can deduct state and local income taxes or sales taxes, as well as property taxes, up to a limit.

Tax Credits:

- **Child Tax Credit**: Available for qualifying children under age 17, this credit provides up to $2,000 per child, with the potential for up to $1,400 of it being refundable.
- **Earned Income Tax Credit (EITC)**: A refundable credit aimed at helping low- to moderate-income workers, with the amount based on income and the number of qualifying children.
- **Education Credits**: The **American Opportunity Tax Credit (AOTC)** and the **Lifetime Learning Credit (LLC)** offer tax relief for qualifying education expenses.
- **Energy-Efficient Home Credit**: Individuals who make qualifying energy-efficient improvements to their home can receive a tax credit for a portion of the costs.

Which is Better: Tax Deductions or Tax Credits?

In terms of direct financial benefit, **tax credits** tend to be more valuable than tax deductions. This is because tax credits directly reduce your tax bill, whereas tax deductions only reduce the amount of income that is taxable, and the savings depend on your tax bracket.

However, this doesn't mean deductions should be overlooked. For example, deductions like the mortgage interest deduction and charitable contributions can provide significant savings for many taxpayers. The key is to evaluate your tax situation and understand how each tool—deductions or credits—impacts your specific circumstances.

For higher-income individuals, maximizing tax deductions through itemizing can be effective, especially if you have significant deductions, such as mortgage interest or charitable contributions. On the other hand, if you qualify for refundable tax credits, they are typically more beneficial because they can lower your tax liability to zero and provide a refund.

amazon

AMAZON - TAX DEDUCTIONS VS. TAX CREDITS

Amazon uses tax deductions and tax credits to optimize its tax strategy

CHALLENGES

- Complex Global Operations
- Significant Investment in Infrastructure
- High Revenue and Operating Costs

OBJECTIVES

MINIMIZE TAX LIABILITY

Amazon sought to reduce its tax burden through both tax deductions and credits while maintaining compliance with global tax laws.

OPTIMIZE FINANCIAL REPORTING

Amazon had ensure accurate financial statements for investors, and tax authorities.

RESULT AND BENEFITS

- Amazon has significant capital expenditures related to its infrastructure, which allows the company to take advantage of tax deductions.
- Amazon combines tax deductions and credits to maximize tax savings.

Long-Term Capital Gains vs. Ordinary Income

The distinction between long-term capital gains and ordinary income is one of the most crucial concepts for investors and taxpayers alike. While both terms refer to types of income, they are taxed very differently, which can have significant implications for your overall tax liability. Understanding these differences is vital for making strategic investment decisions and optimizing your tax planning.

What Are Long-Term Capital Gains?

Long-term capital gains refer to the profits made from the sale of an asset that has been held for more than one year. These assets can include stocks, bonds, real estate, and other forms of investment. The key factor that defines a long-term capital gain is the **holding period**. If you hold the asset for longer than a year before selling it, any profit made from the sale is classified as a long-term capital gain.

For example, if you bought shares of a company for $1,000 and sold them a year and a half later for $1,500, the $500 gain would be considered a long-term capital gain. The tax treatment of long-term capital gains is typically more favorable than that of ordinary income, meaning that you will generally pay a lower tax rate on these gains.

The tax rates for long-term capital gains are based on your taxable income and filing status. For most taxpayers, long-term capital gains are taxed at one of three rates: **0%, 15%, or 20%**. The specific rate you pay depends on the amount of income you earn.

What Is Ordinary Income?

Ordinary income, on the other hand, refers to income that is taxed at the standard rates for wages, salary, and business profits. This includes income from employment, self-employment, interest, dividends, and short-term capital gains. **Short-term capital gains** occur when you sell an asset that you have held for one year or less, and these gains are taxed at the same rates as your ordinary income.

Ordinary income is subject to tax rates that range from **10% to 37%**, depending on your income level. These rates are higher than the tax rates for long-term capital gains, which is why holding investments for a longer period can be financially beneficial for investors.

For example, if you earn $60,000 in salary and $2,000 in short-term capital gains from stocks sold within one year of purchase, the $2,000 is considered ordinary income and taxed at your regular rate, not the lower long-term capital gains rate.

How Tax Rates Differ: Long-Term Capital Gains vs. Ordinary Income

One of the primary reasons long-term capital gains are so favorable is the difference in tax treatment. For instance, let's consider a single taxpayer who has a total taxable income of **$50,000**. For **ordinary income**, the tax rate could be anywhere from 10% to 22%, depending on the exact breakdown of that income.

However, if that same taxpayer were to sell an asset that they had held for more than one year, the profit from that sale would fall under long-term capital gains taxation. For taxable incomes of $50,000, the long-term capital gains rate would be **15%**.

The table below outlines the long-term capital gains tax brackets for 2025 based on your filing status:

Filing Status	**0% Capital Gains**	**15% Capital Gains**	**20% Capital Gains**
Single	$0 to $47,025	$47,026 to $518,900	$518,901+
Married Joint	$0 to $94,050	$94,051 to $583,750	$583,751+

As seen, long-term capital gains are taxed at much lower rates than ordinary income, which is one of the main benefits of holding onto assets for longer periods before selling.

Why Does Holding Investments Longer Make Sense?

Investors often face the temptation to sell assets quickly, especially when they see prices rising. However, the decision to hold onto an investment for longer than a year can result in significant tax savings due to the lower long-term capital gains tax rates. By postponing the sale of assets until the one-year mark, investors can benefit from the 0%, 15%, or 20% tax rates on gains, depending on their income.

For example, let's say you bought stock for $10,000 and sold it for $15,000 after six months. The $5,000 profit would be taxed as ordinary income. If you had held the stock for one year, that same $5,000 profit would be taxed at the long-term capital gains rate, which could save you hundreds of dollars in taxes.

Moreover, long-term investing encourages better decision-making by focusing on the company's growth potential rather than short-term market fluctuations. This approach can lead to higher returns over time, as opposed to frequently trading in and out of assets, which can be both costly and tax-inefficient.

When Does Short-Term Capital Gains Come Into Play?

While long-term capital gains are generally more advantageous, there are situations where short-term capital gains may be necessary or preferable. Short-term capital gains occur when assets are held for one year or less. These gains are taxed as ordinary income, and the tax rate can be as high as 37% for individuals in the highest tax brackets.

Active traders, for example, often engage in short-term investments, aiming to profit from quick market movements. In this case, while the taxes are higher, the potential for quicker profits could justify the tax burden. Additionally, some investors may find themselves in a situation where they need to liquidate assets quickly to cover expenses, making short-term gains inevitable.

In these cases, it's important to weigh the potential for profits against the higher tax costs. Investors should consider their personal financial situation and risk tolerance before making short-term trades, and tax planning should be part of the decision-making process.

Managing Long-Term and Short-Term Capital Gains

Given the different tax treatments of **long-term** and **short-term capital gains**, it's essential to manage your investments strategically. For those looking to minimize taxes, holding assets for more than a year can significantly reduce the amount of taxes paid. However, for those who engage in short-term trading, it's important to be aware of the higher tax rates on short-term gains and plan accordingly.

Tax-efficient investing strategies include:

- **Holding assets for over one year** to qualify for long-term capital gains.
- **Tax-loss harvesting**: Selling losing investments to offset taxable gains.
- **Utilizing tax-advantaged accounts**, such as IRAs or 401(k)s, where capital gains may not be taxed in the current year.

Understanding the difference between long-term capital gains and ordinary income is a fundamental part of tax planning for investors. By recognizing the benefits of hold**ing investments for longer periods, individuals can take advantage of favorable long-term capital gains tax rates. This strategy not only reduces tax liability but also encourages better long-term financial decisions. However, for those who trade more frequently, it's important to understand the impact of short-term capital gains taxes and plan accordingly. Ultimately, tax-efficient investing requires a balance between managing gains, expenses, and taxes, and understanding these concepts is essential for maximizing investment returns over time.**

Why Business Entity Type Matters for Taxes

Choosing the right business entity is one of the most crucial decisions an entrepreneur or business owner will make. Not only does it affect liability, governance, and operations, but the type of entity you select can also have significant tax implications. The structure you choose can determine how much you pay in

taxes, how you are taxed, and how you file your business taxes. Understanding the differences between business entities and their tax treatments is essential to optimizing your tax position and managing financial responsibilities effectively.

Types of Business Entities and Their Tax Implications

There are several types of business entities, each with its own tax treatment. Let's explore the most common ones:

Sole Proprietorship

A sole proprietorship is the simplest form of business structure, where the business is owned and operated by one individual. From a tax perspective, the owner and the business are considered the same entity. This means that the business itself does not pay taxes directly; instead, all profits and losses are passed through to the owner's personal tax return. The income is reported on Schedule C attached to the owner's personal tax return (Form 1040).

The primary tax advantage of a sole proprietorship is simplicity. However, the downside is that the business owner is personally liable for the business's debts, and they are taxed at the individual income tax rates, which could be higher than corporate tax rates. Additionally, the owner must pay self-employment tax on the business's net income, which includes both Social Security and Medicare taxes.

Partnership

A partnership is an arrangement where two or more individuals share ownership of a business. Like a sole proprietorship, a partnership itself does not pay taxes; instead, profits and losses are passed through to the individual partners. Partnerships must file an informational tax return using Form 1065, and each partner receives a Schedule K-1 showing their share of income, deductions, and credits. This information is then reported on the individual partners' tax returns.

Partnerships offer flexibility in profit distribution, allowing partners to agree on a share that differs from ownership percentages. However, each partner is personally liable for the partnership's debts, and like sole proprietors, they must pay self-employment taxes on their earnings.

Limited Liability Company (LLC)

A Limited Liability Company (LLC) is a hybrid entity that provides the legal protections of a corporation with the tax benefits of a partnership or sole proprietorship. An LLC can choose how it wishes to be taxed. By default, single-member LLCs are taxed as sole proprietorships, and multi-member LLCs are taxed as partnerships, meaning they pass through profits and losses to the owners' personal tax returns. However, LLCs also have the option to elect to be taxed as a C Corporation or S Corporation if they choose.

LLCs provide the benefit of limited liability protection, meaning owners (members) are not personally responsible for business debts. This makes them a popular choice for small businesses. LLCs also have more flexibility than corporations in terms of structure and taxation. However, members must still pay self-employment tax on earnings unless the LLC elects corporate taxation.

Corporation (C Corp)

A C Corporation is a separate legal entity from its owners, meaning it is taxed separately. Corporations file their own tax returns using Form 1120 and are subject to corporate income tax on their profits. The profits of the corporation are taxed at the corporate tax rate, which is currently 21% as of 2025.

The downside of a C Corporation is the potential for double taxation. This occurs when the corporation pays taxes on its income, and then the shareholders pay taxes again on any dividends they receive from the corporation. However, corporations can take advantage of various deductions and credits, making them appealing for larger businesses. They also provide the best protection against personal liability for the owners.

S Corporation

An S Corporation is similar to a C Corporation in that it provides liability protection and is a separate legal entity. However, an S Corporation enjoys **pass-through taxation**, meaning that the corporation itself does not pay taxes on its income. Instead, income, deductions, and credits are passed through to the shareholders, who report them on their individual tax returns. S Corporations are limited to 100 shareholders, and shareholders must be U.S. citizens or residents.

S Corporations avoid double taxation, which is one of the biggest advantages over C Corporations. Shareholders of S Corps are not subject to self-employment tax on their share of the corporate income, making S Corporations a favorable option for many small businesses and entrepreneurs. However, like LLCs, S Corporations have more strict requirements and limitations on ownership and the types of shareholders.

Key Factors to Consider When Choosing a Business Entity

Tax Rates

The structure you choose determines your business's tax rate. For example, the C Corporation tax rate is fixed at 21%, while sole proprietors and partnerships are taxed based on individual income tax brackets. Choosing the right structure can significantly affect your tax rate, and in some cases, a business may prefer the S Corporation or LLC structure for its potential to avoid double taxation and reduce the personal liability exposure that comes with a sole proprietorship or partnership.

Self-Employment Tax

Sole proprietors, partners, and LLC members are subject to self-employment tax, which covers Social Security and Medicare taxes. This can be a substantial tax burden, especially for high-earning small business owners. On the other hand, S

Corporation shareholders are not subject to self-employment tax on their share of the profits, which can result in significant tax savings.

Liability Protection

An important factor when choosing a business structure is liability protection. LLCs, S Corporations, and C Corporations provide limited liability protection, meaning that the personal assets of the owners are generally protected from business debts and lawsuits. In contrast, sole proprietors and partners are personally liable for any debts or liabilities incurred by the business.

Flexibility in Management

LLCs and partnerships offer more flexibility in how they are managed. For instance, LLCs can be managed by their members or by appointed managers, while partnerships allow for different profit-sharing arrangements. Corporations, on the other hand, have a more rigid structure, with required formalities such as shareholder meetings and board elections.

Chapter 8: Accounting for Investors

GAAP: Understanding Generally Accepted Accounting Principles

Generally Accepted Accounting Principles (GAAP) refer to a set of rules, standards, and guidelines used to prepare financial statements. These principles are designed to ensure consistency, transparency, and comparability of financial information across companies, helping investors, regulators, and other stakeholders assess the financial health of businesses.

GAAP plays an essential role in the financial reporting process. It provides a framework that governs how businesses should record, summarize, and report their financial transactions. These principles help maintain consistency across industries and ensure that financial statements are truthful and reliable.

The Importance of GAAP in Financial Reporting

The primary goal of GAAP is to facilitate clear communication between companies and stakeholders by presenting financial data in a consistent manner. For investors, this means that they can compare financial statements from different companies with ease, making informed decisions based on uniform accounting practices. Without these standards, financial reports would be highly subjective, leading to confusion and potentially misleading investors.

GAAP applies to various forms of financial reporting, including the balance sheet, income statement, and statement of cash flows. It governs the recognition, measurement, and presentation of various financial elements such as revenues, expenses, assets, and liabilities. This ensures that financial statements reflect a company's true financial position at any given point in time.

Key Principles of GAAP

GAAP is built on several fundamental principles that guide accountants in recording and reporting financial transactions. These principles include:

1. Principle of Regularity: This principle asserts that accountants must adhere to established rules and regulations when preparing financial statements. This ensures that the financial information presented is accurate and consistent with accepted standards.
2. Principle of Consistency: Consistency in financial reporting is key to producing comparable statements. Accountants must use the same methods and principles from one reporting period to the next unless there's a valid reason for changing them. Any changes in accounting practices must be disclosed.
3. Principle of Sincerity: Accountants must strive to present the financial position of the company in a truthful and accurate manner. The intent is to reflect the company's financial reality without manipulation or exaggeration.

4. Principle of Permanence of Methods: This principle stresses the importance of consistency in the application of accounting methods and techniques. **Accountants should use** established methods over time, making only necessary adjustments based on valid changes in business operations or financial conditions.
5. Principle of Non-Compensation: Both positive and negative aspects of financial information should be presented without offsetting one another. For example, a company's gains should not be compensated by its losses.
6. Principle of Prudence: This principle encourages accountants to adopt a cautious approach when reporting financial information. It suggests that liabilities and expenses should be recognized as soon as they are foreseeable, while revenue should be recognized only when it is realized or assured.
7. Principle of Continuity: This principle assumes that a company will continue its operations indefinitely unless there is evidence to the contrary. This assumption affects how assets and liabilities are reported.
8. **Principle of Periodicity**: Financial information should be reported in regular, consistent periods (e.g., quarterly or annually). This allows stakeholders to assess the company's performance over time.
9. **Principle of Materiality**: This principle dictates that financial statements should reflect all material information, or facts that could influence decisions made by the users of those statements. In other words, any significant financial data that might affect users' understanding of the company's financial health must be disclosed.
10. **Principle of Utmost Good Faith**: This principle encourages transparency and honesty in all financial dealings, ensuring that all transactions are fully disclosed and accurately reported.

GAAP vs. IFRS: Key Differences

While GAAP is primarily used in the United States, other parts of the world follow the International Financial Reporting Standards (IFRS). IFRS is a set of international accounting standards issued by the International Accounting Standards Board (IASB). The differences between GAAP and IFRS can affect how financial information is reported, particularly for companies operating in both markets.

Rules-Based vs. Principles-Based: GAAP is rules-based, which means that it provides specific guidelines for how financial transactions should be reported. In contrast, IFRS is principles-based, meaning it provides broader guidelines that allow for more interpretation in specific cases.

Inventory Accounting: GAAP allows the use of the Last In, First Out (LIFO) method for inventory accounting, which can lower taxable income in times of rising prices. IFRS does not allow LIFO, instead preferring the First In, First

Out (FIFO) method, which may result in different inventory valuations and tax implications.

Revenue Recognition: Under GAAP, revenue is recognized when it is realized and earned, while IFRS allows for more flexibility, permitting revenue recognition once a contractual agreement is established.

Development Costs: Under IFRS, development costs are capitalized as intangible assets if they meet certain criteria, whereas GAAP treats these costs as expenses in the period incurred.

Financial Statement Presentation: In GAAP, unusual or extraordinary items are shown separately in the income statement, while in IFRS, these items are generally included in the income statement without special classification.

The Role of GAAP in Ensuring Transparency

For investors, one of the most significant benefits of GAAP is that it ensures transparency in financial reporting. By adhering to these principles, companies provide consistent and reliable data, which investors can use to assess a company's profitability, solvency, and overall financial health.

GAAP promotes **consistency** across financial reporting, making it easier for investors to compare companies across industries. This is particularly important when analyzing stocks, bonds, or other investment opportunities. With a standardized accounting framework, investors can more confidently make informed decisions about their investments, knowing that the financial statements are consistent, comparable, and reliable.

By understanding the purpose and application of GAAP, businesses can ensure that their financial statements are in compliance with legal standards, while investors can be confident in the reliability of the information they are using to make investment decisions.

The Four Accounting Principles and Assumptions: A Deeper Dive

Accounting is a cornerstone of financial reporting, providing essential insights into a company's performance. The Generally Accepted Accounting Principles (GAAP) offer a standardized framework for businesses to follow when reporting their financial data. Among the core elements of GAAP, four key principles stand out as foundational, guiding the process of accounting and ensuring consistency in financial reporting. These principles work in tandem with certain underlying assumptions to form a robust accounting framework. In this comprehensive dive, we explore the four primary accounting principles and the four assumptions that shape financial reporting.

The Four Accounting Principles

1. **Principle of Regularity**

   The principle of regularity asserts that accountants must adhere to established rules, regulations, and standards when preparing financial statements. This means that all companies must follow GAAP's prescribed methods for recording and presenting their financial information. Regularity ensures that financial data is presented consistently, making it easier for stakeholders to compare the financial health of different businesses. This principle not only provides uniformity but also builds trust with investors and regulators, ensuring that the reports generated are reliable and credible.

For instance, a company must consistently apply the same method of calculating depreciation each year. If a company switches from straight-line depreciation to declining balance depreciation without justification or explanation, it would violate the principle of regularity, creating confusion and potential discrepancies in reporting.

2. **Principle of Consistency**

   Consistency dictates that once an accounting method or principle is adopted, it must be used consistently over time. This helps avoid discrepancies in financial statements and ensures that financial reports reflect comparable data across periods. The consistent application of accounting methods allows analysts, investors, and other stakeholders to make reliable, year-to-year comparisons of a company's performance.

Changes in accounting policies or methods can be made, but they must be disclosed in financial statements. If a company changes its revenue recognition method, for example, it must provide a rationale for the change and describe its impact on the financial results. Failing to maintain consistency could confuse investors, as it would appear as though the company's performance is inconsistent, even if it's due to reporting changes rather than actual fluctuations in financial health.

3. **Principle of Sincerity**

   The principle of sincerity emphasizes that accountants should strive to provide an accurate and truthful representation of a company's financial position. This principle encourages transparency, ensuring that the financial data presented does not mislead stakeholders. The sincerity principle is about maintaining integrity in financial reporting, with the objective of presenting a company's true financial condition.

For example, companies must ensure that they report both their assets and liabilities accurately, reflecting the actual state of affairs. If a company were to deliberately underreport liabilities or overstate revenue, it would be violating the sincerity principle and engaging in fraudulent reporting, undermining the reliability of its financial statements.

4. **Principle of Permanence of Methods**

The principle of permanence of methods highlights that once a company establishes its accounting methods and procedures, those methods should be maintained consistently over time. The idea is that accounting practices should be stable to provide a reliable basis for comparison. If a company changes its methods of calculation or reporting frequently, it creates inconsistency, which makes it difficult for investors or analysts to evaluate its long-term performance.

A good example of this principle is seen in the treatment of fixed assets. If a company chooses a method to depreciate its assets (e.g., straight-line depreciation), it should continue to apply this same method for future accounting periods. Changing depreciation methods without adequate explanation could undermine the ability to make accurate long-term performance assessments.

The Four Accounting Assumptions and Their Impact

While the principles guide the practices of accounting, assumptions form the bedrock that allows accountants to make reasonable judgments when preparing financial reports. These assumptions are fundamental to understanding how companies operate and how their financial statements are prepared. Let's explore these assumptions in detail.

1. **The Going Concern Assumption**
   The going concern assumption presumes that a company will continue its operations indefinitely unless there is evidence to the contrary. This assumption is fundamental to the preparation of financial statements, as it allows accountants to treat assets and liabilities in a manner that assumes the company will continue to function. For instance, under this assumption, companies do not need to immediately liquidate assets at market value but can instead record them based on their ability to generate future income.

If a company is deemed unlikely to continue as a going concern—for example, due to severe financial distress or bankruptcy—its financial statements must reflect this. Assets may need to be valued at liquidation prices, and liabilities may need to be classified as current liabilities.

2. **The Economic Entity Assumption**

The economic entity assumption posits that a company's financial records must be separate from the financial records of its owners or other businesses. This principle ensures that financial statements reflect only the activities and transactions of the company, not personal assets or liabilities. It establishes that the company's financial performance should be reported independently from that of its owners or any other organization to avoid confusion or conflict of interest.

For example, if an owner of a small business takes out a personal loan to invest in the company, this loan should not appear on the company's balance sheet. Instead, it is treated as a personal liability of the owner, ensuring that the company's financial records are not mixed with personal finances.

3. **The Monetary Unit Assumption**

   The monetary unit assumption asserts that all financial transactions should be recorded in a stable currency, and it assumes that the purchasing power of that currency remains relatively constant over time. In practice, this means that a company's financial reports will not account for inflation or changes in currency value unless specifically stated.

While this assumption simplifies financial reporting by using a single unit of measurement (typically the domestic currency), it can create challenges in times of significant inflation or currency devaluation. For example, in hyperinflationary economies, the value of the currency may erode rapidly, making it difficult to compare financial performance over time without adjusting for changes in purchasing power.

4. **The Time Period Assumption**

   The time period assumption dictates that financial reports should cover specific periods, typically quarterly or annually. This assumption allows for the systematic tracking of a company's financial performance over time. By dividing the life of a business into time periods, accountants can produce periodic financial statements that help stakeholders monitor a company's progress and make timely decisions.

For instance, the annual income statement reflects a company's performance over the entire year, but a quarterly income statement provides a snapshot of how the company is performing within a shorter time frame. This assumption allows for timely adjustments and evaluations, but it also introduces the potential for short-term volatility to obscure long-term trends.

Why These Principles and Assumptions Matter

The four accounting principles—regularity, consistency, sincerity, and permanence of methods—are essential for providing transparency, reliability, and consistency in financial reporting. They ensure that financial statements reflect a company's true financial position and performance over time, allowing stakeholders to make informed decisions.

The four accounting assumptions—going concern, economic entity, monetary unit, and time period—provide a framework that allows accountants to record and report transactions in a standardized manner. These assumptions simplify the accounting process and ensure that financial statements provide meaningful and consistent information to stakeholders. They also enable financial reports to reflect the business reality in a way that is understandable and actionable.

In essence, the accounting principles and assumptions form the foundation of financial reporting. They provide the rules and the assumptions that guide accountants in preparing financial statements that investors, regulators, and other stakeholders rely on to assess a company's financial health and make informed decisions. Without these principles and assumptions, financial reporting would be chaotic, inconsistent, and ultimately unreliable.

The Two Accounting Constraints

In accounting, constraints are guidelines or limitations that help ensure financial reports are useful, reliable, and practical. These constraints are an integral part of Generally Accepted Accounting Principles (GAAP) and are designed to balance the need for accurate financial reporting with the realities of cost, time, and practicality. There are two main accounting constraints that guide the preparation of financial statements: the cost-benefit constraint and the materiality constraint. While they may seem simple, these constraints play a crucial role in ensuring that financial reports are both informative and cost-effective.

1. Cost-Benefit Constraint: Balancing Accuracy with Practicality

The cost-benefit constraint is perhaps one of the most pragmatic and fundamental concepts in accounting. It recognizes that providing financial information comes with costs—whether it is in terms of time, resources, or financial investment—and that these costs must be justified by the benefits the information provides. Essentially, if the cost of gathering and reporting certain financial data exceeds the benefits that stakeholders would derive from having that information, then it is acceptable not to include it in the financial statements.

For example, a small business may find it impractical and expensive to implement a complex accounting system just for tracking minor transactions. If the benefits of having that information, in terms of better decision-making or increased investor confidence, do not outweigh the implementation costs, the company may decide to forgo tracking such details.

The cost-benefit constraint helps companies avoid spending excessive amounts of money or time on financial reporting that will not significantly impact decision-making. This ensures that the financial reporting process remains efficient and aligned with the company's resources. For instance, detailed reports on minor expenses, like office supplies, may be disregarded if they would not materially affect the company's financial health or stakeholders' decisions.

A good example of this constraint in action is when a company decides not to break down minor expenses like small office supplies in its financial statements, as the cost of tracking and reporting these expenses would outweigh the benefit of providing this information to users of the financial statement.

The cost-benefit constraint thus aims to maintain a balance between the resources required for accurate reporting and the usefulness of the information provided. It ensures that financial reports are neither too costly nor unnecessarily cumbersome for companies to prepare while maintaining the integrity of essential data.

2. Materiality Constraint: The Significance of Information in Decision-Making

The materiality constraint is another key concept in accounting that ensures financial statements focus on information that is significant enough to influence decisions. According to this constraint, information is considered material if its omission or misstatement could affect the decisions of users of the financial statements. In other words, not every transaction or event needs to be reported in exhaustive detail. Instead, the focus is on those transactions and items that are substantial enough to impact decision-making.

Materiality in accounting considers both quantitative and qualitative aspects. **Quantitative materiality** refers to the size or amount of the transaction in relation to the company's overall financial position. For example, a $1,000 expense may be considered immaterial for a large corporation with billions in revenue but could be material for a smaller company with limited financial resources.

Qualitative materiality, on the other hand, pertains to non-financial factors that might influence stakeholders' decisions. For instance, a minor legal issue or a regulatory violation may not result in a significant financial impact but could be material if it affects the company's reputation or its ability to operate within legal frameworks.

The materiality principle is subjective and can vary depending on the context and the size of the company. Large multinational corporations, for instance, may not consider a $10,000 discrepancy as material, but for a small business, the same discrepancy might be significant enough to warrant further investigation and disclosure.

For example, a company that discovers a small error in its accounting records—say, an overstatement of $100—may decide not to correct it if it's deemed immaterial to the overall financial statements. The rationale here is that the cost of correcting the error may outweigh the benefit of making the correction, as the error would not significantly impact a decision-maker's assessment of the company's financial health.

On the other hand, a $100,000 discrepancy could be considered material and would need to be addressed promptly to avoid misleading stakeholders. A material event or transaction, such as a large acquisition or a major lawsuit, must always be disclosed in the financial statements due to its potential impact on financial performance and stakeholder decisions.

The materiality constraint allows companies to exercise judgment in determining which items need to be reported in detail, ensuring that financial statements remain focused on the most significant information without being burdened by trivial details.

Why These Constraints Exist

Both the cost-benefit and materiality constraints exist because they acknowledge the reality that accounting is a practical discipline. These constraints aim to ensure that financial reporting is not only accurate and relevant but also cost-effective and manageable. If these constraints were not in place, companies would be required to provide excessive amounts of information, much of which would be of little use to decision-makers, while also incurring unnecessary costs in gathering and reporting that data.

For instance, the cost-benefit constraint prevents companies from spending excessive resources to collect information that would have little to no impact on stakeholders' decisions. In the same vein, the materiality constraint ensures that the focus remains on significant information that can guide decision-making, rather than getting bogged down in minute details that offer limited insight.

By adhering to these constraints, businesses can provide meaningful, reliable financial statements without overburdening themselves with the task of reporting every minute detail. These constraints strike a balance between ensuring accuracy and efficiency, providing the necessary information for stakeholders to make informed decisions, without overwhelming them with unnecessary data.

The Interplay Between the Two Constraints

While the cost-benefit and materiality constraints are distinct, they often work in tandem to help companies produce clear and useful financial reports. For example, when a company determines whether to report a particular expense, it might first consider whether the information is material to the decision-making process. If it is, the company would then assess whether the cost of reporting it is justified by the benefit it provides to stakeholders.

In a real-world scenario, a company might find that reporting a minor expense is both material (because it affects an important aspect of financial performance) and beneficial (because the cost of reporting it is low). In this case, the company would report the expense in the financial statements. However, if the expense is immaterial, and the cost of reporting it would exceed its benefits, the company would choose not to disclose it.

What Investors Are Really Looking for in Financial Statements

Investors rely heavily on financial statements to assess the health, profitability, and potential of companies in which they are considering investments. These statements, which include the balance sheet, income statement, and cash flow statement, provide a detailed picture of a company's performance, its financial position, and its ability to generate cash. However, financial statements are only useful if investors understand what they are looking for, as raw numbers alone cannot tell the full story.

While different investors may have specific areas of focus based on their individual goals, there are several key aspects that most investors prioritize when reviewing a company's financial statements.

1. Profitability

One of the primary things investors look for in financial statements is the company's ability to generate consistent profits. Profitability indicates a company's capacity to sustain operations, expand, and reward its shareholders. Investors assess profitability through key metrics such as:

- **Gross Profit Margin**: This metric indicates how much money a company makes from its core business operations after subtracting the costs of goods sold (COGS). A higher gross profit margin suggests the company is effectively controlling its production costs and pricing its products or services competitively.
- **Operating Profit Margin**: Operating income, derived from a company's core business activities, shows how efficiently a company is running its operations before interest and taxes. A high operating profit margin signals a company's operational efficiency.
- **Net Profit Margin**: Net profit margin is the final measure of profitability, calculated by dividing net income by total revenue. A higher net profit margin suggests that a company is successfully converting revenue into actual profit, which is crucial for sustaining dividends and funding growth.

Investors scrutinize these profitability metrics to ensure the company has a viable path to generating long-term returns. Profitability is often a sign of strong management, a good business model, and the ability to weather economic downturns.

2. Liquidity and Solvency

Liquidity and solvency provide insights into a company's financial stability and its ability to meet short-term and long-term obligations. These metrics are especially critical in assessing the risk associated with investing in a particular company.

- **Current Ratio**: This ratio compares a company's current assets to its current liabilities. A ratio higher than 1 indicates that the company has enough assets to cover its short-term obligations. A low current ratio could suggest liquidity problems, which might concern investors about the company's ability to survive short-term financial challenges.
- **Quick Ratio**: The quick ratio is a more stringent test of liquidity, as it excludes inventory from current assets. This is important because inventory can be less liquid, and investors want to see if a company can meet its obligations with its most liquid assets. A quick ratio greater than 1 is typically considered a good sign.
- **Debt-to-Equity Ratio**: This ratio measures a company's total debt in relation to its shareholders' equity. It is a key solvency ratio used by investors to evaluate the company's financial leverage. A high debt-to-

equity ratio could indicate that the company is highly leveraged, meaning it relies heavily on debt to finance its operations. While some debt is necessary for growth, too much debt can increase the risk of insolvency, especially if economic conditions change.

Investors pay close attention to these metrics to understand whether a company is in a healthy financial position and capable of weathering economic and market fluctuations. High liquidity and low debt levels typically signal a lower-risk investment, which is especially important for risk-averse investors.

3. Cash Flow and Capital Efficiency

Cash flow is one of the most important aspects of financial health that investors assess. A company can appear profitable on paper but still struggle with cash flow if it cannot convert its earnings into actual cash.

- **Operating Cash Flow**: Operating cash flow shows how much cash is generated from a company's core operations, excluding investments and financing activities. Investors look at this number to determine if a company is truly generating enough cash from its business to cover its operations, repay debts, and fund growth.
- **Free Cash Flow**: Free cash flow is the cash remaining after a company has paid for capital expenditures (e.g., purchases of equipment or infrastructure). This figure is crucial because it represents the cash available to return to shareholders in the form of dividends or share buybacks. A company with strong free cash flow has more financial flexibility and the ability to invest in growth opportunities.
- **Cash Flow from Investing and Financing Activities**: Investors also look at how a company is investing and financing its activities. For example, heavy investment in property or equipment may signal growth, while excessive borrowing may be a red flag. Likewise, companies that are buying back stock or paying down debt may be signaling confidence in their future prospects.

The strength of a company's cash flow provides investors with insights into its ability to fund operations, expand, and provide returns to shareholders. Positive free cash flow, in particular, is a sign of financial strength and resilience.

4. Efficiency and Return on Investment

Investors are keenly interested in how efficiently a company is using its capital to generate returns. High returns on investment indicate that the company is effectively managing its resources to produce profits.

- **Return on Equity (ROE)**: ROE measures the return generated on shareholders' equity. A high ROE indicates that the company is effectively using shareholders' capital to generate profit. For investors, a consistently high ROE can be a sign of good management and a potentially profitable investment.

- **Return on Assets (ROA)**: ROA measures how efficiently a company uses its assets to generate profits. This ratio is particularly important for capital-intensive industries where large investments in assets are required. A high ROA indicates that the company is generating more profit with less capital, which is appealing to investors.
- **Return on Investment (ROI)**: ROI is another key measure for assessing how effectively a company uses its capital to generate returns. Investors are interested in ROI because it reflects the overall profitability of their investment.

High efficiency and strong returns typically suggest a well-managed business capable of maximizing the value of its resources. Investors look for these signs as indicators of a company's long-term viability and growth potential.

5. Risk Factors and External Indicators

Beyond the numbers in the financial statements, investors also consider the broader context in which a company operates. This includes external factors such as market conditions, industry trends, and regulatory environments, as well as internal factors like competitive advantages and management quality.

Investors typically review:

- **Management Discussion and Analysis (MD&A)**: The MD&A section of a company's annual report provides qualitative insights into the company's operations, strategy, and future outlook. This section helps investors gauge the management's vision for the company and any potential risks or opportunities that may not be immediately obvious from the financial statements alone.
- **External Risks**: This includes risks from the market, competition, economic conditions, and other external factors that could impact the company's performance. Investors closely monitor how companies address these risks and position themselves to navigate challenges.
- **Industry-Specific Metrics**: Some industries have their own key performance indicators (KPIs) that investors track. For example, in the tech industry, metrics like user growth, customer acquisition costs, or product development cycles may be key indicators of future growth potential.

By considering these external and internal factors, investors can assess the overall risk profile of the company and its potential for growth.

6. Investor Sentiment and Market Conditions

Finally, investors look at how the market values a company's stock or other securities. Stock price performance, valuation ratios like price-to-earnings (P/E), and investor sentiment play a critical role in the decision-making process. A company with a high stock price and favorable valuation may signal market confidence, but investors also need to consider whether the stock price is overvalued relative to the company's financial performance.

Investors rely on financial statements to gain insights into a company's financial health, profitability, liquidity, cash flow, efficiency, and potential for growth. By evaluating these key areas, they can make informed decisions about whether a company aligns with their investment goals and risk tolerance. Understanding how to read and interpret financial statements is essential for any investor looking to assess the true value of a company and its prospects in the market.

How to Choose the Right Investments

Choosing the right investments is one of the most critical decisions an individual or institution can make. The right choices can lead to substantial financial growth, while poor investment decisions can result in significant losses. To make informed and strategic investment choices, it's essential to evaluate various factors, understand your financial goals, risk tolerance, and be aware of the market's broader conditions.

Investing is not about following trends or taking wild risks; it's about aligning investments with your long-term objectives, whether they are to generate passive income, accumulate wealth, or preserve capital. This article will explore key principles and strategies for selecting the right investments.

1. Define Your Financial Goals

Before diving into any investment opportunities, the first step is to clearly define your financial goals. What are you hoping to achieve through investing? Your goals will shape your investment strategy, influencing your risk tolerance, time horizon, and the types of assets you choose. Common investment goals include:

Wealth accumulation: Building wealth over time, often through growth-oriented investments such as stocks or real estate.

Income generation: Seeking regular cash flow from dividends, interest, or rental income, often from bonds, dividend-paying stocks, or real estate.

Capital preservation: Protecting your initial investment, typically through low-risk assets like government bonds or savings accounts.

Retirement savings: Preparing for retirement, which typically involves a combination of growth and income-generating assets like 401(k) plans, mutual funds, and index funds.

Understanding your specific financial objectives helps you identify the right investment vehicles and makes it easier to determine how much risk you're willing to take.

2. Assess Your Risk Tolerance

Risk tolerance refers to how much risk you are willing to take with your investments, which can vary based on your personal preferences, life stage, and financial situation. Understanding your risk tolerance is crucial because it determines the types of investments that align with your comfort level.

Low Risk: If you are risk-averse or closer to retirement, you might prefer investments that are more stable, like bonds, blue-chip stocks, or real estate. These assets tend to offer lower returns but are less volatile.

Moderate Risk: If you are willing to accept some risk for higher potential returns, you might consider a balanced portfolio that includes a mix of stocks, bonds, and real estate.

High Risk: Younger investors with a longer time horizon may be willing to take on higher levels of risk in exchange for the potential for higher returns. This might include investments in emerging markets, high-growth stocks, or speculative assets like cryptocurrency.

It's important to honestly assess your comfort with market fluctuations and your ability to withstand potential losses. Keep in mind that risk tolerance can change over time, so regular reassessments are essential as your financial situation evolves.

3. Understand Different Asset Classes

The next step in choosing the right investments is understanding the various asset classes available. Each asset class behaves differently under various market conditions, and it's crucial to choose those that align with your financial goals and risk tolerance. The primary asset classes include:

Stocks: Stocks represent ownership in a company and are typically growth-oriented investments. They have the potential for high returns, but they are also subject to significant price volatility. Stocks are ideal for investors looking for growth over the long term and are willing to accept the associated risk.

Bonds: Bonds are debt securities issued by governments or corporations. When you buy a bond, you are essentially lending money to the issuer in exchange for interest payments over a fixed period. Bonds are generally considered safer than stocks, but they offer lower returns. Bonds are a good choice for income-seeking investors or those looking to preserve capital.

Real Estate: Investing in real estate involves purchasing properties for rental income or capital appreciation. Real estate can be a stable investment option and provides diversification, but it requires more hands-on management and has lower liquidity than stocks or bonds.

Mutual Funds and ETFs: These investment vehicles pool money from multiple investors to buy a diversified portfolio of stocks, bonds, or other assets. They are a good option for investors who want diversification without the need to pick individual stocks or bonds. Mutual funds and exchange-traded funds (ETFs) are great for investors seeking passive, long-term growth.

Commodities and Precious Metals: Commodities like oil, gold, and agricultural products can serve as hedges against inflation or economic instability. However, they can be highly volatile and may require specialized knowledge to invest in effectively.

Cryptocurrency: Cryptocurrencies, such as Bitcoin and Ethereum, have become popular alternative investments in recent years. However, they are highly speculative, with significant price fluctuations and regulatory uncertainties.

A well-diversified portfolio often includes a mix of these asset classes, which helps to spread risk while achieving targeted returns. Understanding the unique features of each asset class will help you make informed decisions about where to allocate your capital.

4. Diversification

Diversification is one of the key principles of sound investing. It involves spreading your investments across different asset classes and sectors to reduce risk. The idea is that different assets perform differently under various market conditions, so if one asset class performs poorly, another might perform well, thereby balancing the overall risk.

For example, if you invest solely in tech stocks, your portfolio may experience substantial volatility if the technology sector faces a downturn. However, if you diversify by including bonds, real estate, and international stocks, your portfolio becomes less reliant on the performance of a single sector, thus reducing overall risk.

Diversification can also be achieved within an asset class. For instance, if you are investing in stocks, you can diversify by owning stocks from different sectors, such as healthcare, finance, and energy, or by investing in various geographic regions, such as the U.S., Europe, and emerging markets.

5. Research and Due Diligence

Before making any investment, thorough research and due diligence are critical. This includes analyzing the financial health of potential investments, understanding their business models, evaluating management teams, and assessing market conditions.

- **Financial Health**: Look at key financial metrics, such as revenue growth, profitability, debt levels, and cash flow. Financial statements, such as the balance sheet, income statement, and cash flow statement, are critical in this analysis.
- **Business Model and Market Potential**: Understand how the company generates revenue, what its competitive advantages are, and whether its business model is sustainable. Consider how the company fits within its industry and what external factors could affect its performance, such as technological changes or regulatory shifts.
- **Management Team**: The strength of a company's leadership team is

critical to its success. Look for experienced and capable executives with a proven track record of making good decisions and creating value for shareholders.

- **Valuation**: Ensure that you are not overpaying for an asset. Tools such as the price-to-earnings (P/E) ratio, price-to-book (P/B) ratio, and price-to-sales (P/S) ratio can help you assess whether a stock is undervalued or overvalued compared to its earnings, book value, or sales.

In addition to analyzing individual investments, it's important to monitor broader market conditions, such as interest rates, inflation, and economic growth, as these factors can influence the performance of your investments.

6. Consider Investment Horizon and Liquidity Needs

Your investment horizon—how long you plan to hold an investment before needing access to the funds—plays a significant role in choosing the right investments. If you are saving for a long-term goal, such as retirement, you can afford to take on more risk and invest in assets that may be volatile in the short term but have high growth potential in the long term, such as stocks or real estate.

If, however, you need access to your investment in the short term, such as for a down payment on a house, you will likely want to invest in more liquid, lower-risk assets, such as money market funds or short-term bonds.

7. Stay Informed and Adjust Your Portfolio as Needed

Investing is not a one-time decision. To achieve long-term success, you must regularly monitor your portfolio, stay informed about market trends, and adjust your holdings as necessary. Market conditions and your personal circumstances may change, and your portfolio should evolve accordingly.

Reviewing your portfolio periodically allows you to make sure that your investments continue to align with your goals and risk tolerance. This might involve rebalancing your portfolio by buying or selling certain assets to maintain the desired allocation.

Choosing the right investments requires a comprehensive understanding of your financial goals, risk tolerance, and the different types of investments available. Diversification, thorough research, and regular monitoring of your portfolio are essential strategies for long-term success. By following these principles and aligning your investments with your unique financial objectives, you can build a strong foundation for achieving financial growth and stability.

Conclusion

Key Takeaways for Beginner Accountants

Starting a career in accounting can be overwhelming, given the vast landscape of regulations, principles, and best practices. However, the core foundations of accounting are relatively straightforward once understood. As a beginner accountant, it's essential to grasp the fundamental concepts that will guide your day-to-day tasks and ensure your success in the field. Below are key takeaways that can help you navigate your journey.

1. Understand the Importance of Financial Statements

As a beginner accountant, you will often deal with three key financial statements: the balance sheet, income statement, and cash flow statement. These documents are crucial in reflecting a company's financial health, providing insights into its operations, and helping stakeholders make informed decisions. The balance sheet offers a snapshot of what a company owns and owes at a particular point in time, while the income statement shows performance over a period, detailing revenues and expenses. The ca**sh flow statement tracks the movement of cash** in and out of a business, helping managers understand liquidity and cash position.

Mastering how to prepare, analyze, and interpret these financial statements is one of your first and most important tasks as an accountant. Understanding the relationships between these documents is equally important, as the data flows from one statement to the other, and discrepancies can reveal significant issues with a company's financial practices.

2. Focus on Accuracy and Attention to Detail

Accountants deal with numbers, and those numbers must be accurate. Inaccuracy, even in seemingly small amounts, can lead to errors in financial reporting, which can ultimately have significant repercussions, including legal implications, loss of trust, or financial penalties. A key skill in accounting is the ability to pay close attention to details. Developing this skill **early will ensure you can spot discrepancies, audit trails, and ensure compliance with regulations such as GAAP (Generally Accepted Accounting Principles) or IFRS (International Financial Reporting Standards).**

Accuracy isn't just about adding numbers correctly; it also involves understanding the processes and methods used in each calculation. Learning to track, verify, and cross-check your entries is essential in ensuring that the final figures presented in reports are correct.

3. Learn the Fundamentals of GAAP and IFRS

Whether you're working with a U.S.-based company or an international firm, it's crucial to understand the relevant accounting standards that govern financial reporting. In the U.S., GAAP is the standard, while globally, IFRS is more widely used. As an accountant, you should become familiar with both and understand when and how they apply.

These standards are not merely guidelines but rules that all accountants must follow to ensure consistency, comparability, and transparency in financial reporting. Learning about concepts like revenue recognition, expense matching, and the presentation of assets and liabilities will help you understand the logic behind accounting practices and help you interpret and apply these standards effectively.

4. Develop Strong Organizational Skills

Accounting involves a large volume of data, which needs to be sorted, categorized, and stored in an organized manner. Whether you're working with physical records or digital spreadsheets, being able to stay organized is essential. An accountant often handles various financial documents, files, and reports, each with its own set of details. If these records are not well-maintained and easily retrievable, it can lead to confusion and inefficiency.

Invest time in learning tools like Excel, QuickBooks, or other accounting software to help you manage and organize financial data. Staying on top of deadlines, managing multiple projects at once, and handling a variety of tasks simultaneously will help you maintain a smooth workflow.

5. Always Prioritize Ethical Practices

Ethics in accounting is paramount. As an accountant, you will be privy to sensitive financial information, and you must always act with integrity. Adhering to ethical standards ensures that the financial data you report is reliable and trustworthy, not only for internal use but also for external parties like investors, government regulators, and creditors.

In addition to following legal guidelines, it's important to ask the right questions, challenge any questionable practices, and seek clarification when needed. Ethical decision-making should be a fundamental part of your work ethic. It's also crucial to stay updated with industry-specific regulations and laws.

6. Master the Tools of the Trade

In today's digital world, accounting is increasingly being handled by software tools that can help automate many tasks, from managing transactions to preparing financial statements. Familiarizing yourself with accounting software, such as QuickBooks, Xero, or SAP, will improve your efficiency and allow you to perform your tasks more effectively.

Additionally, learning spreadsheet software like Excel is essential. Excel remains the go-to tool for accountants due to its powerful functionalities, including pivot tables, functions, and financial modeling tools. A solid understanding of these tools can help you work faster, reduce errors, and ensure consistency across documents.

7. Practice Time Management

Accounting professionals often work with tight deadlines. Whether you're closing the books for the month, preparing for an audit, or meeting tax filing deadlines, managing your time efficiently is key. Organize your work into manageable tasks, prioritize based on urgency, and avoid procrastination. Balancing multiple tasks while maintaining accuracy is a valuable skill that will serve you well in your career.

Good time management also means balancing your professional workload with personal time to avoid burnout. In a field that can sometimes be intense, it's important to maintain a healthy work-life balance.

8. Know the Tax Implications

Taxation plays a significant role in accounting, and understanding the tax implications of financial transactions is crucial. Whether it's corporate tax, VAT, or individual income tax, knowing the rates, rules, and deadlines for tax submissions is important for accurate financial reporting.

You should be aware of the tax laws that affect your company and learn how to calculate taxable income, handle deductions, and comply with tax regulations. For many accountants, specializing in tax accounting can lead to opportunities for growth and advancement.

9. Understand the Role of Internal Controls

Internal controls are the policies and procedures that ensure the integrity of financial reporting and safeguard a company's assets. As an accountant, you must understand how to design and implement these controls to prevent fraud, errors, and financial misstatements.

Strong internal controls help create transparency, reduce risk, and ensure that all transactions are appropriately authorized and documented. This might include verifying that assets are safeguarded, reviewing financial processes, and ensuring accuracy in reporting.

10. Continuous Learning and Professional Development

Accounting standards and regulations change over time, so continuing education is key to staying relevant in the field. Professional certifications, such as becoming a Certified Public Accountant (CPA), can enhance your career prospects. Additionally, attending workshops, webinars, and pursuing online courses can help you stay updated on the latest accounting technologies, tax laws, and financial practices.

Accounting is a dynamic profession, and embracing ongoing learning will keep you prepared to adapt to new challenges and opportunities as they arise.

Key Takeaways for Beginner Accountants:

1. **Master Financial Statements**: Understand the balance sheet, income statement, and cash flow statement.
2. **Accuracy Matters**: Precision is key to preventing costly mistakes.

3. **Learn GAAP and IFRS**: Grasp accounting principles and standards for consistency.
4. **Stay Organized**: Efficient record-keeping leads to smoother workflows.
5. **Uphold Ethics**: Integrity is the foundation of a successful accounting career.
6. **Use Accounting Tools**: Familiarize yourself with accounting software and Excel for efficiency.
7. **Manage Time Wisely**: Meet deadlines while maintaining accuracy and quality.
8. **Know Tax Laws**: Understand tax implications for accurate financial reporting.
9. **Focus on Internal Controls**: Protect assets and ensure transparent financial reporting.
10. **Commit to Learning**: Keep up with changing accounting standards and pursue certifications.

Next Steps: Continuing Your Financial Education

As you conclude the foundational stage of your accounting or financial education, it's important to recognize that learning in this field is an ongoing process. The financial landscape is constantly evolving with new regulations, technologies, and best practices. Here are some practical next steps to continue developing your skills and advancing in your financial career.

1. Pursue Professional Certifications

Certifications can greatly enhance your credibility and career prospects. For accountants, the Certified Public Accountant (CPA) designation is one of the most respected and widely recognized qualifications. It provides a comprehensive understanding of accounting principles, tax laws, auditing, and financial reporting, making you a valuable asset to any company. Beyond the CPA, consider certifications like the Certified Management Accountant (CMA) or Certified Internal Auditor (CIA) to further specialize in management accounting or auditing.

To become certified, you'll typically need to meet education and experience requirements, followed by passing the relevant exams. Many organizations also value specialized certifications related to specific industries or software (e.g., QuickBooks or tax law certifications).

2. Stay Updated on Regulatory Changes

Accounting standards and tax regulations often change, and it's critical to stay current to ensure compliance in your work. Follow updates from authoritative bodies such as the Financial Accounting Standards Board (FASB), International

Accounting Standards Board (IASB), and Internal Revenue Service (IRS). These bodies release new standards, regulations, and tax updates, and following them will help you maintain an up-to-date knowledge base.

You can subscribe to newsletters or attend webinars hosted by these organizations, and also consider joining professional groups or associations like the American Institute of CPAs (AICPA). Being part of these communities will help you stay on top of the latest trends and developments.

3. Use Online Learning Platforms

Online learning platforms offer a wealth of resources to further your accounting education. Websites like **Coursera**, **Udemy**, and **LinkedIn Learning** provide access to accounting courses, webinars, and tutorials taught by experts in the field. Many of these platforms offer courses on advanced topics such as forensic accounting, management accounting, financial modeling, and budgeting. These courses can help you broaden your skills and specialize in areas of accounting that interest you the most.

4. Gain Practical Experience

While theoretical knowledge is essential, real-world experience is just as crucial. Seek out internships or part-time positions in accounting or finance. Many universities and colleges also offer practical training programs that partner with accounting firms or businesses. By gaining practical experience, you'll develop a deeper understanding of accounting software, industry-specific practices, and the nuances of financial reporting. In addition, this experience will make you more attractive to potential employers as you move forward in your career.

5. Specialize in a Niche Area

Once you have a solid understanding of general accounting principles, consider specializing in a niche area that interests you. Some popular specializations include tax accounting, forensic accounting, auditing, management accounting, and international accounting. Specializing in a niche area allows you to deepen your expertise and stand out in the job market. Specializations often require further certifications and education, but they can open doors to more rewarding and high-paying positions.

6. Build Networking Skills

Networking is vital in any profession, and accounting is no exception. Attend industry conferences, seminars, and local accounting association meetings to meet others in the field. Building relationships with fellow accountants, business owners, and financial professionals can lead to valuable opportunities for mentorship, collaboration, and career advancement. Professional networking is also an excellent way to exchange ideas, learn new practices, and stay updated on industry trends.

7. Learn Financial Software and Technology

In today's fast-paced digital world, being proficient in financial software is essential. Tools like QuickBooks, Sage, and Xero are widely used in the accounting industry for managing financial records, reporting, and tax filing. Familiarity with software like Microsoft Excel—which remains indispensable for financial analysis—will also enhance your job performance. Additionally, as automation and artificial intelligence become more prominent, learning how to leverage these technologies in accounting will be a crucial skill for future accountants.

8. Read Industry Publications

Make it a habit to read industry publications like The Wall Street Journal, Accounting Today, The Journal of Accountancy, and Financial Times. These resources offer insights into the latest trends, case studies, and expert opinions, which will deepen your understanding of the financial sector. Subscribing to professional journals and reading accounting blogs will help you stay informed about the broader financial landscape and gain knowledge of various financial markets, economic trends, and changes in financial regulations.

9. Develop Soft Skills

While technical accounting skills are essential, don't overlook the importance of soft skills like communication, problem-solving, and critical thinking. As an accountant, you'll often need to explain complex financial concepts to non-financial stakeholders. Being able to communicate effectively and clearly is key to ensuring that others understand financial reports and decisions. Developing these interpersonal skills will make you a well-rounded professional and a more valuable team member.

Final Thoughts and Resources for Ongoing Learning

Accounting is an ever-evolving field that offers numerous opportunities for growth and specialization. Whether you are a beginner just starting your journey or a seasoned professional looking to expand your knowledge, continuous learning and professional development are essential for long-term success.

By pursuing certifications, gaining practical experience, and staying updated on the latest industry trends, you can ensure that you remain competitive in the field. Networking with other professionals and specializing in areas that interest you will open doors to exciting career opportunities.

To make ongoing learning easier, here are some resources to help you stay ahead in your accounting career:

1. **Online Courses:** Websites like Coursera, LinkedIn Learning, and Udemy offer a variety of accounting and finance courses.
2. **Professional Associations**: Joining groups like AICPA or CIMA can provide networking opportunities and access to exclusive educational

resources.

3. **Industry Publications**: Subscribe to journals like Accounting Today or The Journal of Accountancy for updates on accounting standards and industry news.
4. **Podcasts**: Listen to accounting-focused podcasts like The Accounting Best Practices Podcast or The Accounting Influencers Show to learn from experts in the field.
5. **Webinars and Conferences**: Participate in webinars and attend conferences hosted by professional organizations to expand your knowledge and connect with other professionals.

Accounting is a dynamic and rewarding profession that requires continuous learning, technical expertise, and strong ethical practices. By following the above steps and using available resources, you'll be well-equipped to navigate your career path and continue to grow as a financial professional.

www.ingramcontent.com/pod-product-compliance
Lightning Source LLC
Chambersburg PA
CBHW031323230926
51848CB00001B/69